He Must Increase; I Must Decrease

A Journey to Restoration, Identity, and Purpose

JEFF CROPPER

ISBN 978-1-68526-131-3 (Paperback)
ISBN 978-1-68526-132-0 (Digital)

Scripture quotations are taken from the Holy Bible, New International Version®, NIV®. Copyright © 1973, 1978, 1984, 2011 by Biblical, Inc.™ Zondervan Publishers. www.zondervan.com.

Covenant Books
11661 Hwy 707
Murrells Inlet, SC 29576
www.covenantbooks.com

Contents

Preface

My journey to the completion of this assignment from heaven began with no idea whatsoever on my part of its ultimate purpose. As you will discover, I was simply driven to rise early each day and then to be still, to wait, and to listen. Eventually the desire to write down what my Father was placing within my heart, my mind, and my spirit impassioned me.

Along the way, the Holy Spirit spoke to me through several different means. Many times, He led me to scriptures as well as explanatory resources, which helped me better understand and discern the truth that He was purposing for me to share. On other occasions, He placed songs in my heart the lyrics of which demonstrated and expounded upon a teaching that He desired for me and others to receive. On, yet, other instances, He guided me to writings and teachings, which originated with Him and were then penned, under His anointing, by His spirit-filled servants.

It wasn't until many months into my pilgrimage that even a glimpse of its eventual purpose was revealed. By the time my Father's plan became unmistakably clear, most of what He desired to say had already been written.

At that point, I was faced with the daunting—to me but not to Him—task of retracing the steps of my journey for the purpose of acknowledging those servants to whom He had led me for help, understanding, direction, and inspiration in the completion of His calling (Hebrews 13:20–21). That process was time-consuming, difficult, and at times stressful but always faith- and trust-building.

Just as He promises, He never left my side. He is always faithful to complete the good work that He began. With His guidance and help, I have arrived at the place where it is my heartfelt conviction and belief that He is pleased to complete this good work.

To those of you who have, unknowingly, played a role in this assignment by obediently, passionately, and faithfully penning the lyrics to a song, or by writing words of encouragement, instruction, or explanation, please accept my heartfelt gratitude and thanks. I have done my sincere best to give credit to and to acknowledge each of you herein. And if there is anyone who I have overlooked or missed, please know that I am genuinely apologetic. It neither was nor is my intention to do so.

I did not start with what is before you in mind. What I did begin with was a passion to know Jesus as completely, as intimately, and as deeply as He would allow. He has and continues to bring that to pass. As you will see, He has perfectly captured my heart and changed my life.

This journey/assignment began with Him. Its every step has been guided by His hand, and it shall be completed to His glory, His honor, and His praise. That is what He has placed in my heart, what has inspired and driven me. Thank you!

Introduction

For some time now I have been reading two books entitled the *Newness Advantage* and the *Nature of Freedom*. They are written by Graham Cooke and are part of the Letters from God Series. The books are unique in that they present as a collection of letters written from God's perspective and designed to enlighten and empower believers at all stages of their relationship with Him. At the end of each letter, the reader is presented with a number of thought-provoking questions purposed to encourage deeper contemplation of the content presented.

During the same time, my wife, Megan, gifted me a journal and encouraged me to begin to write my thoughts on paper. Throughout my life, I had never been one to chronicle anything. No diaries, no journaling, no note cards during church services. It wasn't that what I was hearing or thinking lacked significance but was mostly a product of an innate capacity to retain information without writing it down. Now I found myself presented with questions that I wanted to answer, in writing, and a book full of clean, white, lined pages to do so on.

At some point during the month of May (2019), I finished the books and consequently ran out of questions to answer. With no intention of continuing to develop my writing prowess, I placed my partially used journal on a shelf and moved on to other, what I thought to be, more important undertakings. God had a different plan. The Bible teaches that His ways are not our ways and His thoughts are not the same as ours (Isa. 55:8). This is a truth that I had seen play out time and time again in the lives of other believers. One that I was about to witness firsthand in my own life.

The year 2019 was both a trying and an amazing season of my journey. God was using troubles that I was experiencing with my health as a perfect opportunity to increase my faith by teaching me to trust in and surrender to Him. He had my full and complete attention. I was all in, and my Father knew it. The Holy Spirit was my constant companion, whispering truth and promises into my receptive ears. The life-changing pilgrimage that God had planned for me had begun.

For some time I had been rising early and sitting in the quiet stillness of the morning hoping to hear from my Father. I think I mentioned that it was also an amazing season of my journey. Incredible because He met me there every single day. He never missed one. He promises to be with us always, wherever we go, and I for one will carry the banner and wear the T-shirt that proclaims so.

Not only did He show up faithfully, He also prepared a table for me, right there in the middle of my battle. And if that wasn't enough, He sat and communed with me there. Not out of some sense of pity or obligation but because He wanted to. Because He likes, no, He adores me. How is this so? This was all new to me. It was just the beginning.

While all of this was wrecking me in the most amazing of ways, as my sister-in-law Ruth puts it, there sat my journal on the shelf quietly awaiting its moment of divine appointment. It did not have to tarry for long. Soon I came up with a brilliant idea (at least that was what I thought). Why not write down what I was experiencing, both the great and the not so great? For what reason, I really had no idea. The Holy Spirit is funny that way. He will allow us to take what is His and believe that it is ours, even though it never was—all for the purpose of preparing and empowering us to fulfill the divine calling prepared by God in advance for us.

With no concept whatsoever of the magnitude of what was happening, I found myself exactly where God wanted me to be. Not surprisingly, I was there eagerly and willingly. Armed with pencil and journal and a determined resolve to write down only that which my Father, through His Spirit, spoke into my spirit and my mind, I pressed on. What followed can be found here.

Beginning at a conservative pace and then gradually ramping up the production, the Holy Spirit, for a period of approximately eighteen months, faithfully spoke truth over and into me and then guided my hand as I documented the same in what had become one of my most precious possessions, my new journal.

Sometimes the messages came in dreams, other times by way of songs in the night. Often they arrived via scriptures or other Holy Spirit inspired writings. Mostly, they were presented as I waited and listened at the altar where we gathered each morning. Rarely were they ambiguous or unclear. Like everything else that comes from God, they were always right on time. Never too early nor too late.

Until about a month ago, I proceeded with only one purpose and intention in mind. Show up, commune with and listen to my Father, and then write down that which the Holy Spirit directed. You will find, and I will reiterate on the pages that follow, that the one being ministered to first and foremost was the one with the pencil in his hand.

I acknowledge that there were instances where I was allowed a glimpse of the ultimate purpose for what was transpiring before me. However, making every effort to keep pride from entering, I strived to avoid giving any consideration to the same. That is, until God opened my eyes to the concepts of clear vision and audacious faith during the latter days of my assignment. As you will discover, it was then, at just the perfect time, by way of a book entitled *Sun Stand Still* by Pastor Steven Furtick, that my Father revealed how His hand had divinely ordered each step of my journey and birthed a vision of how He would continue to do so going forward. (*Sun Stand Still* is an incredible writing with an anointed message. I would greatly encourage you to read it [Furtick 2010].)

The pages that follow will first provide you with a glimpse of my life leading up to the moment during the spring of 2019 when I was inspired to begin writing down that which God had imparted and then carry you through a year-and-a-half-long journey during which my identity and purpose in Jesus became abundantly clear. Along the way, my sincere belief and my genuine prayer is that God will reveal to you how deeply He loves you and how precious you are to Him; that the realness of His power and majesty will captivate your heart and your spirit; that you will come to realize that His presence and His favor are yours to possess, in abundance; that He, His beloved Son, and His powerful Holy Spirit desire to become everything for and to you; that They are all that you will ever need; and, finally, that the words spoken by John the Baptist and written in the Gospel of John chapter 3 verse 30 will resonate with you and become your daily declaration: "He must increase; I must decrease."

Let's Start with Some Background

Billy Burton Cropper was a kinda skinny young man who was as outgoing and friendly as he was handsome. He had a personality that would light up and take over a room when he entered it. There was rarely a time that he was at a loss for words. Shirley Lane, on the other hand, was quiet and reserved. She was one of thirteen children (yes, you read that correctly) born to Charles and Elizabeth Lane, entering somewhere in the middle of the pack. She was smart and drop-dead gorgeous. When she entered a room, no one noticed her personality because they could not see beyond her beauty.

Billy Burton first laid eyes on Shirley on New Year's Eve of 1956. He was immediately smitten. As he tells the story, he was instantly determined to first kiss and then marry her. After Shirley made him work pretty hard, he was successful on both counts. They were married on November 15, 1957. Why is all of this important you ask? Because Billy Burton and Shirley were not brought together by chance or by fate. They were enjoined by the hand of God to be my mom and dad. A gift for which I am blessed and forever grateful to my Father.

Less than a year later, on September 29, 1958, in Milford, Delaware, I joined the family. As I write this I am sixty-one years of age. My brother Bill and sisters Tamara and Vicki joined Mom, Dad and I one, four, and seven years later, respectively. The early years of my life could best be characterized as traditional and normal. I know that it is cliché, but life really was so less complicated for a child during the sixties. No video games, no cell phones or computers, no cable television (our TV was black and white and had only two channels) and no Air Jordans. We went to school, worked from an early age, and enjoyed simple things like camping and ice skating on the

1

local millpond. My parents worked hard, loved us greatly, and provided everything that we needed. Growing up, I would have told you that we were wealthy. It wasn't until many years later as an adult that I grasped the realization that we were not. That is what an amazing job of parenting my mom and dad did and one of the reasons that I know that God's hand was upon us.

My father had to work a lot, and my sisters took up much of my mother's time and attention, leaving my brother and I to navigate life together. I will be forever grateful that such was the case. During that season, God formed a depth of loyalty and an unbreakable bond that has served to carry and strengthen each of us to this day. Whether we were reenacting the World Series in the front yard with a Wiffle ball and bat; embarking on bike adventures; listening to WKBW in Buffalo, New York, on the radio; hanging out at Uncle Jake's general store; fighting (mostly with each other) or engaging in more mischievous enterprises, we did it together. Much of who I am today was rooted and formulated during those years.

In 1964, my family moved to a large Victorian-style house located in Bishopville, a small town on Maryland's Eastern Shore. I did most of my growing up there. My mother has lived nowhere else since, while my dad did so until February 2001 when he went to live in one of those mansions that Jesus has prepared for His followers.

That same year I began my formal education at Bishopville Elementary School, a six-room schoolhouse. My class had six students, and there was one teacher for every two grades. We did have a cafeteria that served amazing food (lots of mashed potatoes and gravy). Before you start judging me, know that I never had to walk miles barefoot, in the snow, to attend school; and we did have pencils and paper as opposed to stones and chisels. I learned greatly and progressed from those humble beginnings to Berlin Middle School and then to Stephen Decatur High School, from which I graduated in 1976. (Both had many more than six students per class.) It was on to college and the next season of my life.

Before delving into my college experience and beyond, there is one additional important subject to address: my faith experience. For as long as my mind will allow me to recall, my mother took me and my siblings to church. I have this picture burned in my brain of my mom on her knees beside her bed praying. I did not know what she was saying, but I was fully aware of Who she was saying it to and that she did so every night. It left an indelible impression on me.

As for my dad, he did not initially attend church with us. To be completely accurate, he did not go into the building with us. He would drop us off at the church, go somewhere that remains unknown to me, and then pick us up after the service. All of that changed when one of my sisters asked him the reason that he did not come inside with us. Having no good answer, my father attended church regularly with the family from that point forward. Out of the mouths of babes.

The church that we attended was very ceremonial with an orderly, ritualistic style of worship. Being young and impressionable, I followed along without giving much thought to the truth of or the basis for what was being expounded. At times, I did get a sense that something inside of me did not completely line up or agree with what I was being taught. However, I quickly discarded any such thoughts and moved forward with life.

That is, until my sophomore year of high school. It was then that I met a young man by the name of Grant, who would not only become my closest friend throughout high school but in addition, the person through whom God would launch my faith journey into flight. Grant was a born-again believer who loved Jesus and would not hesitate to tell you so. Even though I had no idea what that meant, Grant had an early birthday, a driver's license, and a Ford Pinto. He met all the necessary requirements to become my bud.

The catch to my growing friendship with Grant was that if I wanted to ride in his car with him, I had to go where he went, and in Grant's case, that meant church. Not knowing what lay before me, I agreed. Since I still had to attend church with my family on Sunday morning, I went to church with Grant on Wednesday or Sunday evening or during special services called revivals. For those of you who know anything about these particular gatherings, you are aware that I was being thrown into the deep end of the pool, head first.

It did not take long for me to discern that there was something different at my new best friend's place of worship. The minister talked a lot about Jesus and the Bible and sin and hell, and when he did, his voice grew louder and more stern. He also spoke of love and forgiveness and salvation and eternal life. Funny thing was that, as foreign as it all sounded, my attention was grabbed and my curiosity peaked. There was something real and genuine about it. I went back many more times, and as I did, I began to notice that at the end of each service, the minister would invite anyone who wished to receive Jesus into their heart to be their Lord and Savior to come forward. While I never did take him up on his offer, my heart pounded within me each time. Seeds were being planted. The Holy Spirit was preparing me and drawing me to my Father and to His Son.

More Lead-Up (The College Years)

During the fall of 1976, my parents, my siblings, and I all piled into our Chevy window van with wood paneling on each side and set out for Morgantown, West Virginia, and my freshman year of college. Being the oldest child and the first on either side of my family to pursue an education beyond high school, it was both an unfamiliar and an emotional experience for all of us. The females cried a lot while my dad and my brother did not, although I think that they had to fight the urge. Morgantown is six hours west of Bishopville, so when the van drove back toward Maryland without me in it, reality set in, and then I cried.

That first year I stayed in my room most of the time and studied, only leaving temporarily to go to class, to eat, and to attend football and basketball games. That lifestyle resulted in good grades, little fun, and kept me free from the normal temptations of college life. I neglected to mention in the prior chapter that during high school, I steered pretty much clear of drugs and alcohol. An accomplishment that can be attributed to playing sports, hanging with Grant, and spending time with my one and only girlfriend. My every intention was to continue that lifestyle during this next season of my life. For one year at least, my plan was a success.

Year two began with the walls of my grand scheme developing some cracks and the temptations of college life gaining territory. The relationship with my high school sweetheart had by now fallen victim to distance and the allure of many, many attractive and available coeds. I also began to buy into the old adage that goes something like this: "Oh, come on, what will one drink hurt? Everybody does it." Problem is that, it wasn't long before neither one drink nor one girl was enough. I was all in—and I do mean all in.

5

Incredibly, I continued to go to class and to study and was able to maintain the GPA that usually results therefrom. By this time, I was fully acclimated to college life and thriving therein. I graduated in the spring of 1980 and prepared to pursue my lifelong dream of becoming an attorney. Jeff's life plan was moving forward, full throttle. I was on the increase, and there was very little evidence of Jesus anywhere in the picture.

Prior to graduating, I was hired by the university to serve as a resident assistant during my junior year. I was assigned to a huge four building complex called Towers. Each Tower had ten floors with approximately fifty freshmen on each floor. There were two male and two female dormitories all connected on the ground floor.

Not long into the fall semester, my attention was drawn to a freshman coed who was the most amazingly beautiful woman I had ever laid my eyes upon. Instantly, she held captive my every thought. I could barely focus on anything else. After much contemplation, I engineered a plan by which I could make her acquaintance. Once successful, I never looked back. Her name, you ask? It was Megan. We began to date and remained together throughout college. She is now my wife and the mother of our children. We have been together ever since.

After three grueling years of law school, still in Morgantown, and two bar exams, Megan and I were married in Ocean City, Maryland, on October 1, 1983. We took up residence in my hometown of Bishopville. Happy, ambitious, and much in love, we ventured into the future together—her, a special education teacher, and me, practicing law—with high hopes and expectations.

This would be an appropriate spot to interject a couple of updates. My parents continued to be well, living in that same house in which I had spent the majority of my life. My brother, Bill, had fallen prey to the drug-and-alcohol culture and was living a high-stakes lifestyle in Florida. My sisters were embarking upon their college experiences, soon to be married themselves. Megan and I continued to engage in the social scene, but only on weekends, and lived a life far removed from the one described by that preacher at my good friend Grant's church. That was all about to dramatically change.

Speaking of Grant, our relationship dissipated after we each headed off to college. Then, after graduating, we reconnected; and Megan and I, along with our children, were blessed to be able to spend time with Grant, his wife, Dawn, and their daughters, Amy and Emily. Several years later, at a seemingly way too early age, he went to be with Jesus. I carry the thought that God had a vacancy in His army, and Grant possessed all the necessary qualifications for the position. Maybe he has even been assigned to minister to an old high school best friend.

During the month of November 1985, Megan; my sister Tamara; her husband, Michael; and I ventured to Morgantown for a football weekend. For two days we engaged in much frolicking and revelry. As we traveled back to Maryland, I began to experience severe chest pains. So much so that immediately upon our return, Megan and I headed for the emergency room. After a battery of tests, which lasted for days and weeks (not spent in the hospital), my symptoms were diagnosed to be stress related. It would be an understatement to say that I was not satisfied. Did these people not know that I was dying? Were they going to just stand by while I perished? Somebody was totally not getting it, and I soon discovered that it was not the medical professionals.

Sometime between October 1983 and November 1985, I had been watching television one evening when my attention was drawn to an advertisement for a free book entitled *Power for Living*. I immediately got up, called the number provided, and ordered the book. I had no real idea why. (You will hear me say that a lot.) When it arrived, I put the book on the shelf and forgot about it. That is until my health dilemma during the fall of 1985.

With seemingly nowhere else to turn, I took the book off the shelf and read it completely through in one sitting. It laid out the plan of salvation clearly and concisely. Almost immediately, every word that God had spoken into me ten years earlier at Grant's small church rushed back into my heart, my mind, and my spirit. The seeds that lay dormant for so long instantly began to germinate, and the answers to many questions at once became crystal clear. It was Jesus! I needed a Savior, and He was right there with open arms waiting for me. With just the two of us present, I asked Him to come into my heart and save me from my sins. He did both. I had been set free. I was a new creation, a child of God.

Being fully convinced of the realness of what had occurred, I was now faced with a dilemma that appeared the size of one of those Towers that I lived in during college. How was I going to explain this to those closest to me? Being born again was not only a foreign concept within the circles that I existed, but it was pretty much frowned upon as well. As I would soon learn, God writes better stories for our lives than we do. He had this, and He had me exactly where He wanted me. Don't go away. The story that He was writing was just beginning to unfold and was only going to become more interesting.

The GPS Recalibrates

It was not long before I sat down with Megan and laid out the details of my life-changing experience. I could tell that she had pretty much no idea what I was going on about. My wife had been raised in the same denomination that I had, so the concept of being born again was new to her. However, I could also see the love and acceptance in her eyes, and she would confide in me later that she knew that something genuine and real had taken place in me. We began attending a Bible-based church similar to the one that I went to with Grant, and it was not long before Megan also had given her life to Jesus. Soon after, we were both baptized.

This next part blows me away even as I write it now. I had immediately begun to pray for Jesus to capture the hearts of my entire family, honestly believing some to be too far outside of even His divine reach. Boy, would He show me. A few months later, I received a call from my brother. We had very limited contact during that time, so the call was out of the ordinary to start with. It only got more so. It didn't take long for me to realize that something was different. Bill was having a difficult time explaining the purpose of his call to me, a fact that completely changed when he declared these words: "I feel like someone has lifted a refrigerator off of each of my shoulders." I knew right then that my Father had radically answered my prayers.

I was witnessing the immeasurable power and love of Jesus up close and in a huge way for the first real time, and it far exceeded the limitations of my human mind. My brother giving his heart to Jesus reminded me of Paul's conversion. Although he never imprisoned or took the life of any of God's children prior to being saved, it was not beyond him to ridicule, criticize, or even humiliate believers when-

9

ever the opportunity presented itself. His lifestyle was about as far removed from the teachings of Jesus as one could be. Bill's conversion not only profoundly impacted me, but it had a similar effect on many others. He has been walking with and serving Jesus ever since. He pastors a church in Maryland and has influenced people's lives for the kingdom of God in far too many ways to document here.

Within a few months, my entire family had asked Jesus to be their Lord and Savior. God was on the move in the Cropper family. The seeds planted years earlier were reproducing five, ten, even a hundredfold. Our Father was pleased; the enemy was not. While hardships and trials were on the horizon, Jesus was on the throne of my life—at least for the foreseeable future.

Armed with a completely different perspective, Megan and I continued with life. We worked, we prayed, we fellowshipped with other Christian couples, and we attended church. We did our best to grow as believers by studying God's Word and by serving Jesus as He led us. Our lifestyle had changed because our hearts had been transformed.

On January 13, 1988, we were blessed with the birth of our son, Daniel. Any of you who have children are fully aware of the extent to which the arrival of a child impacts and changes your life. Nothing prepares you for the experience of raising and caring for another human being, especially one so helpless and fragile. Every thought, every emotion, and every decision that you make now revolves around this precious gift from heaven. Any consideration for yourself exits stage right. But make no mistake; the loss of sleep, the dirty diapers, the excessive crying, and the lack of anything me related are all minor sacrifices to make when compared to the indescribable love and joy that these little blessings bring into our lives. The child-rearing years in the Cropper household had begun.

On July 23, 1990, God blessed Megan and I with our second child and our first daughter, Sarah. I have these great stories that I like to tell about the hospital birth experiences of each of my children. My wife would be mortified if I related either of them here, so I will refrain from doing so. Suffice it to say that neither was routine or without excitement. I will mention that Sarah's collarbone was broken during her introduction to the world. Had that happened with Daniel, we would have been devastated, but by this time, we were experienced pros at this having-babies thing. (I cannot wait to see the look that will be on Megan's face the first time she reads what I just wrote.)

We took our precious daughter home, and she soon recovered from her birthing incident. At the risk of alienating my son, I have to say that Sarah was a much easier baby to care for than he was. Maybe it was that Megan and I had now been there and done that. Once! Actually, I do not believe that any experience that we had gained made that much difference. Sarah was just a pleasant, peaceful baby who required less maintenance than Daniel. I love them both more than I can put into words and would not change either of our experiences in raising them—just stating facts.

Up to this point, we continued to live in Bishopville in a new home that we had built around the time that Daniel was born. That changed in November of 1991 when we moved into another home in Snow Hill, Maryland, a town located about twenty-five miles to the south. Snow Hill is the county seat for Worcester County, and I was working there, so it only made sense to make the move. It was a town of about 2,500 residents with good schools and a few more amenities than we had previously been accustomed to. It would be our home for the next twenty-five-plus years and the place where we raised our children; created memories; pursued our careers; and strived, not always successfully, to serve our God.

In February of 2001, my father passed away. By that time, he had given his heart to Jesus and, although in ill health, was serving Him in any way possible. I love my earthly father deeply, and it blessed me greatly to have served our Lord side by side with him. I cannot wait to see my dad in his new, perfect body and to worship Jesus along with him.

The children quickly grew older and taller and began to pursue the gifts and the passions that God had planted within them. Daniel loved baseball and was really good at it. Sarah was a beautiful dancer. They both excelled in school, were positive role models, and brought us great joy. Each also shined in their respective interests, which both blessed and occupied Megan and I. There are very few greater joys in life than helping and watching your children succeed at something that they love. At the same time, very few things are more energy and time consuming.

Between work and travel and the everyday demands of life, Megan and I were left with little time for each other and, more importantly, for our precious Lord. It would be fair to say that each began to receive less and less of our attention to the detriment of both. Please do not misunderstand what I am saying. I loved and continue to love both of my children with all my heart. There is little to nothing that I would not have done or would not now do for either of them. What I lost sight of is that my Father loves them even more and that what I needed to do was to completely surrender them to Him, trusting that He would protect them and work out all things, not only for their good but for mine as well; to allow Him to become greater in their lives and mine while I became less. I was doing just the opposite with my children as well as in every other aspect of my life, and it would only become more so the case.

Daniel graduated from high school in 2006 and headed to the University of North Carolina Wilmington (UNCW) on a baseball scholarship. His baseball career was skyrocketing and would lead to him playing professional baseball for five years. Being a loving father and a huge baseball fan, I became absorbed in my son's budding career. Between games and travel, little time was left over for anything but work. While in college, Daniel met Hannah, who became his girlfriend and then, after baseball, his wife. I consider Hannah to be my third child and my second daughter. I love her as if she were my own. In my eyes, she is exactly that.

Sarah graduated from Snow Hill High School in 2008 and, after a brief stop at Salisbury University, ended up at the same school as her brother, UNCW. She secured a great job and a college degree and made her mother and I beyond proud. While I was spending most of my time with Daniel, Megan was doing likewise with Sarah. They grew to be best friends. A bond that continues to this day. Along the way, our daughter met and fell in love with Shane, who also played baseball at UNCW. They were married in Cancun,

Mexico, in January of 2019. You can do the math. Shane became my fourth child and my second son, and I love him equally with the other three. All our children now live near us in the Wilmington, North Carolina, area.

With the nest in Maryland empty, my wife and I threw ourselves even more deeply into our jobs while at the same time routinely traveling to North Carolina and planning for retirement and the future. By this time, Megan had over twenty-five of the thirty years necessary to retire completed. She was counting the days until her dream of relocating to Wilmington could become a reality. I, on the other hand, had put in thirty plus years of service and was eligible to retire. Unlike my wife, I was very uncertain that ending my working career was what my heart desired. I was still very entrenched in the "Jeff must increase" mode, giving little or no consideration to what, if any, impact my actions and decisions were having on Jesus and His Father's kingdom. I had fully acceded to the throne.

I have come to realize, to my astonishment, that during the "Jeff first" season of my life, Jesus never took His eyes off me. I can point to instances during that time when, even though I paid zero attention to it, He was right by my side pursuing me and rescuing me, not allowing me to stray completely from the plan that He had spoken over me before I drew my first breath of air. All of that was about to change in a divine way. My spiritual GPS was about to recalibrate to a route that I never saw coming. Just a couple of more stops before my journey to restoration, identity, and purpose begins. It will not be long now.

Almost There

Fast-forward to the fall of 2016. Megan has less than two years until her target retirement date of June 16, 2018, and she is in full-blown planning mode. There is a house in Maryland to sell; financial plans to be finalized; and a yet unknown home in North Carolina to purchase, among many other details to attend to. My wife had a clear vision of where God was leading her. I, on the other hand, did not. However, that was about to change in a way that I never saw coming.

The Worcester County (Maryland) legal community was by this time abuzz with the news that two of its three circuit court judges would be retiring within a few months. For me, the news was interesting but did not provoke any career change aspirations, at least not immediately. As with many other decisions, both before and after, my Father had a different story to write.

To add to the other ingredients of my life's mix during this time, the Holy Spirit was engineering a spiritual awakening deep within me. For the majority of my journey with Jesus, I had struggled with the doctrine of "once saved, always saved." My unwillingness to accept this teaching absolutely stemmed from a complete lack of understanding of God's unconditional love for His children and the depth and magnitude of what occurred at Calvary. Jesus declared, "And this is the will of Him who sent me, that I shall lose none of all that He has given me, but raise them up on the last day" (John 6:39).

That settled the matter for me. His Word was all that I needed. I am now fully convinced that my eternal destination is secure. Armed with the truth of God's love for me and Jesus's declaration found at John 6:39, I am now certain that my Lord never abandoned me, not once. That even during the seasons of my life when I had placed my interests and wants above His plan and purpose, He never took His eyes off me, regardless of how disappointed and/or hurt He was by my choices. While I sat on the throne of my existence, Jesus, who rightfully belonged there, continued to pursue and rescue me. Why would He do such a thing? Because He adores me and because His Father had a plan and a purpose for me to fulfill. Step number one was to get my attention. He was quickly gaining it.

Regardless of the direction that I chose to take with my life, God's Spirit never stopped speaking to and reminding me of the Way that I should be traveling, the Truth that I should be following, and the Life that I should be living. So when something that is going to seem "out there" to many of you began to occur in my life during the fall of 2016, it captured my complete attention. When the numbers 9 and 29 began to appear everywhere before me, and I do mean everywhere, instead of ignoring them, I began to search for what the Spirit of God wanted to say to me. (I am fully aware of the fact that some, if not many, of you are about now considering putting this down and writing me off as having lost any marbles that I had to have had to make it this far. That is certainly your choice to make. I would simply say, please do not! I promise that if you will trust God and stay with me, He has something incredible and life altering for you.)

I began by looking within each book of the Bible, both Old and New Testaments. I examined every scripture in any chapter that could have possibly unlocked the mystery of 9 and 29. I found nothing. I looked again to no avail. I prayed for God to show me, and when He did not, I begged Him for the same with a similar result. Filled with frustration and doubt, I reverted to the only option remaining, the one that my Father wanted me to pursue all along: I waited, and I listened.

Megan and I were attending my brother's church, The Uprising in Salisbury, Maryland. We had been doing so for around twenty years. At the beginning of each year, the leaders and the elders of the church would declare a twenty-one-day fast, a time set aside to commit to God the firstfruits of our lives for the coming year. As we sat waiting for church to begin on one Sunday in late December 2016, I experienced one of the most spiritually significant moments of my life. On the two huge screens in the front of the sanctuary was an announcement for the upcoming 2017 fast. It said something like this: "Join us for our annual 21 day fast to be held from January 9, 2017 through January 29, 2017." I stared in amazement. It was like I could not speak. Megan must have noticed and asked what was wrong. I just pointed at the screens. She knew immediately what was happening. She was the only person that I had confided in. My wife is a spiritual warrior. She will disagree with that statement, but I see it clearly every day. She loves Jesus, and she is 100 percent committed to Him. She got what was happening.

The Holy Spirit had revealed the meaning and the purpose of 9 and 29. Now my next step was to commit to fasting and praying and waiting for God to speak to me and point me in the direction that He had already established for me to travel.

While God was moving, so was the judicial selection process. I was being greatly encouraged by many friends and colleagues to throw my hat into the ring. It was highly flattering, and I was beginning to listen and consider the possibility. I was also determined to only move in the direction that God pointed me.

The fast arrived, and filled with excitement and anticipation, I dove wholeheartedly in. I prayed, I read, I fasted, and I listened. Then I did the same all over again. I got nothing. Twenty days passed and no revelation. On the evening of January 28, I went to bed, having reminded God of that which He was already well aware: time was running out. He was in no way concerned. He had everything completely under control. I drifted off into a deep sleep. At somewhere around 3:00 or 4:00 a.m., I was abruptly awakened with only one thought in my mind: Isaiah 42. I jumped out of bed, ran to the room where I spent time with my Father, and frantically opened my Bible. This is what I read:

> Here is my servant, whom I uphold, my chosen
> one in whom I delight; I will put my Spirit on
> him and he will bring justice to the nations. He
> will not shout or cry out, or raise his voice in the
> streets. A bruised reed he will not break, and a

smoldering wick he will not snuff out. In faithfulness he will bring forth justice; he will not falter or be discouraged till he establishes justice on earth. In his law the islands will put their hope." This is what the Lord God says—he who created the heavens and stretched them out, who spread out the earth and all that comes out of it, who gives breath to its people, and life to those who walk on it: "I the Lord, have called you in righteousness; I will take hold of your hand. I will keep you and make you to be a covenant for the people and a light for the Gentiles, to open eyes that are blind, to free captives from prison and to release those from the dungeon, those who sit in darkness. I am the Lord; that is my name! I will not give my glory to another or my praise to idols. See the former things have taken place, and new things I declare; before they spring into being I announce them to you. (Isa. 42:1–9)

There are sixteen more verses in chapter 42. I did not believe that I needed to read any further. I had my answer. No need to read any further. I should have! God directed me to all of Isaiah 42, not just the portion that suited my plans. (Over a year later, God specifically spoke Isaiah 42:16 over me: "I will lead the blind by ways they have not known, along unfamiliar paths I will guide them; I will turn the darkness into light before them and make the rough places smooth. These are the things I will do; I will not forsake them.")

I am not certain whether I made a wrong turn at this point or not. What I have become convinced of is the truth of God's Word that states that the steps of a righteous man are ordered (Ps. 37:23 and Prov. 16:9). Through Jesus, I am declared by God to be righteous (2 Cor. 5:21). Therefore, I believe that I was exactly where God wanted for me to be, and as you will see, I arrived there by way of the precise path that He had set out for me.

Armed with my Isaiah 42 revelation and bursting with excitement, I could not wait to tell Megan and/or anyone else who would listen. And just for the record, I am aware that Isaiah was prophesying about Jesus in chapter 42. God made that clear to me soon after leading me there on January 29. I still believed that He was speaking this particular Word over me at this particular time. I also believed that my next step had been set before me. I was convinced that my Father wanted me to be a judge. As you will hear me say time and time again, His plans are not always what we believe them to be. But they are always better than ours and for our good.

I submitted my application to the Judicial Nominating Commission and threw myself into the highly political, time-consuming, energy-draining appointment process. I believe that nine other attorneys submitted their applications. I made it through the first round of interviews, which narrowed the field to five candidates for two positions. One of those applicants was my dear friend Peg. Peg had applied twice prior and had not been appointed either time. I deeply wanted her to receive one of the appointments and was convinced that she would. So in my mind, I was competing with three other candidates for one appointment. While I was not as politically connected as a couple of my fellow candidates, I was convinced that I had something, or someone, special on my side.

By the end of the summer of 2017, the judicial appointment process had stalled waiting for interviews with the governor to be scheduled. The relocation to North Carolina, on the other hand, was proceeding full steam ahead. Our house in Maryland had sold in record time, and we had signed a contract to have our new home in North Carolina built. Megan was about to begin her final year of teaching, and we had made the move to a rental townhouse at the beach in Ocean City, Maryland.

At the same time, the Holy Spirit continued to be at work in my life. I was drawing nearer and closer to God, and He was doing likewise to me. (Take a look at James 4:8.) He was increasing, and I was decreasing. With my heart still very much set on and believing that I would soon be a judge, my relationship with my Lord was being restored. Jesus was being returned to His rightful place on the throne of my life.

I had my interview with the governor on December 20, 2017, almost exactly one year after having received the 9 and 29 revelation from God at my brother's church. He was friendly and warm, and it was an awesome experience to spend some time with him. I thought that it went well. The next day Megan and I drove to North Carolina to spend Christmas with the children and wait for a decision. Regardless of the outcome, God had begun to put into place the details of the story that He had written for me long ago. I had an inexplicable peace.

On December 27, in the parking lot of a dry-goods store in Wilmington, North Carolina, with Megan and Sarah by my side, I received the call and the news that I did not receive an appointment. I was disappointed (I have to admit that I shed some tears with my wife and my daughter) and a bit numb but, surprisingly, not devastated. Over the days that followed, one of the hardest things to do was to interact with those who had so passionately supported my candidacy. You learn who the people are that care the most about you through an adventure such as the one I had experienced. In my case in particular, you also learn a lot about your God and how much He adores you; and it becomes abundantly clear that wherever it is that you are going, He will be right there with you, hopefully increasing while you decrease.

It was now 2018, and there was one last hurdle to jump before my God-ordained destination would be set. My dear friend Peg had received one of the appointments. I was overjoyed. Peg had served as the county's judicial master/magistrate for many years. Her appointment had created a vacancy that had to be filled. I hesitantly applied. Unlike with the judicial application, I did not earnestly seek God's direction this time around. I should have. The good news about our Father is that He will redirect us when we stray off course, even if we are unaware that we have done so.

The ultimate responsibility of choosing Peg's replacement fell upon one of my best friends, Judge Brian Shockley. During the entire application/interview/hiring process, my hesitancy persisted. I will never forget the day that Brian called me with his decision. He never struggles for words. He did that day. He told me what I have been trying to say here for the last couple of paragraphs: that he did not believe that my heart was into taking the position. He could not have been more correct.

What Brian probably didn't know, and what I was beginning to become more keenly aware of, was that God had a different plan, a better story for His child, Jeff's life. There would be no more recalibrating of the GPS. I was headed to North Carolina and the beginning of an amazing journey to restoration, to identity, and to purpose.

On June 16, 2018, Megan and I made our final trip from Maryland to North Carolina and moved into our new home. We were filled with great joy and excitement. By this time, God was teaching me and preparing me daily. For what? I still had no idea. (There it is again!) I just knew that He had ascended to the throne of my life where He belonged.

Over the next eleven months, Megan and I got settled into our new surroundings. We joined and became connected at an amazing church. We began serving at an incredible urban/homeless ministry. We became involved in a Bible study group in our neighborhood and began cultivating relationships with many people whom God had placed in our lives.

All the while, the Holy Spirit had begun the process of guiding me to my rightful place in my Father's kingdom. Some days it was rich beyond words while others it was extremely difficult and painful. (While God was using some health issues as a means by which to establish my faith and trust in Him, Satan was constantly shooting flaming arrows of untruth in my direction to fuel fear and doubt.) Regardless of which voice I heard on any particular day, one truth remained constant: "All things work together for the good of those who love the Lord and who are called according to His purpose" (Rom. 8:28). By this time, my love for my Father and His Son Jesus was becoming firmly established. Wherever He was leading me, I would never be alone, never be forsaken, always be loved, always be protected, and always be covered. With what you have read as a backdrop, I began to write in my journal as I was led.

What follows are 236 entries from my first journaling/writing experience. A compilation of thoughts, messages, prayers, truths, and teachings spoken by God to and over me through the Holy Spirit, the purpose of which I believe was to reveal true identity and real purpose in Him. Consume them however He directs. Whether you are led to receive them over the course of a year or more, as they were given to me, or during a shorter period of time, my prayer is the same: I ask that our Father will open your heart to the reality, the depth, and the richness of His immeasurable love for you while simultaneously opening the eyes of your spirit to the better story that He has written for your life. We will talk again when you are finished.

God Restores Relationship, Instills Identity, and Reveals Purpose

May 5, 2019

It is Sunday morning, and I continue to face the difficulties that come with my leg injury. Satan continues his attack upon me while God covers and comforts me, keeps me, and encourages me. My Father reminds me that I overcome by the blood of the Lamb and the word of my testimony (Rev. 12:11). He sent me this, from my friend and brother Arzie: "Be joyful in hope, patient in affliction, faithful in prayer" (Rom. 12:12). Then He allowed me the privilege of sharing His words and His promises of encouragement from Psalm 46:1–2; Isaiah 41:10; and Joshua 1:9 with a friend. All the while He was strengthening and encouraging me likewise. He is beyond words amazing! Along this journey of almost two years, He has never left my side, and while it has at times been hard, I would not change one second of it. It has brought me to a place of love and trust, a place of His favor, His presence and His promises; to a place of knowing my identity and the privileges afforded me in Jesus; to a place of surrender and of service; to a place of truth and of hope; to the place where I belong!

May 9, 2019

The presence of God is surely with me this early morning, speaking His truth and His will into my spirit and my heart. It is an indescribable privilege to experience the presence of my Father, and

I want to soak it in, to absorb every last word that He is speaking to me. What I am hearing is that it has to be *all* about Him and *all* about His Son; that He must increase and I must decrease; that my service to Him and for Him must originate from Him; that it cannot be of my doing; that if I am to fulfill His purpose, I must be in communion with Him. I must put aside *all* else and seek to enter into His presence, to sit with Him and to listen to Him. All that I shall receive from Him requires His divine impartation each and every day. Those that He loves, He calls; and those that He calls, He equips; and those whom He equips must experience His presence. They must be in relationship with Him. That is where I long to be.

May 10, 2019

This morning a seemingly great weight has come to rest upon my shoulders. Many difficult, trying matters weigh on my mind. And then, as I arrive at this place, I am quickly reminded that what is weighty to me is but mere handiwork to my Father. Glory be to His name that He is not only able but greatly desirous of bearing my burdens. There is nothing that is outside of the reach of His glory, outside of the realm of His power, or outside of the cover of His majesty. All that He requires of me is my trust, my willingness to surrender, and my determination to be still and to wait and to see what He has done and what He will do. To exercise the faith which has been so lovingly, so mercifully, so graciously and so generously given to me. It is so little for me to give in light of how much that He offers in return.

May 13, 2019

So many times I choose to see the circumstances of my life through the lens of my sight and to have God do likewise. Rather than seeing or attempting to see as He does, I place Him into the box of my sight, of my understanding, of my wishes. Such an approach is not His will for me and does not lead me down the path that He has prepared. Knowledge is His gift to me and greater than gold. I must not only receive it but gain it and walk in it. It leads to understanding, which in turn leads to relationship. With relationship comes God's presence and favor, out of which flows trust, peace, and fulfillment. I have before me a decision. It is really my Father's decision to make; but it directly involves me, my path, my trust, my faith, and my surrender. I long to hear His voice on this. Maybe I already have. I am determined to hear from Him, to trust Him, and to allow Him to write this story. He will not fail me. He never does!

May 14, 2019

This would appear to be a big day in my journey with my Father. A decision looms in my life that my God has already made, and that I must do my best to discern. Like most of these types of situations, the answer would not appear to be abundantly clear, and that is where faith enters. I am convinced that the actual path that I choose to take is not as important to my Father as is my trusting Him in making the decision. He is more interested in shaping me, in having me grow, in changing my mindset, and in increasing my faith than He is in what I actually do. He will see to it that the mission is completed with or without me. He just desires my heart, all of it. Of this I am certain: He will love and adore me regardless. He will be with me always, wherever I go. He will not forsake me. I am His, and that will never change.

May 16, 2019

The decision that loomed over me has been made. God's better story is being written, and while I do not know it in its entirety (and may never will), I am at peace that it is His story and that it will work to the advancement of His kingdom in people's lives. God has and continues to birth the "new" in me. He is providing me with an upgrade and receiving it is a glorious experience. I am not the same person that I was when we moved here one year ago. I think differently, see differently, act differently, pray differently, worship differently, and serve differently. In a word, I "live" differently. I have come to understand that God, through the Holy Spirit, is sanctifying me, setting me apart for Him and for His glory. I used to be so afraid of that word. Now that I understand what it entails and grasp its purpose, I no longer fear it. Instead, I am embracing the experience.

May 17, 2019

You may have noticed that I do not write here every day. Only when I am responding to God's voice and then only under the inspiration of the Holy Spirit. Recently, the pace of the Spirit's movement in my life has changed. It would appear to be a time for me to wait and to listen, to sit at Jesus's feet and allow Him to speak to me and refresh me before my next assignment, to receive from Him the bounty of His provision. It is so much easier for me to give to others than it is to receive for myself. But because I am learning of who I am in the kingdom and in my Savior and what that means for me, it is becoming easier to accept and to walk in the rewards and the benefits of my relationship with my Father. So for now, I will be still and know that He is my God, I will wait and see His goodness, and I will listen for every word that comes forth from His throne.

May 18, 2019

It is Saturday, and unlike most of my mornings, recently there seems to be some distractions. I try not to let them interfere with this precious time with my Lord, but I am only partially successful. It reminds me of how easily our focus is diverted. When things in life are not so dire, we are prone to go on our merry way, unattentive to our desperate need for Jesus. It is at such times that I am so very thankful for the Holy Spirit, who gently, and maybe sometimes not so gently, reminds me of how utterly helpless and hopeless I am without my Lord and Savior. It also calls to mind just how necessary the trials and difficult times are. While they are not easy, they convince me of God's great love for me and of my need for His presence and His favor. They teach me to trust in and to surrender to Him. I am thankful for such times and long to arrive at a place where I do not need them to be drawn to His bosom. But until such a time, I will endure these storms, blessed by the assurance that my Jesus walks through them with me.

May 24, 2019

It is Friday morning, and God has spoken three instructions from His heart into mine this day. First, He reminds me that He desires to commune with me, to hear from me, to speak with me and guide me, and to do so always in times of joy and ease as well as in seasons of difficulty. It is the nature of my flesh to neglect my Lord when all is well, but that is not the desire of the Spirit that dwells within me. I long to give God my all no matter the circumstances surrounding me, and I beg that His Spirit would prompt me to do so. He is worthy of my full attention, my complete devotion, and my utmost praise, *always*! That is my goal, my intention, my heart, what I strive for. He is also reminding me to be a doer and to be intentional to that end. It seems like such a simple objective, but it is not—at least, not for me. Therefore, I need to be nudged, maybe even pushed. Praise His name that He is faithful to do so, every day, if necessary. Lastly, He is encouraging me to be faithful with the gift that He has placed inside of me, to give back to His kingdom from that which He has entrusted me to manage, to be certain to honor Him with the gift that has been so graciously bestowed upon me. There they are, three messages from my Father, each lovingly spoken to equip me to fulfill the plan that He ordained and purposed for me long ago.

May 30, 2019

It is Thursday morning and I felt led to place some thoughts on paper. Yesterday we had our first "Rooted" leader training. I met Kim, Daniel, and Christian and reconnected with Filipe and Kevin. These are truly men of God and brothers in Christ. God has brought us together to teach and train us for His next assignment: teaching and encouraging discipleship and then pointing and leading followers of Jesus to the next step of their journey. It is a calling of high honor and great privilege, and I am blessed to be embarking upon it with these men. My prayer is that God would ordain every word that comes from my mouth and every thought that enters into my mind during this and every other season of my life. That it would always be about Him and never about me, and that should it become otherwise, that the Holy Spirit would quickly correct me and redirect me back to where I am called to be. That He would increase, and that as He does, I would decrease.

June 2, 2019

I am reminded this morning of the greatness of my Lord Jesus. He is everything good. He is like a lion in His power, the Lion of Judah. He is like a rose in His beauty, the Rose of Sharon. He is like a lamb in His meekness and humility, the Lamb that was slain for my sins. He is like the driven snow, pure and spotless. He is like a king, full of majesty and honor, the King of kings. He is like a brother, accountable, faithful, loving, and compassionate. One that will never leave me. He is my everything. He is my all in all. He is my Savior. He is my friend, and He adores me. He never leaves my side. All that He has is mine. He withholds nothing from me. He is my Sufficiency. He is my Healer, my Provider, and my Deliverer. He is everything to me, and I love Him so very much!

June 6, 2019

It is an amazingly beautiful morning, and the presence of God's creation is an undeniable testimony to His majesty and His greatness. Magnificence that is captured by the words of a song that the Holy Spirit has placed in my heart and on my lips this morning:

> Holy, Holy, Holy! Lord God Almighty, early in the morning our song shall rise to Thee. Holy, Holy, Holy! Merciful and mighty, God in three persons, Blessed Trinity. Holy, Holy, Holy! Only

Thou art Holy, there is none beside Thee. Perfect in power, in love and purity. I bow before Thee, King of Glory, Holy are you Lord! None beside Thee! Perfect in power, my God forever, You were and are and You will be. (Shane and Shane 2018)

The song is entitled "Holy, Holy, Holy (We Bow Before Thee)." It is an old hymn that we sang in church almost every Sunday as I was growing up. I did not pay much attention to the lyrics until recently when I heard a remake by two of my favorite contemporary Christian artists named Shane and Shane. I was blown away! What an amazing expression of the greatness of our God and Father. What an incredible declaration of praise to and worship of the One who is truly holy, who is truly perfect, and who is truly worthy. I bow before Thee, my King of Glory, because You are perfect in power, perfect in love, and perfect in purity. Because there is none beside Thee. But mostly, because You are holy, holy, holy!

June 8, 2019

It is early on Saturday; and I have awakened to the presence of my God; His Son, my Savior; and His Spirit that dwells within me. I am filled with joy and peace and rejoicing in God's great love for me. I was reminded yesterday of His mighty hand that is upon me and of His great favor that is over me. First, He saw me through a difficult visit to the dentist. It ended up being an uneventful experience because my Father was with me and made a rough place smooth, just as He promised He would. A trip to the dentist may seem like a small thing, but I have come to understand that everything that involves His children is of significance to our God. Then seemingly out of nowhere, He greatly encouraged me through a couple of hours that He ordained for me to spend with my neighbor Dennis. He allowed me to see Dennis's heart as He sees it, to see that Dennis is His child whom He loves and that the Holy Spirit dwells within him, that He has placed us together to encourage one another and to point others toward His Son. He does that for and with His children. He unifies us and makes us one. Jesus prayed that we would be one as He and His Father are one (John 17:11 and 23). He purposes our paths to cross that He may strengthen and encourage us through one another before being dispatched to serve as witnesses of the redeeming, life-changing love and power of His Son. Our God truly is amazing!

June 12, 2019

I am reminded very clearly this morning of God's mighty presence being with me and of His powerful favor being my companion. That because I have received His Son and surrendered to His will, He has ordered my steps and placed me in the palm of His hand. I am overwhelmed and full of great joy by virtue of the revelation that He has chosen me and set me apart to be His child and thus to serve and please Him; to be His ambassador and point people to Jesus. That He would die for me and take away my sin is amazing enough, but that He would go a step further and freely give me His righteousness truly defines His love for me. The reality of these gifts is now embedded inside of me. The Holy Spirit has grafted them into my heart and into my spirit and brought them to life within me. I am new, I am changed, I am His, I am chosen, and I am loved—now and forevermore. All glory and honor and praise be to His name!

June 13, 2019

Last evening I gathered with my "Rooted" brothers and received a Word from God regarding our eyes and our vision. It came from Matthew 6:22–23 and spoke of viewing things singularly through the light of God's Word in order that no darkness may enter in. This morning, while examining that scripture passage, the Holy Spirit took me through Matthew 5, 6, and 7 (The Sermon on the Mount). And as He did, I was convicted by the words of Jesus. I was shown that there are things in my life that do not line up with His teachings and that I must, with the help of the Holy Spirit, make changes. As always, His admonitions were not harsh or critical but were given firmly, blanketed in His great love. Joshua 1:8 states, "Do not let this Book of the Law depart from your mouth, meditate on it day and night so that you may be careful to do everything written in it." Father, please increase my faith and fill me with the truth of your Word that no darkness, but only light, would be found within me. "Sanctify them by the truth; your word is truth" (John 17:17).

June 16, 2019

Today is Father's Day, a day to celebrate and honor fathers everywhere. It brings to mind my two fathers. First, my earthly father, who I miss and love greatly. I cannot wait to see him again in the presence of our Lord Jesus. Then there is my heavenly Father, who is the greatest of and the model for all fathers. He is the only perfect example of what a good father should be. The manner in which He provides and protects, teaches and guides, and forgives and loves equips us with the template for what every father should look like. His compassion, His faithfulness, His loyalty, His devotion, His understanding, His wisdom, and His tenderness are all qualities that I strive to emulate. He is the Father of all fathers. And on this Father's Day, I choose to honor, to worship, to exalt, and to glorify Him. For He truly is a good, good Father and worthy of my praise. "My Father, Who art in Heaven, Hallowed be Thy Name..." (Matt. 6:9).

June 19, 2019

Some days I feel led to journal my thoughts while other days I do not. Today my mind and my spirit are flooded with love, praise, and worship for my Father, for His Son, and for His Holy Spirit. While my affection for Them is incessant, at certain times those emotions would seem to flood my heart. This is such a time. They are ever present and right on time, not too early and never too late. Their guidance, Their counsel, and Their provision are all perfect and exactly what I need. There is great power and an endless reservoir of compassion in Their presence. I am reminded that I can do all things because They strengthen me. What an indescribable privilege and honor it is to be Theirs and to be loved by Them. What amazing joy floods my soul when I hear Their voice. I love Them with all of my heart; and out of that love is birthed a passion to serve Them, to please Them, and to be with Them. This morning I pray for boldness and intentionality of purpose as I walk with my Father, His Son, and the Holy Spirit through this life. They are worthy of my utmost!

July 1, 2019

I come to this place, as led by my Father, when He speaks something specific into my heart through His Spirit. Today is such a day. Recently I have been more keenly aware of God's great mercy and overwhelming grace in and over my life; of how He has protected me, spared me, and saved me from the pestilence that arrives by day, and by night, as well as from the enemy's snare (Ps. 91). I rejoice that He has done so in order that I may testify of His great faithfulness. That the seasons change, as do I, but He remains unchanged forever. The magnitude and outpouring of His love for me are as great and as plentiful as ever it was or as ever it will be. Life's cares and trials give me need for His river of grace, which is inexhaustible and always available to me. Generations come, and they go, but God's grace remains the same. I have been purchased with that grace. My path is not my own but my Lord's to direct and navigate. Oh, what peace and joy that truth brings. Would it be that I should never wander to any other source for any other thing (Spurgeon 1995, 366).

July 4, 2019

"So that when the day of evil comes, you may be able to stand your ground, and after you have done everything, to stand" (Eph. 6:13). The enemy is attacking me and making every effort to steal my joy and to stir up fear and doubt within me. Just when I feel strong and secure, I am made aware of my weakness and my great need for God's strength during every moment of every day. The Holy Spirit reminds me to put the Word of God that I pass on to others into practice in my own life. He reassures me of who I am and to Whom I belong, as well as of the great benefits and privileges that are afforded to me as a result thereof. He encourages me that He has already won the battle and that all that is required of me is to stand upon that and every other promise that comes from Him. That He loves me perfectly, which casts out all my fear. Right on time, He gently and compassionately confirms that I am His and He is mine and that He has me squarely in the palm of His mighty hand. Glory be to His name!

July 12, 2019

It is early on Friday, and it is very quiet. As is often the case when I awake, my mind is fertile ground, and Satan wants to occupy as much of it as I will allow. The great news is that from the moment that my eyes open and my thoughts begin, Jesus is right beside me, just as He promised, upholding me, warring for me, guarding and strengthening me, being my ever-present help. There too is the Holy Spirit, reminding me of all that He has taught me, assuring me that I am a child of the Most High God and that as a result thereof, I am adored and the benefactor of each and every one of the benefits and privileges afforded to His Son. Then I am allowed a glimpse of my Father, standing *large* above everything with His arms reached out over me, covering me and speaking these words: "Fear not you who are favored among men for I am with you always, wherever you go. My rod and my staff shall comfort you. Goodness and mercy will follow you all of the days of your life. We will dwell and abide together both now and forevermore." And I am at peace.

July 19, 2019

My heart is filled with the knowledge of the overwhelming great love that my Father has for me. Out of that adoration, He continuously teaches me who I am in Him—that I am a reflection, a mirror image, of His Son Jesus whom He loves beyond measure and to whom He has given everything. The kingdom is His in all of its splendor. We are His in all of the beauty that comes from Him. He has revealed to me that which He sees in me and thus who I am in

Him. I am loved; I am adored; I am forgiven; I am able; I am blessed; I am delivered; I am provided for; I am His heir, His child, His reflection, His servant, and His messenger. Because of who I am and out of His great love for me, He has placed a desire in my heart to share all of this with everyone and anyone who will listen. What an amazing calling! Praise be to His name!

July 21, 2019

"Be still and know that I am God..." (Ps. 46:10). There are times when it is necessary to quiet our minds and all that is around us and there to wait upon our Father. Should He choose to impart His wisdom, knowledge, or a specific directive into our hearts, our minds, and/or our spirits, how blessed we shall be. But I have discovered that the true gift of such moments is to be found in the peace and overwhelming reassurance of His presence. In the humbling revelation that the God of *all* things has not only come to be with me and commune with me, but that the desire of His heart is to do so, great joy floods my spirit. Indescribable love envelops me. All doubts, fears, concerns, and worries evaporate away. Whatever burdens me is rendered powerless. I long to dwell in this place forever, and at some point, I will do just that. But until then, I am refreshed, sustained, and empowered by His presence. How greatly blessed I am!

July 25, 2019

Last evening I once again spent time with my brothers in our "Rooted" group. What powerful men of God they are, and oh, how it blesses me to share Jesus with them. When we are together, God is present and the Holy Spirit reigns. There is much encouragement and wisdom and knowledge dispersed. Our Father has called us to advance His kingdom together in this season of our lives. Regardless of our different stages of life, when we are together, we are united for this one single cause: to point people to Jesus. It is a great privilege and a high honor to join with them and to serve our Lord and Savior, Jesus Christ. Today I have been called to meet with the pastor who is responsible for the "Rooted Experience" at our church. I sense that God has another assignment for me, and regardless of what He is calling me to, I am highly honored and greatly excited. May the Spirit of God be my guide.

July 26, 2019

Here I am one day later so that I may share the amazing good news that my God and Father bestowed upon me yesterday. I know that my mind cannot fathom the plans that He has for me, nor the enormity of His love for me, nor the benefits and privileges that flow therefrom; but with each passing day, He is revealing those treasures to my heart in greater abundance. The last year has been difficult at times, and yet it has been the absolute best year of my life! Through the trials, I have come to know with certainty how deep and how wide is the love of Christ for me, how great and how real His promises are for me, and how firmly I can place my faith and my trust in Him. I now know that He has plans for me, and yesterday, I learned that part of those plans will be to coordinate the "Rooted Experience" at our church. It is a big calling, but one that He has equipped me for. Once again, He has blessed me beyond my imagination. Praise be to His name!

August 4, 2019

It is early, and as I sit in the quiet stillness and wait upon my Lord, I am reminded of what great things He has done in my life. I am led to recollect His love and compassion over me as well as His ever-present faithfulness and devotion to me and to those that I love. I call to mind His beauty and His power and His grace and mercy. His gentleness, kindness, patience, and goodness reign over me and follow me all the days of my life. He adores me, and the Holy Spirit has taught me what that means for me. It proclaims that I am forgiven, I am redeemed, and I am His righteousness. I am chosen by Him to be His child and His heir. I have been set apart from before time to fulfill a purpose that He set in place just for me, and I am equipped specifically and divinely for such calling. I am holy because He is holy and because He says so. I am His, and I am greatly blessed. All of this is certain in my heart and brings forth praise and worship; honor and glory; exaltation for my God and Father, for my Lord and Savior, and for His Holy Spirit. Shout hallelujah, oh my soul!

August 8, 2019

I am stirred to write what is swirling in my spirit this morning. God, through His Spirit, is moving within me. I sense and I believe that He is beginning to usher in something new and meaningful and purposeful in my life, and I want more than anything to receive it. However, I discern that I am to be still and to wait for His further instruction and confirmation. So with great excitement and anticipation, I will wait. I am not overwhelmed or afraid or intimidated. To the contrary, there is a discernible peace about me. I am filled with joy, humbled by my Father's love for me and by His desire for me to fulfill that which He has already declared over me. I am determined and destined, chosen and called to please Him, to serve Him and to serve others. A new assignment, an upgrade is coming. Excitement and anticipation fill me. I can't wait, but I will.

August 9, 2019

Just about two years ago, God, through His Holy Spirit, spoke His will over me; and thus, truth was declared in my life. And I began a journey that had been set for me since before time. I had no idea where that path would lead or what it would entail. I only knew for certain in that moment that what was happening was real and that it was of God and, as I would come to fully comprehend, He would be with me every step of the way. The two years since have been sometimes difficult, sometimes scary, and sometimes painful but always for my good; and through them, I have been changed completely. I now know for certain who I am and to whom I belong as well as what that means for my life. My Father's promises, revealed to me by His Holy Spirit, are now my daily guide. And while where exactly His plan will take me has yet to be fully revealed, I have come to understand and to trust that my path will be perfectly ordered and limited only by His will for me.

August 13, 2019

I am fully convinced and divinely assured of my identity in and through my Lord and Savior, Jesus Christ. I know with certainty that I am adored by my Father, that I am not hidden, that there has never been a moment that I was forgotten. He knows my name, and it is written upon His hand. And yet there are times when I find a sullen, maybe even sad, aura about myself. Uncertain of where it comes from, I am troubled by the possibility that it is generated by my lack of faith or trust in what I have been led to write. Then my Father, as He always lovingly does, reminds me that without sorrows, there would be no need for Jesus; without anguish, no need for grace; without my Lord, I am nothing. My complete dependence is upon Him. When He is present, my troubles withdraw. When I behold Him, all doubts and fears subside. I am His, kept and preserved by Him, by Him and Him alone. So I welcome the quiet sullen times that serve as a reminder of the One to whom I belong and upon whom I depend. Glory be to His name!

August 20, 2019

Do you not know? Have you not heard? The Lord is the everlasting God, the Creator of the ends of the earth. He will not grow tired or weary, and His understanding no one can fathom. He gives strength to the weary and increases the power of the weak. Even youths grow tired and weary, and young men stumble and fall; but those who wait (hope) upon (in) the Lord shall renew their strength. They will soar on wings like eagles; they will run and not grow weary, they will walk and not be faint. (Isa. 40:28–31)

I have been directed to this Word from my Father by the Holy Spirit. As soon as I finished writing it down, my eyes were directed to the bottom of the next page in my journal where it is written as well. (If you are questioning whether God is speaking something to you, just keep your eyes and your ears open. Oftentimes, He will reveal and confirm that it is in fact Him.) God truly desires to speak to me and to give me direction through this passage this morning. This is what I hear Him saying, "You may not always understand My ways or the direction in which I am leading you, but rest assured that I am with you always, that your provision is secure and that you are Mine." So I will do as He directs, even when I do not understand. I will wait on Him, and while I do, I will trust Him and His great love for me and place my hope in Him. I will allow Him to increase while at the same time I am decreasing.

August 21, 2019

Last night I was given a dream in which my mother was at a table with me and we were preparing to eat. She asked me to pray, and I began to recite a mundane, very normal prayer. As I did, she became very agitated and asked could I not give a meaningful, heart-felt prayer. I was immediately awakened, and a sadness fell over me because many times this is exactly what I give to my Father. I fail to provide Him with what He so richly deserves, which is my best. I fail to give Him the firstfruits of my worship; the firstfruits of my heart, of my time, of my service, of my devotion, or of anything else that is rightfully His. Do you get what the Spirit of the Lord is saying? I did. And I do. And that is why I was saddened. He deserves so much more! He gives me nothing but His best; the least that I can do is render the same to Him in return. The part that overwhelms me is that He is not angry with me. He continues to love me, and out of that adoration, He gently reminds me of what is important. It is *Him*!

August 27, 2019

This morning I am moving around a lot as I prepare to leave later today to travel back to Maryland for a visit with family and friends. All of this movement is opposed to a normal morning for me, which is spent with my Lord waiting and listening for the Holy Spirit to speak to me, to teach me, and to guide me down the path that my Father has ordered for me. The beautiful thing is that as I scurry about occupied with the things of life, He just quietly waits for me. With a smile on His face, He does not chastise or criticize me. Instead, He patiently waits, pouring out His compassion on me because He adores me and because He knows that in the midst of all the noise, I feel likewise about Him. I still see Him because He is always there. What I am saying is that my God is faithful. Every day He is faithful to me. He never changes, and I can count on that. So can you.

August 29, 2019

I sit in quiet peaceful solitude at my brother's house in Maryland. I am reflecting on several things. First, God's presence in my life. No matter where I am He is there. ("I will be with you wherever you go.") And with Him, He brings His grace, His mercy, and His love; and He pours each of them over me. His peace envelopes me, and His joy encourages me. Next, He gently reminds me of this: "He opposes the proud but gives grace to the humble" (1 Pet. 5:5), and that a fine line exists between the two. He has done such great things in my life, and as I share those blessings with others, I must be careful and aware to do so in a manner that points to Him, exalts Him, and glorifies His Son. He encourages me by revealing His pleasure in my exuberance and my excitement. Then He shows me that others receive the good news more willingly when it is delivered humbly with no perception of pride whatsoever. I am so thankful for my Father's patience with me. He is so very good!

August 30, 2019

I continue to be in Maryland this morning, sitting in my mother's home in Bishopville. As I quietly commune with my Father, I am led to reflect upon my past life here and how so much has now changed. Our existence on earth is like that, constantly changing, and then we are no more. On some level, it is sad and depressing, but in my spirit, I am at peace. Because, as the changes occur, I am made more keenly aware that my Father remains the same. He never changes. Regardless of where I find myself on this journey, His presence is with me, and it is unflappable. He is faithful every day. I can count on His love and compassion greeting me every morning and His provision seeing me through every circumstance. I am His, and He is mine, and that does not change. It is forever constant, and it guides me along this journey of changes until I take my rightful place of dwelling in His house forever.

September 1, 2019

It is Sunday, and my time in Maryland is quickly coming to an end. As always, my steps are numbered, and my path set before me. I have been afforded the opportunity to speak with and to see many of those who God has made dear to me and placed under my care (1 Pet. 5), and it has blessed me greatly. Tomorrow I return to North Carolina where God has placed me, where His plan and purpose for my life are unfolding, and where those who I love most greatly reside. There, a storm (Dorian) is looming, a danger is approaching, and an opportunity presents itself: a chance to trust in Him that calms the waters and stills the seas; an opportunity to receive His peace, His protection, and His provision; and to worship Him and stand upon His promises.

> This I call to mind and therefore I have hope, because of the Lord's great love we are not consumed, for His compassions never fail, they are new every morning, great is His faithfulness. I

say to myself the Lord is my portion therefore I will wait upon Him. The Lord is good to those who place their hope in Him, to the one who seeks Him. (Lam. 3:21–25)

Storms will come, and storms will go. But the love, compassion, goodness, and faithfulness of the One who calms the winds and quiets the seas will remain steadfast forever. His hand of protection will be upon His children. Therefore, as for me and my house, we will trust the Lord our God.

September 3, 2019

By my Father's ever-present grace, I am safely back in North Carolina. I asked Him not only for a safe journey but for a peaceful one as well, and He did not fail me with regard to either request. He never does. As I sit here in my quiet place, I feel a great peace. This is where He greets me every day. This is where He has taught me to trust Him. This is where He prepares a table for me and where He sits and communes with me. While He is with me wherever I go, this is our special place. Here I have built an altar and invited Him to join me. Here I worship Him. Here I exalt Him. Here I glorify His name. It is in this place that I surrender to Him and to His will. It is an amazing place, not because of its location but as a result of His presence. And what overwhelms me most is that He desires to be here with me. He adores me—me who is so unworthy on my own and yet who is completely worthy and deserving through the blood of His Son. It is so very good to be here. Praise be to His name!

September 5, 2019

As hurricane Dorian approaches, I find myself at peace and desirous of putting what my Father has placed in my heart on paper. I find that desire to be my passion of late. Each morning I feel a longing to express, outwardly, what God is pouring into me. Honestly, since my return from Maryland, I have not felt well in my body. It would appear that the enemy is attempting to instill fear and discouragement in me by way of what I feel physically and what I see with my eyes. But the Holy Spirit is teaching me to walk by faith and not by sight, and so therefore, I declare, "Praise be to my Lord and Savior, Jesus Christ! The enemy will not succeed in his ploy to steal my joy or to destroy my peace. I am at ease because 'Greater is He who is in me than he that is in the world'" (1 John 4:4). My Father has spoken His Word over me and surrounded me with His great and many promises, and therefore, I will not fear. I am His child, and He adores me. His presence is with me, and His favor is upon me, and therefore, the gates of hell cannot prevail against me! That is what He has placed in my heart this day.

September 8, 2019

Most mornings I do my best to wait upon my Lord before writing in this blessed place. To be still and to listen for Him to speak to me. Today that is not necessary. My heart, my mind, and my spirit are overflowing. Last evening, Megan and I went to see the movie *Overcomer*. It was amazing and so very anointed. The Spirit of God was present in that theater, and I was overwhelmed. I still am. It is in moments like last night and this morning that my Father takes me to a new place, a deeper place, a sacred place of experiencing Him. I never want to leave that place, and I long for as many people as possible to experience it along with me—especially those whom I love and care for deeply, those who have been placed beside me and under my care. In the movie, two of the main characters are asked to put into words who they believe that they are. At first, they are unable to do so, at least not with much conviction or passion. But as the movie unfolds and they find themselves surrendering more to the Holy Spirit, all of that changes. The eyes of their hearts are opened to the truth being imparted into their spirits, and then they receive the revelation that they are who their heavenly Father declares them to be. And who exactly is that? For months now the Holy Spirit has led me to, and then not allowed me to leave, the book of Ephesians, especially the first three chapters. I have felt a burning desire to share

Paul's words therefrom with anyone who will listen. In the movie, a young lady is led to the first two chapters of Ephesians to discover who it is that God says that she is. There He proclaims that she is "blessed"; she is "holy"; she is "blameless"; she is "predestined"; she is "His daughter"; she is "redeemed"; she is "forgiven"; she is "chosen"; she is "included in Christ"; she is "marked with a seal, the Holy Spirit"; she is "alive in Christ"; she is "raised up with Jesus and seated with Him"; she is "saved"; she is "God's workmanship"; she is "near to God"; she is "a citizen of Heaven"; she is "a member of God's household"; she is "a child of God"; she is "His." And you and I too are *all* of these things. When asked, "Who I am?" my answer now and henceforth will be decisive and clear: "I am who God says I am, and I will not be defined in any other way." My identity is in Him, both now and forevermore. Yours can be as well. You have got to see this movie.

September 10, 2019

For much of my life I have desired to be the focus of attention, both in my earthly existence and on my spiritual journey. I have longed to be showered with the praises of men in both arenas. In doing so, I possessed no understanding of the damage inflicted or of the responsibility and the burden imposed by such a wish, nor did I perceive from where such an objective arose. Recently, through the grace of my Father, the Holy Spirit has shown me that my place in the kingdom derives its origin from the throne of heaven and was set in place before I took a breath. I have also been made aware that any attempt on my part to proceed or exist outside of that calling will not only result in complete failure but will most likely lead to harm to myself and/or others. Needless to say, this is an area of my life in which both repentance and sanctification are necessary and ongoing. The most encouraging revelation has been the realization that my assignment, my calling—in whatever form it presents itself—is of the utmost importance to my Father and to His kingdom, and therefore, He will patiently prepare and equip me to successfully fulfill it.

All that is required of me is for my will to be decreased while His is increased. It is a plan that, with the Spirit's help, I am embracing.

September 12, 2019

Those whom God has called He has equipped for His purpose in the calling. Of this truth, I am certain, and on this promise, I strive to stand. And yet at times, I find anxiety attempting to enter into my thoughts. Oh, how weak and feeble I am. He has shown me that when my focus is on myself and even more so on the thoughts, the opinions, and the approval of others and not on Him, then I open the door for negativity, fear, and worry. The truth is that I know from where my help comes from—it is from Him and Him alone. I am fully aware that there is only one opinion that matters, and it is my Father's. In addition, I know precisely what His opinion is of me. He adores me. He desires to be in a relationship with me. He chose me, weak and feeble me. He also called me to a specific place and purpose, one for which He has prepared me. A plan during the completion of which He will always be by my side. So what does it matter what anyone else may say or think? In You, Jesus, I will find my importance, my significance, and my purpose. Therefore, in You, Lord, I will place my trust.

September 14, 2019

Not certain of what exactly my Lord would have me to place here this morning, but feeling the direction to do so, I opened to this page. There I find the passage below ("Lord my God, I cried to You for help, and You restored my health" [Ps. 30:2]); and I am reminded of my place, my state of mind, my journey of restoration with Jesus of approximately one year ago. Engulfed with and paralyzed by fear, sadness and despair, and virtually broken by the same, I was in need of something, a revelation of truth that was yet unknown to me. I began to search everywhere for answers. I desperately looked for help, for hope, for strength. When every turn produced more fear and despair, I cried out to the only One who could rescue and save me—the One who was there all of the time, the One who was pursuing me, the One who adores me, the One who desired to be with me and who had a plan for me. You know His name. He is Jesus. So this morning, I declare my praise for and my worship of Him and express my heartfelt thanksgiving to Him through the words written by King David in verse 2 of Psalm 30: "Lord my God, I cried to You for help, and You restored my health." Glory and honor be to Your name!

September 17, 2019

Lord, I am overcome with the need to worship You, to praise and to exalt your holy name, because You alone are worthy and because You have filled my heart with an overwhelming love for You. All glory and honor I bring to You. Little do I have to offer. So I bring my sacrifice of praise, my heart filled with adoration, and my gift of surrender; and I place them at Your feet. Lord, You are beautiful. Your face is all I see, for when Your eyes are on this child, Your grace abides in me. My cup runneth over. Holy, holy, holy Lord God Almighty. Early on this morning, my song shall rise to thee. Only Thou art Holy, there is none beside Thee. You are perfect in power, in love and purity. Oh Lord, You are my God, You are my Father, and I am Your chosen child. You adore me and are faithful to me every day. What then shall I say? What then shall I do? I shall worship You. I shall exalt you and praise Your name. That is my passion. For that purpose, I was created and given breath. Oh, that not one day should pass in which I would neglect to fulfill that calling.

September 18, 2019

Today is a significant day in my life for the following reasons. First, it is my wife's sixtieth birthday, and I am drawn to pause everything and consider the amazing gift from God that she is to me. Her faith in and her love and passion for Jesus, first; her children, second; and me, a close third blesses my life each and every day. Her patience, her prayers, and her support have undergirded me for forty of those years. I love her with all of my heart and thank God for placing her by my side on this journey. Next, my mother and my sister, Vicki, are here for a visit; and that brings me great joy. It is a wonderful gift from God to simply spend time with those that we love so deeply. Finally, tonight is the kickoff of the "Rooted Experience" at our church and the beginning of a season during which God has promised to fulfill a portion of His plan and His purpose for my life. My hope and my prayer is that He will continue to teach me to trust Him and to know with certainty that His presence and His favor are with me and upon me wherever I go.

September 19, 2019

Yesterday was a day of great blessing in my life and a reminder that my Father is with me always. His presence and His favor never leave me. He is faithful to me every day, and He never fails me. Megan's birthday was blessed; and even though we were not able to spend much of it together, our love for each other, which is a gift from God, was ever present. The "Rooted" kickoff had God's hand upon it. He took my anxiety level, which was higher than I would like to admit, and turned it into peace and joy just as He promises that He will do if we only ask and cast our cares upon Him. He did something that I never saw coming and, through it, allowed me to share my heart for Him with those gathered. He is so incredibly amazing! This morning I am overjoyed by and with the people, His people, that He has surrounded me with and allowed me to enter into relationship with Jesus beside. It blesses me greatly and brings me immense comfort. God is *so good*!

September 24, 2019

God's calling upon one's life is a matter of great significance and something not to, in any way, be taken lightly. I have come to know that of our own auspices, we are not able to complete the task. I am likewise convinced that He who calls equips His children for the assignment and that such provision always comes by way of the Holy Spirit. Without God's Spirit, we are of little use to the kingdom of

God. Loved and adored, yes; productive, not so much. But surrendered and open to the Holy Spirit, we are assured of and endowed with power. Power to boldly serve as our Father's witnesses wherever He leads us. Not only does the Spirit of God empower us, but He gently corrects and redirects us when our flesh attempts to distract us from our appointed purpose. Oh, that we would know His voice so intimately that we would ignore and flee from any other.

September 27, 2019

The Holy Spirit has directed my thoughts to the concept of joy this morning. So what do I know of this idea known as joy? I know that it comes solely from the Lord, that it is the foundation of my strength, and that it is a fruit of the Spirit. That is to say, that it is a gift that we receive from God when we accept His Son into our hearts and ask Him to save us from our lost state of sin. I also know that it is different from happiness, which the world and/or the flesh have to offer. I know that happiness is temporary and fleeting while joy is eternal and fulfilling; that while sorrow may momentarily intervene in our lives, joy is always there waiting to restore us in the morning; and that where our Father is, there is joy unceasing, which means that heaven is and will be filled with it. Finally, I know that for most of my life, I have experienced little or no joy. I had times of happiness that were fleeting and unfulfilling, but no joy was present. And how do I know this, you ask? Because now I have joy. And why do I know that I have it now, you inquire? Because now I have Jesus. Want to upgrade your happiness to joy? Get Jesus!

September 29, 2019

From time to time, but not often, thoughts enter into my mind of sinful times in my past life. These thoughts are extremely detailed and clear and give rise to intense sorrow, shame, and sadness. Even feelings of guilt attempt to worm their way in. I wonder what I could have been thinking and how I could have allowed myself to be overcome by the influence of such evil forces. It reminds me that standing alone, I am no match for these princes and minions of darkness. I tell myself that I lost my way, and in fact, that is true. But what I really lost was my connection to Him, who is the Way. I turned away from my first love and, in so doing, forfeited His presence and His favor, His covering, and His protection. Now for the Good News. He never lost sight of me. He pursued me and then rescued and reclaimed me. Why did He do such a thing? Because I am His. He cleansed me of that sin and declared me righteous forever. In His eyes, it is as if I did nothing wrong. His Word promises that He doesn't even remember my wrongdoings. Hallelujah! So I rebuke those thoughts that the enemy sends, as well as Satan himself, in the name of He who is my Lord—Jesus, Savior of the world.

October 2, 2019

"In his heart a man plans his course, but the Lord determines his steps" (Prov. 16:9). I have also heard it said that the steps of a righteous man are ordered. Therefore, because Jesus has made me righteous, my steps are set before me by God. I am convinced of this because He said so, but also because where He takes me I would not fashion to go on my own. I planned to stay in Maryland; He brought me to North Carolina. I planned to play golf and relax; He set my feet to serve Him and to do so actively and vigorously. I planned to have an easy path; He needed to train me up in the way I should proceed, and thus, adversity became my companion. I searched for small assignments; He had larger plans for me. I wanted to be in control while He desired surrender. I wanted to choose who I encountered and stood beside; He had others in mind. He has a plan for me, a glorious plan, and now all that I desire is to fulfill it: to serve Him, to serve His people; to complete His purpose for me; and to please Him every day.

October 4, 2019

Recently I have been reminded of just how vulnerable I am to the enemy, and to my flesh, when I am not completely connected and surrendered to my Father. I have resided in both a place of full surrender as well as a place of total self-dependency and, with the help of the Holy Spirit, have come to recognize each. Here are some observations regarding both. When attempting to rely on myself, I did not possess a true, clear realization of my great vulnerability. Now, after having walked in complete surrender to God, I know when I am being pulled down and drawn backward and just what danger lies in that place. It is then that I must press in and lean on Jesus, the author and perfecter of my faith. I also realize that when I am in a place of surrender, walking in the presence and with the favor of my Father, I am prone to believe that I will never be tempted to leave that place. When I do so, I am being deceived and placed at risk of being rendered vulnerable all over again. "Be careful when you think you stand, lest you fall!" (1 Cor. 10:12). The enemy still prowls; therefore, I will strive to press in and to lean on Jesus. He is the One who is fully able to keep me and carry me through.

October 8, 2019

At this time a year ago, my Father had me in such a different place. I found myself struggling with fear and leaning on my own understanding. I searched for answers everywhere from anyone except the only One who actually had them. Finally, crushed and broken, I cried out to Jesus. And He, who was there all of the time, took me by the hand; and we began the most amazing, the most incredible, the most marvelous journey. He replaced my fear with peace and taught me to trust. He turned my sadness into joy. He revealed my Father's heart for me and showed me who I am in Him. He transformed me into a new man, birthed in His image, while simultaneously crucifying the old me. He gave me His plan for my life and purposed it into action. He changed me completely. It wasn't always easy, but He never left my side, and while I do not know what tomorrow or next week or next year will bring, I am certain of this: He will be with me wherever He leads me, and where He leads, I will follow.

October 10, 2019

In case there was any doubt, which there was not, yesterday God revealed to me once again, very clearly, that He knows exactly where I am at all times and that He is intimately aware of what I need, when I need it, and that it is Him. His presence and His favor are all that I require and the perfect gift that I long for. They are what my spirit, my heart, and my soul crave. They sustain me, they encourage me, they motivate me, and they reassure me. They fuel and restore me; they are everything to me. And while I know that God is with me always, wherever I go, sometimes it is necessary and good to receive a special encouragement or an intimate visitation from the Holy Spirit, in whatever form He chooses, to reinforce my Father's promise of His presence and His favor. I love Him with all my heart, and I know that He adores me every day. But all the same it is good to receive a divine reminder from time to time. How often and when, you ask? I will trust Him to make that decision because His timing is always perfect. My vote is for as often as possible.

October 13, 2019

It is my Father's daily purpose to reveal to me who I am to Him; to convince me that I am the same to Him as is His precious Son, Jesus, which renders me cherished by Him as well. That as a result of the Cross, not only am I entitled to the same relationship with Him as Jesus possesses, but that He desires that very thing. That such was the purpose for sending His Son. For me! My Father has created a place for me, and it is one of complete and total freedom through His Son. I am completely new. The old me is no longer. And while all of this has been and is being divinely revealed to me each and every day, some days it seems more intensely evident. Today is such a day. A day when the reality and the truth of who I am in the kingdom of God, coupled with His immense love for me, floods my spirit with joy and with peace. A time when a heartfelt desire to pass the truth of His love onto others wells up within me and reminds me of how greatly thankful I am to be afforded the opportunity to do so. Thank you, Father, for the privilege and the honor of serving as a witness to the magnitude and the truth of Your love to those who You have divinely placed in my path.

October 15, 2019

I awoke this morning with a seemingly unexplainable heaviness draped over me. In the quietness I did what the Holy Spirit has been teaching me and sat on the back porch being still, waiting and listening. Soon two things occurred. First, there came an amazing chorus of singing from what sounded like hundreds of birds. It was as if they were praising God in unison at morning's first light. It was truly incredible! Then these words flooded my spirit: "Put on the garment of praise for (instead of) the spirit of heaviness." I had heard this before; however, I wanted to find it in Scripture. I did so in the book of Isaiah:

> And provide for those who grieve in Zion—to bestow on them a crown of beauty instead of ashes, the oil of gladness instead of mourning, the garment of praise instead of despair. They will be called oaks of righteousness, a planting of the Lord, for the display of His splendor…they will receive a double portion… (Isa. 61:3)

That is me, and that is for me this morning from my Father. These lyrics from the song "The Lord Is My Salvation" (Shane and Shane) fill my mind and my spirit: "Glory be to God the Father, Glory be to God the Son, Glory be to God the Spirit, the Lord is my salvation."

This morning He has bestowed upon me a garment of praise to replace the spirit of heaviness. My heavy burden has been lifted and replaced with a heart filled desire to worship my Father with gladness and to give glory, honor, and praise to Him that is my salvation. How awesome is that!

October 17, 2019

I had a conversation recently with a man of God who is well versed in religious doctrine and the various theological factions within God's church. We discussed two in particular. It is important for me to note that each of these groups are followers of Jesus and would appear, to me at least, to espouse the belief that eternal life and salvation are to be attained through the gift of the redeeming blood of Jesus Christ. Aside from that common ground, there seems to be little agreement. It is not necessary here to detail the divergent theological ideologies but only to say that one faction's focus could be characterized as "experiential" with the other as "legalistic." The attention given here is a result of the small amount of confusion that was birthed by this discussion. Confusion that is only being addressed because of the elements of biblical truth present in each faction. This is what the Holy Spirit is saying to me in this regard. "God is not the author of confusion, but of peace..." (1 Cor. 14:33). He is love. He has given me His Spirit to guide me into all truth. I have come to know and trust His voice, and He has never failed me. So in this time when the enemy of my soul attempts to use confusion to distract my focus, I will all the more listen to and stand upon each and every word that comes from the mouth of my Father. He will reveal to me and provide me with exactly what it is that I need to fulfill His plan and His purpose for my life. How do I know this? Because He promised: "His divine power has given us everything we need for a godly life through our knowledge of Him who called us by His glory and goodness" (2 Pet. 1:3). Listen for and then follow God's voice, and when you do, any and all confusion will disappear.

October 20, 2019

> In repentance and rest is your salvation, in quietness and trust is your strength... (Isa. 30:15)

> Be still and wait patiently for Him... (Ps. 37:7)

Be still and know that I am God… (Ps. 46:10)

Listen to His voice and hold fast to Him. For the Lord is your life… (Deut. 30:20)

Let the wise listen and add to their learning… (Prov. 1:5)

My sheep listen to my voice… (John 10:27)

Yet the Lord longs to be gracious to you; He rises to show you compassion. For the Lord is a God of justice. Blessed are all who wait for Him. (Isa. 30:18)

Be still, wait, listen. It is these three directives from God, through the Holy Spirit, that are occupying my heart, my mind, and my spirit. And while it is contrary to my human nature to do so, I am discovering never-before-experienced peace in the midst of each. It is in these actions that I am learning that the presence of God dwells, and that therein is the place where He desires for me to reside. It is the place in which my soul longs to be. Today's message: be still, wait, and listen; for it is there that you will find the Lord.

October 23, 2019

There are times in this journey to which I have been called—as a matter-of-fact, most of the time—when my heart is filled with great joy and peace. There it is easy to walk out and exercise my faith and to worship and shout praise to Him to whom I owe everything and love with every fiber of my being. Then there are the other more difficult times—times such as I find myself experiencing now, times when I am under attack and my flesh attempts to rise up against me, times when I am weak as fear tries to work its way in. A year ago I would have been paralyzed. But now I am not. Have I somehow gotten stronger? The answer is a definitive yes and an absolute no.

No, I am not myself more able to ward off these fiery arrows of the enemy. But yes, I am capable of overcoming them by virtue of my knowledge of and my trust in the One who is fully able to do so. Do not be misled. This is a hard place—this place of trust and surrender, this place of instruction and development. Unlike a year ago, today I am not afraid. Armed with the great and mighty promises of my Father, I now know who I am and, more importantly, who He is to and for me. So this I declare: "I am still confident of this: I will see the goodness of the Lord in the land of the living." I will "wait for the Lord." And I will "be strong and take heart and wait for the Lord" (Ps. 27:13–14).

October 25, 2019

My thoughts turn to this place at and this time during which I come each day to be with my Father. It is such a special place, the most important place, to me. A holy place, a sacred place, a place of transformation and revelation, a quiet place, a place of favor where my Father speaks to and teaches me, guides and directs me. I am reminded of men of God who built altars in such places, so I searched and discovered that in order to live by faith, we must build an altar. To do so means that we offer everything that we are and all that we have to God. Before we would attempt anything for Him, God would say, "I want you. I want you to put all that you are and all that you have on an altar for me." Such is real fellowship with God, real worship of Him. From a human viewpoint, this would seem foolish. Some will declare us crazy and fanatical. Why would you forsake everything for someone or something that you cannot even see? If you have been called by God and have built an altar before Him, then you already know the answer to that question. Building an altar means that we realize that we are here on earth for God, that our life is for Him, and that He is our life. So we put everything on the altar. At the point in our journey where we declare, "God, everything is for You. All that I am and all that I have is Yours," that is where real consecration occurs. In a spiritual sense, it is there where we build an altar. And while at that sweet moment in time we have no idea what our declaration of surrender involves, the One to which it is made does. It is of His doing; it is His calling; it is He who proclaims, "I want you!" Therefore, it is He who begins the good work in us, and it is He that will complete it. As for my part, I have built an altar for Him, a place where I will come each day and worship Him, where I will have real fellowship with Him, where I will surrender all that I am and all that I have to Him. Praise His mighty name!

October 26, 2019

It is really early on Saturday; and I sit here in my quiet place, being still, waiting upon, and listening for God to speak to my heart. I very much am in need of His compassion this morning, so I will wait patiently, for it never fails. It is new every morning. I am bolstered by His great love for me and the assurance that He is with me always, wherever I find myself, and that His faithfulness is so very great. In my flesh, I feel somewhat discouraged, afraid, and concerned. Something is warring against my body. My lungs are uncomfortable in a way that is not normal, and they have been for several days. All the same in my spirit, this is what I hear:

> Be strong and courageous. Be not afraid, do not be discouraged, for the Lord your God will be with you wherever you go. (Josh. 1:8)

> I will turn the darkness into light before them and make the rough places smooth… I will not forsake them. (Isa. 42:16)

> The Lord is good to those whose hope is in Him… (Lam. 3:25)

> Without faith it is impossible to please God for those who come to Him must believe that He exists and that He rewards those who earnestly seek Him. (Heb. 11:6)

I have faith. It is God's gift to me, and this morning I choose to exercise it by standing upon the promises found in His Word.

October 29, 2019

Job 35:10 says, "But no one says, 'where is God my maker, who gives songs in the night...'" Oftentimes, but in particular during difficult periods, I have discovered that my Father does in fact place a song or songs in my heart as I sleep. I had not experienced this gift of assurance and encouragement until recently, and I must say that it is amazing. First, that the God of heaven would be aware of me and of my plight, and then that He would come to me in the stillness of my rest and undergird and uplift me with a song. *Wow*! And to no surprise, the song is always just what I need. Last night was no exception: "Build My Life" by Housefires and Pat Barrett.

> Holy, there is no one like You, There is none beside You; Open up my eyes in wonder and show me who You are and fill me with Your heart and lead me in Your love for those around me. And I will build my life upon your love, it is a firm foundation; And I will put my trust in You alone and I will not be shaken.

He loves me beyond measure, and I am to build my life upon that love and to trust in that love and not be shaken. That is what He wants me, and you, to hear and to know at this place in our journey. He is so good to us!

October 30, 2019

This journey of faith that my Father has called me to has changed my life. Not only have I come to understand and grasp His great love for me and who I am to Him, but I have also discovered that the learning and growing process is sometimes very hard. In the beginning of my sojourn, the difficult times overwhelmed me.

Fear was a constant companion. But with each trial, I have come to know that I am never alone. Jesus does not leave my side. If you have been reading along with me, then you are aware that recently there has been such a time for me and that, of course, there too has been His presence. I awoke this morning to a text from my beloved friend Arzie, which included Romans 15:5 ("May the God who gives endurance and encouragement give you a spirit of unity among yourselves as you follow Christ Jesus..."). A perfect Word for where I find myself from the One whose timing and wisdom is always spot on. And last night as I slept, another song, "Fear No More" by Building 429. Again, just what I needed!

> This isn't what I choose, But it's where I'm finding You, When I'm broken and undone, Your mercy's just begun, You overcome my doubt, Your hands are reaching out, You hold me through the storm, And I will fear no more...

Just a taste. The rest is every bit as amazing because He is exactly the same. Father, thank you for your endurance and for your encouragement.

November 2, 2019

To completely trust someone or something has to be one of the most challenging goals of one's journey. At least, that is the case for me. I find it easy to say the words "I trust you" but very hard to actually live out that trust. For to trust someone as our Father, His Son, and the Holy Spirit require of us means to wholly and to completely surrender to them; to hand over the reins of your life; and to not only believe but to be certain that they have got you, that they love you, and that they will not fail you. Trusting Jesus and surrendering to Him is so much more than saying "I trust you." It is living and acting out that trust. One who trusts believes with no doubt that he or she is taken care of and, out of that assurance, walks in peace, in joy, in goodness, in patience, in faithfulness, in goodness, in kindness, in gentleness, and in self-control. I strive and I long to trust my Lord in such a way each and every day.

November 3, 2019

I remember speaking with a dear friend and brother once about how hard the mornings could be when we are facing a difficult trial in our lives. You wake up, after having been afforded a brief reprieve from the struggle while you sleep, hoping that somehow the pain and heartache have passed you by, only to find them sneering directly at you as your eyes catch a glimpse of morning's first light. My friend was struggling with the prospect of having his son taken from him; and each morning, until God divinely intervened, he awakened to that harsh, paralyzing possibility. We agreed that the mornings present a parallel in that, while sometimes difficult, they also present the most blessed moments of our journey. Special, because it is then and there that our Beloved Jesus awaits. I can envision the huge smile upon His face as He lovingly waits in the quiet stillness of the first part of the day for my friend and for me and for all of His church to awaken, patiently anticipating and longing to commune with each of us. It was, and continues to be, His overwhelming love that saw my friend through such a very hard season in his journey. It is that same unmatched adoration that carries and helps each of us navigate through the issues of this life. Oh, that I would never lose sight of how greatly He adores me and that His compassions never fail; that they are new every morning; that He is faithful every day; that He will be with me always, wherever I go; and that He will not forsake me. Never forget!

November 5, 2019

It is so very important to seek God first in every moment of this journey that we are on, to be under the guidance of the Holy Spirit always. That might sound like a "duh" statement, but if we do not consciously remind ourselves to ask God for His direction and His will, then it becomes so easy to fall into the "old man" habit of leaning upon our own understanding. When we do so, we miss God's purpose for our lives and the blessings that flow there from. We cease to act as His disciples and to advance His kingdom here on earth. We no longer are glorifying and edifying He who is so completely worthy of the same. Of late, the Holy Spirit has gently reminded me of this very truth; and in my heart, I am driven to ask for forgiveness should I have, at any time, placed my will before His or put my agenda first. I am not even sure how I arrive at such a place of pursuing my increase over my Father's. In my heart of hearts, I just want Jesus and nothing else will do. Yet there I am, out on an island, advancing my own plan without seeking any guidance from the One sent to direct my every step. I am so grateful that His eye is always watching me. Thank you, Holy Spirit, for nudging me back to where I need and want to be: at His feet, serving Him only.

November 8, 2019

I have noticed of late this passion, this overwhelming desire within me, for God's Word. I have loved the Scriptures from the beginning of my journey with Jesus, but this is more. When I awake, the first thing that my heart desires is to delve into my Bible, my devotionals, and/or anything else from which God speaks. I have to confess that my prayer life has suffered somewhat as a result of this intense desire that the Holy Spirit has placed within me. I have asked why and have very clearly come to understand that it is a longing to hear from my Father that drives this passion. It is like sitting at His feet and hearing the very words come from His mouth. It produces a closeness that the spirit within me craves while at the same time teaching me, equipping me, preparing me, and sanctifying me for what lies ahead—for glorifying my Father. It is such an amazing place to be. "Sanctify them (me) by the truth Father, Your Word is truth" (John 17:17).

November 10, 2019

I arose this morning feeling ill in my body. In the past that would cause me concern and stress, but today there is a calmness and a peace about me, a feeling that can only come from one place. I sensed God's Spirit instructing me to be still and to listen; to wait upon Jesus, my Lord to come to me. Then I read the passage below, "My health may fail, and my spirit may grow weak, but God remains the strength of my heart; He is mine forever" (Ps. 73:26), and I was encouraged. For so long I have relied upon my own strength—that is, until the last year and a half when God has completely captured my heart. And now He reminds me that my reliance is no longer to be on me but on Him. With each passing day, I can say with confidence that my help comes from the Lord, that He is the "strength of my heart." Not me, not my lifestyle, not my habits, not doctors or medicines, or anything else that this world has to offer. Just Jesus and Him alone. All that is here will pass away, but He is mine forever. While I am here, He will be my refuge and my strength. His mercy and goodness will always be with me, and then afterward, I know for certain that I will dwell in His house forever.

November 12, 2019

The Holy Spirit is speaking to me as clear a message of truth as I have ever received. He is saying, "Your Father knows exactly where you are and is intimately aware of what you are going through. He sovereignly and divinely placed you there. He did so out of His great love for you in order that your faith, which is more precious than gold, can be grown and increased to the fullness that is necessary for Him to fulfill His divine purpose in your life. He knows that the journey is marked by rough and dark places, by trials and tribulations, and that it is hard at times. He wants you to know that He loves and adores you and that He is working it out for your good. His eye is never off of you. He has a great and mighty plan for your life and it will be completed to His glory." That is what the Spirit of God is saying to me this day. Know that our Father is no respecter of persons. What He gives to one He has for all His children. Therefore, receive the word of the Lord today and walk in it. It is spoken not only for me, but for all His children.

November 14, 2019

My mind is racing with so many thoughts, and I am not sure what it is that my Father desires for me to write here. Such uncertainty leads me to recall that He has never failed to impart to me exactly what He wants for me to hear. Not once has God withheld the truth that He wills to be spoken over my life, nor has He neglected to provide the message that He purposes that I share with others of His children. I have been afforded the privilege of knowing His voice and of having been taught where to most frequently find it. I have learned that most often in quietness and stillness, He comes to me. That as I wait and as I listen, when it is His great pleasure to do so, His presence envelopes me. His timing is perfect, and His purpose becomes clear. Oh, what a high privilege and a great honor it is to be in the presence of and to be led by the Most High God. Benevolences that are for all of God's children. Want to experience them for yourself? Simply find a quiet place and invite your Father, His Son Jesus, and His Holy Spirit to join you there. Then be still, wait, and listen for Him to speak to you, believing and expecting that He will. It may be through a scripture or by way of a devotion or some other Holy Spirit-led writing. Your mind may be flooded with the lyrics of a song that has touched your heart. It could come through the encouragement from or ministering of a fellow believer or even from a voice ordained from heaven. Regardless of the means by which it arrives, trust and believe that it will come. Our Father's heart is to be in relationship and in communication with His children. He created us for that reason. Avail yourself of His presence. Seek to hear His voice. I promise you that He will hear and respond to you. He wants to give you the kingdom. All you have to do is ask.

November 18, 2019

I feel the Holy Spirit speaking to my heart regarding faith. Faith is the essence of things hoped for and the evidence of things not seen (Heb. 11:1). Without faith, it is impossible to please God because those who come to Him must believe that He exists and that He rewards those who earnestly seek Him (Heb. 11:6). We are to walk by faith and not by sight (2 Cor. 5:7). It is by grace that we are saved through faith (Eph. 2:8). Faith is what we are called to, faith alone. All else our Father takes care of, everything. But faith is not always easy. The disciples walked with Jesus night and day, yet when the storm came, they were overcome with panic. When Jesus was taken, they scattered. When they were identified with Him, they denied any association whatsoever. Yet He was not angry with them. He loved them. He was patient with those that had been given to Him and taught them faith. He does the same for us, for all of His followers and disciples. He increases our faith by increasing Himself. He reminds us of who He is, of what He has done, and of how deeply He loves us. I, for one, am greatly encouraged. Driven to trust and surrender to Him and to walk in His amazing love for me. *By faith!*

November 19, 2019

God is not the author of confusion. His promises are true and certain. Uncertainty only enters into our lives when we fail to stand on and trust in the truth that He speaks over us. Confusion is a tool of Satan, one which he attempts to use in our times of weakness to redirect our focus from the love of our Father and from His promises, which are freely ours. All too often, out of fear and distrust, we take the bait and fall prey to the trap. We take our eyes off Jesus, who has overcome and defeated the enemy, and by doing so, we allow ourselves to be robbed of the joy and peace that were bought for us with a high price at Calvary. Is it any wonder that Jesus called His disciples out time and again for their lack of faith? I am sure that He is doing the same over me even today. The great news is that He did not give up on the twelve closest to Him and He will not give up on me or on you. He is the author and perfecter of my faith, and He cannot fail. He will increase my faith and rid me of any uncertainty or confusion; and by so doing, He will render me less susceptible to the already defeated schemes of the enemy, empowering me to walk in the victory that is already mine. How's that for good news?

November 20, 2019

The greatest and the most blessed gift that the children of God are given is His presence. It is the benefit that should be most precious to each of us and the one to which we should fervently and desperately aspire. It is all encompassing, all loving, all delivering, and all sustaining. It is the place where true peace resides and where joy unspeakable is found. It is an indescribable place that has no boundaries in time and space. It heals all pains and rights all wrongs. It is the very essence of love. It is a gentle place, a kind place, a patient place, a place of abundant grace and mercy, and a place from which faithfulness flows. It is a place where troubles fade away and nothing but being there matters. Most importantly, it is a place to which we are given free access. It is a place where our Father longs for us to be. Simply focus your heart, your mind, and your spirit upon Him and then ask to enter into His presence; and when you do, you will be ushered into joy unspeakable, love immeasurable, and peace like a river. Oh yeah, and you will never want to leave.

November 21, 2019

Paul wrote to the Philippians, "I can do all things through Christ who gives me strength" (Phil. 4:13). And then Jesus said,

> I am the vine; you are the branches. If a man remains in me and I in him, he will bear much fruit; apart from me you can do nothing… If you remain in me and my words remain in you, ask whatever you wish, and it will be given you. This is to my Father's glory, that you bear much fruit,

showing yourselves to be my disciples. (John 15:5–8)

I am certain this morning that what I desire in my heart is to glorify my Father, to be in His presence, to bear much fruit for His kingdom and to be His disciple. Yet I am being clearly reminded that there is no life within me, no fruit to be borne, no good thing apart from that which God imparts through His Holy Spirit. Any holy thought, devout worship, or gracious act without the sanctifying operation of the Holy Spirit avails nothing good. Forgive me, Father, when I have ventured out without your presence and outside of the guidance of your Holy Spirit. That I would attempt nothing without Him, without imploring His blessing. That I would depend on Him alone is my heart's cry (Spurgeon 1995, 652).

November 22, 2019

With each passing day, it is becoming more clear to me what it is that my Father is working and perfecting in me. Circumstances, some of which are very difficult and painful, come my way in order that my faith in and my trust and reliance upon Him will grow to be my very nature. That I will strive to see everything and to respond always in the manner in which Jesus did and, by so doing, would bring glory and honor to my Father. And that thereby I would walk in the fullness of His love. That peace, joy, patience, love, and each of the other fruits of the Spirit would define me. That my life would constantly bear witness to God's greatness and His majesty. That Christ in me would testify to others and be the hope of His glory to each of them. I am learning that I remain very much like a lump of clay on His wheel. But oh, how grateful and blessed I am that He is mindful of me. That He has chosen me to be His child, and that as such, He will never abandon me but will complete the good work that He has begun, to the glory of His name. *Amen!*

November 23, 2019

All too often it is the belief of God's children that troubles, difficulties, and sufferings are initiated to fulfill the purpose of Satan alone. The Spirit of God is showing me, through His Word, that not only is such a belief in error but that it fuels the enemy's ploy by concealing God's true purpose regarding the matter. Paul wrote, "For it has been granted unto you on behalf of Christ not only to believe in Him, but also to suffer for Him..." (Phil. 1:29). In his second letter to the church at Corinth, he again wrote, "For just as the sufferings of Christ flow over into our lives..." (2 Cor. 1:5). What Jesus suffered, He did so willingly and to fulfill the plan of His Father, not of Satan. "If we share in His sufferings..." (Rom. 8:17). Sufferings set into place by God for a divine purpose: "It was fitting that God... should make the author of their salvation perfect through suffering. Both the One who makes men holy and those who are made holy are of the same family" (Heb. 2:10–11). If God made Jesus perfect through suffering and we are of the same family, cannot we expect to receive the same? Paul further declared that "I want to know Christ... and the fellowship of sharing in His suffering..." (Phil. 3:10). And finally, he wrote to Timothy, "But join with me in suffering for the gospel, by the power of God, who has saved us and called us to a holy life--not because of anything that we have done but because of His own purpose and grace" (2 Tim. 1:8–9). Can we not agree that Satan has no part of any plan that glorifies Jesus, advances the kingdom of God, and perfects the salvation of His children? If so, then suffering is to be expected by the saints of God. Peter wrote,

> Dear friends, do not be surprised at the painful trial you are suffering, as though something strange were happening to you. But rejoice that you participate in the sufferings of Christ, so that you may be overjoyed when His glory is revealed... So then, those who suffer according to God's will should commit themselves to their

faithful Creator and continue to do good. (1 Pet. 4:12–19)

The troubles of which Peter speaks are those encountered for a divine purpose; momentary difficulties that we will never have to face alone and that we are to undergo for the advancement of our Father's kingdom; temporary hardships, the reward for which will be indescribable and eternal.

November 26, 2019

This is, in my flesh, a very hard morning. My body hurts in a lot of places. And yet in my spirit, there is peace, the kind that I cannot explain to anyone that has never experienced it. It does not come from me or from anything in this world. It originates and flows from heavenly places, from the throne of God. Just as He promised, Jesus is with me always. I am never alone because He will not leave me or forsake me. He is with me this morning, and He will keep me through this day as well as those to come. As He often does, He placed a song in my heart as I slept. It is entitled "Hindsight" by Hillsong Young & Free.

> I don't need to know what the future says; Cause if the past could talk it would tell me this: My God isn't finished yet, If He did it before He can do it again; So I will trust Him with what comes next, For the God I know is known for faithfulness, my hindsight says I can trust Him with what's next. For the God I know is known for faithfulness. There's more ahead than what's behind me; Cause through the highs and lows and in between God You go ahead of me. Where You call me I will follow. If the water folds beneath my feet, then You'll pull me from the deep.

What an amazing promise! And my Father spoke it directly over me and to me through His Spirit as I slept. How incredibly blessed I am to be His child, to be loved by and chosen by Him, to be a citizen of heaven and a member of His family.

On another front, I have been praying for someone to help lead our neighborhood Bible group. This morning, as I was writing, God heard and answered my request. A member of the group texted me to say that she would lead next week. Taken care of. (Once again, He is mindful of everything in my life!) Father, You are so very awesome—and worthy of my praise. So this morning, in the middle of the storm, I worship You, I bow down before You, and I still myself and know that You are God.

November 28, 2019

Yesterday was a difficult day in my body. I found it hard to get around as Megan, Sarah, Shane, and I are in Asheville, North Carolina. As a result of my physical struggles, my mind goes to places that may be natural to my flesh but not acceptable to my spirit. They are not so much places of fear but of settling. Settling on and maybe even accepting a result that would appear to bring me harm. Like Paul wrote in 2 Corinthians 1:9, I sense the sentence of death (bodily) around me. I need to hear from my Father. And I have. First, my brother Arzie sent me a scripture: "I know the plans I have for you, says the Lord. They are plans for good and not for disaster, to give you a future and a hope" (Jer. 29:11). Good, no disaster, hope, and a future—all promises from my Father spoken over me. That alone would be awesome enough, but our God gives exceedingly and abundantly. So as I open here and begin to write, I glance at the bottom of the page and find the exact same scripture with, of course, the identical promise. Hallelujah! He is so amazing! Just as with Paul, He will deliver me, and He will do the same for you. Just ask. What He does for one of His children, He will do for all of them.

November 30, 2019

We are back in Wilmington, and a great peace covers me as I sit with my Lord at the altar built for Him. He is moving and stirring in my heart and my mind and my spirit. It began last night as I was lying down to sleep. There He allowed me a glimpse of His mighty power and its availability to me, not through any supernatural manifestation but simply by imparting a revelation of the depth and magnitude of His greatness into my spirit and thus into my mind. He is fully aware, and He revealed to me that there is a limit to that which I can grasp at this time. Oh, how sweet it was to receive just a glimpse. Then as I slept, the enemy made a hapless attempt to distract me with past recollections—all of which have long since been covered and atoned for, thus rendering his ploy a miserable failure. This morning God led me to numerous places where He has reinforced His faithful promises spoken over my life and again allowed me a preview of His plans for me. What He is stressing is His great power and my access to it. He wants me to know that through Jesus that power is available to me and that He desires that I not only walk in it, but that I crave it and use it to fulfill my purpose of serving as a priest and a minister of His Holy covenant. Lastly, and most importantly, He reminds me of the absolute necessity of His anointing (His calling and favor) to the successful completion of His plan and purpose for my life. That without it, I will fail. Therefore, I will seek it. I will strive to never go forth without it. I long to know it intimately and pursue it earnestly and tirelessly. The good news is that it comes only from my Father; and He gives it freely, through Jesus, to each who asks (Spurgeon 1995, 669).

December 3, 2019

To my human eyes, this is an unfamiliar and, at times difficult, path that my Father is guiding me down. He is leading me in a way that I have not known. Yet in my spirit, His Spirit is revealing to me clearly that my journey has a very specific purpose. One that, while not absolutely clear, is nonetheless for His glory. Each day He speaks new truths of His great love and His all-encompassing provision over me and into my heart. He is teaching me to trust Him more completely and to walk more fully in His promises. He is changing my mindset to one of peace and joy and patience in every circumstance. Last night as I slept, He gave me another song: "I Surrender" by Hillsong Worship.

> I surrender, I surrender, I want to know You more, I want to know You more, I surrender…
> Lord have Your way, Lord have Your way in me…

Surrender is not easy, but that is what He desires, and so that will be my destination. I am certain that with His help and in His strength, I will arrive there to the glory of His mighty name.

December 4, 2019

"Grace, Grace, God's Grace; Grace that is greater than all our sin" (Johnston 1910). So often I have spoken of God's grace without fully understanding the powerful significance of it. It is God's "unmerited favor," and it is His gift to His children. Think about that. The all-knowing, all-powerful, all-encompassing, glorious God of all things chooses to grant me His favor. *Wow!* I am accepted by Him, and His approval reigns over me. I have to allow that truth to become a part of who I am, of how I see myself, and of the manner in which I present to others. Coupled with this amazing gift of grace is the privilege of righteousness, right standing, with God. How is it that I, wretched, sinful, weak me, can be in right relationship with the God of the universe? Only by way of His Son, through whom I am lifted to a place of sonship, am I given the gift of right relationship with our Father. Along with which comes all the privileges and benefits of being His child. And He is showing me more each day that these gifts of grace and righteousness, combined together, bestow upon me a power that only comes from heaven. A power to preach the Gospel, to see the sick healed, and to resist Satan. This is what my Father is speaking over me, and over you, into my life, and into yours. We have cause for great excitement (Cooke 2017, 51–58).

December 5, 2019

My Father is speaking a very significant truth into my spirit. It is one directed squarely at where He has me at this moment in time as well as to the destination to which He is leading me. While I do not see clearly where He will have me finish this particular journey, I am beginning to see what I will gain along the way: how He wills to transform and renew my mind into the likeness of His Son. The specific truth is found in the Gospel of Mark:

> If anyone would come after me, he must deny himself and take up his cross and follow me. For whoever wants to save his life, will lose it, but whoever loses his life for me and for the gospel will save it. (Mark 8:34–35)

I read this passage, and it hit me directly where I am. While I have read it before, it carried far less significance than it does at this moment in time, for as you know, I am struggling with my health and the notion of losing my life. I believe that my battle is not uncommon to man. However, in my great desire to walk out my faith and to not trust my flesh or my sight, a conflict ensues. I am certain that through this season, God is purposing to teach me and to shape me into the servant and disciple that He has ordained that I become. He calls me to follow Him, and in so doing, He lays out the costs. Unlike Satan who lures us with lies and hidden outcomes, Jesus clearly reveals the troubles and dangers that accompany serving Him. He tells us up front that we shall suffer, perhaps even die. He is not afraid that we should know the worst because the advantages that come with serving Him far outweigh the discouragements. In short, He is teaching me to not dread the loss of my life so long as it is in the midst of serving Him. To be truly willing to lose it, to venture it, to lay it down; for then and only then will I actually "save it." The reward for doing so will be certain and will include a better life. This is what He desires that I receive in my spirit and that I walk out in faith with my life.

December 8, 2019

Our God's timing is perfect, just as He Himself is without flaw. Each morning that I am led to write, He speaks a word of truth that not only teaches and encourages me, but one that arrives at just the right moment in this season of my life. This morning is no exception. The journey upon which He has me has at times been difficult. There have been rough and dark patches. I have not always understood its purpose or where it is leading me; but I have strived with all that I could muster to walk it out, by faith, trusting His promises to me and His love for me. He is showing me that His desire is that I live and walk in His outrageous love for me. Love that will serve as a catalyst for walking joyfully and peacefully through every life situation. Joy and peace that will in turn testify to and pass on His love and His presence to all whom He brings my way. My Father purposes that gladness and tranquility shall resonate from me for all to see. This life is meant to be embraced and enjoyed in a manner that will bring honor and glory and praise to the One from whom we received it. Recently, I have fallen short in this regard, but praise be to His name, He is patiently teaching me. He instructs me daily to "be joyful always; to pray continually; and to give thanks in all circumstances, for this is the will of God for you in Christ Jesus" (1 Thess. 5:16–18). I have not passed the class just yet, but hallelujah, I am learning.

December 9, 2019

It has been over two years since God began me on this journey that has led to this place where I now find myself. It is an amazing place filled with His presence and His favor, His promises and His love. It is a place that I never want to leave and one where I wish I would have arrived sooner. When it began, I had no idea where I was going or who exactly was leading me there. Early on, my Father spoke to me through four scriptures that He sent by way of my wife, Megan. He had not spoken to me through passages of scripture from her before, but He knew that I would listen, and I did. Those four passages—Joshua 1:8–9; Psalm 112:7–8; Isaiah 42:16; and Lamentations 3:21–25 (I would encourage you to read them)— have been with me and served to guide and uphold me every day since. I hear God speak truth over my life through them even now. They are specifically for me and are His constant voice to lead me on every step of my sojourn. Recently, the Holy Spirit clearly revealed to me through Isaiah 42:16 that where I am right now, as difficult as it seems, is just where I am purposed to be and that my Father has led and guided me here. Such revelation frees me and gives me great peace. It honors and humbles me. He knows exactly where I am because He brought me here. *Wow!* I love Him so!

December 10, 2019

Each and every day our Father is revealing His purpose to create a new identity in each of His children. We are His workmanship created in Christ Jesus (Eph. 2:10). He loves watching as we discover what He has already prepared for us to walk in as part of this new identity. He is constantly at work, giving us the desire and the power to fulfill His good purpose, a large portion of which is that we abound in the joy of His magnificent presence. He longs for us to be cheerful, energetic, and full of life in His Son; and He provides everything necessary for us to accomplish the same by and through the power of His incredible Holy Spirit. As we lean on and focus upon the gift of His presence, we grow to a place of counting all our circumstances as joyful, even when they are difficult. Thus, His command to be joyful always, to pray continually, and to give thanks in all circumstances becomes attainable. By rejoicing in and giving thanks for God's plan for our lives, we are able to receive that which He has designed for us to have. We must live in His cheerfulness over us and, in return, reflect the same to the world around us. It is His will that we do so (Cooke 2017, 63–72).

December 11, 2019

I am being reminded this morning by the Holy Spirit of exactly who I am. Yes, I am Jeff Cropper, son of Bill and Shirley; brother of Bill, Tamara, and Vicki; loving husband of an amazing wife, Megan; father of four incredible children, Daniel, Hannah, Shane, and Sarah; friend to many awesome people; retired attorney; volunteer; leader; and disciple. And while each of those are rewarding and important, they do not define who I truly am. If they were all stripped away, what and who would I be? Prior to three years ago, I could not have answered that question without hesitation or doubt. Today my response is both clear and certain. Jeff Cropper is a child of God, and he is who his Father says that he is. Therefore, he is blessed, he is holy, he is blameless, he is redeemed, he is forgiven, he is chosen, he is included in Christ, he is marked with a seal, the Holy Spirit, he is alive in Christ, he is raised up with Jesus and seated with Him, he is saved, he is His workmanship, he is near to God, he is a citizen of heaven and a member of God's household, He is His, and he is adored (Eph. 1 and 2). He is who his Father says that he is, and he will not be defined in any other way. Glory to God!

December 12, 2019

Today God is showing me and reminding me of three particular people that He has divinely placed in my life and of how faith was necessary to receive the gift that each of them represents to me. First, there is my wife, Megan. She is my rock, my closest confidant. She loves me greatly and without condition. God brings me His peace through her, and I would be lost without her. Yet not that long ago, I attempted to walk away from her. Praise God, He would not allow that to happen, and by His will and by faith, she remains with and for me. Next, there is my brother, Kim, a powerful, Spirit-filled man of God who was brought into my life to speak truth over me and to remind me that my Father has a plan for my life. Kim has a straightforward and bold personality, a direct and intentional approach to serving Jesus that, in my flesh, caused hesitation in opening up to him. God revealed the purity of Kim's heart for Jesus to me, and by faith, I am receiving the huge blessing of having him in my life. Lastly, there is my mentor Brett, who God has placed in my life to teach and encourage me. Yet, when I first met Brett, I found it difficult to relate to him and to get to know him. That quickly changed. God had a plan and a purpose for Brett in my life and for me in his, and so by faith, I waited, and now my Father is richly blessing me by and through him. Three amazing children of God sent to be His hand in my life. All of whom I, at times, misunderstood in my flesh; but who, by faith, I have now discovered are serving as vessels of the richness of God's grace and mercy over me. Our Father is reminding us to be slow to dismiss those who enter into our lives for they may well be sent by Him.

December 13, 2019

The Holy Spirit has been flooding my mind, my heart, and my spirit with the concept of faith for the last twelve hours. First, He reminded me of exactly what faith is. It is "being sure of what we hope for and certain of what we do not see" (Heb. 11:1). I am sure that I hope to glorify my Father by serving Him, by pointing people to His Son, and by making disciples of those who choose to follow Him. In addition, although I cannot see how He will allow me to do so, I am nonetheless certain that He has called me to do those very things. I am also certain that He adores me and that He equips those whom He calls. And I know that in all things He works for the good of those who love Him and are called according to His purpose. I truly love Him and am certain that He has called me. He has also reiterated to me that without faith, it is impossible to please Him because those who come to Him must believe that He exists and that He rewards those who earnestly seek Him (Heb. 11:6). He absolutely exists. and He knows that my heart is His. Finally, He led me to Matthew 9:29. where we learn that Jesus is encountered by two blind men who ask to be healed. Jesus asks them if they believe that He is able, to which they respond yes; and then He grants their request, saying, "According to your faith will it be done to you." Clearly, the

Holy Spirit is teaching me the role and the significance of faith in the completion of His calling upon my life. Help me, Lord, to not only hear but to believe and have faith in the words that You are speaking into and over me.

December 15, 2019

There are many things of which I am certain. I know that I am a chosen, blessed, forgiven, redeemed, adored child of the Most High God. And that as a result, I am a co-heir with Jesus to all that is His. That I am entitled to everything good, all that He has bestowed upon His precious Son. That His promises are real and true, and they are mine, spoken over me. All of them. I also know that I have been called to follow Jesus, and that in order to do so, I must deny myself and take up my cross. Taking up my cross is not easy, it entails losing my life for Him and for the Gospel. It leads me to unfamiliar places, venues that are rough and dark. Locations, however, at which I will never be alone. These are places to which He has gone before me and conquered, places where He then calls me to follow Him, places where His purposes for me will be fulfilled and completed, places where His kingdom will be advanced and He will be glorified, and, lastly, places of freedom for me. Liberation from sin and death simply because He is there and because where He is, there is joy and peace and love. That is where He leads me so that is where I will follow. That is where I long to be. Of all of these truths, I am certain. Thank you, Father, for convincing me of each one.

December 16, 2019

God, through His Holy Spirit, is moving mightily in the spiritual realm on my behalf. How do I know that? Because I can feel and sense it and because He is affording me a small glimpse of it in my spirit. That which is happening there, the battle that is being fought, is so much bigger and greater than I could ever imagine or withstand. Battalions of heavenly hosts are warring with Satan's minions over spiritual territory that my Father has for me. The small portions that

He has allowed me to see are mind-blowing and bring great excitement to my spirit. What incredible love my Lord and my God has for me that He would exhaust the forces of heaven to fight my battle and to equip me to complete the calling that He has placed upon my life. Before I even knew that I was in harm's way, He went to win my war. His love became my greatest defense. It leads me from the dry wilderness. It protects and keeps me. And all I have to do is praise, all I have to do is worship, all I have to do is bow down, all I have to do is stay still. He is my Great Defender, and I am certain that the battle is His and that the victory is mine. Shout *hallelujah*! (Battistelli 2018).

December 17, 2019

All too many times, I allow myself to be caught up in and distracted by the things of this life and of this world, whether good or bad. As a result, I neglect the true desire of my heart and of the Spirit that is within me, which is to give glory and honor and praise to the Savior of my soul, to bow down before and to worship the only One who is truly worthy; to give thanks to the precious Lamb who laid down His life for me; to exalt the King of kings who sits on the throne at the right hand of our Father and makes intercession for me continuously; to glorify Him that is my Way Maker, my Miracle Worker, my Promise Keeper and my Light in the darkness; to earnestly thank Him for adoring me, for standing in my place, for making a way for me, for never leaving me, and for pursuing and rescuing me. Forgive me, Lord, for neglecting to give back to You what You so richly deserve: my praise, my worship, and my adoration. Every day it is in my heart. May it also be on my lips.

December 18, 2019

We live in a fast-paced, ever-moving, noisy world. So when our Father instructs us to be still, to wait, and to listen, it is directly contrary to our normal; and it is difficult. Yet He desires and demands our complete and full attention if we are to receive the full richness of His presence, His favor, and His love. He has spoken great and mighty promises over His children, assurances that we will have difficulty receiving or grasping amidst the clamor and the noise of life in the carnal world. However, in the peace and stillness of His presence, we are free and open to not only hear, but to receive the full blessing of each and every one of His promises spoken over and granted to us. It has not always been easy to be still and to wait and then at that place to listen for His voice, but with His help I am doing so. And I am finding that in that place, I am discovering peace and joy unspeakable along with guidance, direction, assurance, and great love. There I am finding Him, and that is what I truly desire, what I truly need.

December 19, 2019

It was brought to my mind this morning that David begins and ends each of the last five psalms with these words, "Praise the Lord." Then I thought of how often those words are found upon the lips of we who believe. (Which is a good thing!) But do we understand? Do we really grasp who it is that we are praising, and why it is that we are doing so? No other persons or beings other than our Father, His Son, and His blessed Spirit are truly worthy of our praise. We do so because we were created by Him, and we are sustained by Them. Jesus gave His life for us, willingly, at the direction of our Father because They adore us and desire that we be with Them. We praise Him because He is worthy but also because that is where He dwells. He inhabits the praises of His people. His presence is everything to us and all that we will ever need. We experience Him when we lift up our voices in praise. I praise Him because I love Him and because He loves me. I worship His name because He is truly worthy of the same and because I was created to do so. I bow down before Him because He is my Lord, just as He was David's Lord. And so, along with him who slew Goliath and who was filled with a heart of praise for his Lord, I declare, "Praise the Lord!"

December 21, 2019

As I arrive at this place where I meet with my Father each morning and sit in the assurance of His peaceful presence, I am led and guided by His Spirit to write these words of gratitude that have been revealed to me by way of David's declarations found in Psalm 33 and Psalm 34. They so accurately proclaim and convey what has been placed in my heart today and every day. I invite you to make them your earnest and heartfelt prayer along with me.

Thank you, Father:
That Your Word is right and true.
That what You say You will do.
That we can stand upon Your promises.
That You are faithful every day.
That Your love for us and Your compassion over
us are unlimited and never fail.
That You are always watching over us.
That You protect and deliver us, You help and
strengthen us.
We praise You Lord and we exalt Your Name.
Your Name is great and mighty and filled with
power.
Power to save, power to heal, power to deliver
and power to sustain.
Power to carry us to You.
Thank You that You hear us when we call on You
and that You answer us. Not because
You have to but because You desire and long to.
That You deliver us from our fears and save us
from our troubles.
That You direct Your angels to encamp around
us.
That You withhold no good thing from Your
children.

That when our hearts are broken and when our
spirits are crushed You draw even closer to
comfort and restore us.

You are such a good, good God. You are the best
Father and so today and every day we thank
You; we praise You; we worship and adore
You; we bow down before You and glorify
Your Holy Name! We surrender our lives to
You!

Amen!

December 23, 2019

During the earlier days of my walk with Jesus, I was intimidated and a bit fearful of the movement and the work of the Holy
Spirit. I now know that those emotions were the product of my lack
of knowledge of God's Word and of my thin understanding of the
benefits and privileges that are mine as His child. For three years
now, my Father has taken me on a journey filled with His presence
during which He has revealed His amazing love for me along with
the promises that flow therefrom. Probably most significant among
those assurances is that of His Holy Spirit. I have learned that God's
Spirit is love and peace and joy and patience and goodness and
kindness and gentleness and faithfulness and self-control; and that,
most importantly, it is not to be feared or to be avoided. With His
Spirit comes freedom and power—freedom to serve and worship my
Father; freedom to call upon His name; freedom to trust and surrender to Him; and power to save, power to heal, power to deliver, and
power to overcome evil. The Holy Spirit is God's gift to His children
and therefore to me. It is the gift of Himself intended for me to walk
in and for me to access as I journey toward fulfilling His plan and
His purpose for my life! So I say, "Come, Holy Spirit, come! Please
come into my life!"

December 24, 2019

"Peace I leave with you, my peace I give you. I do not give to you as the world gives. Do not let your hearts be troubled and do not be afraid" (John 14:27). These words, spoken by Jesus to His disciples, are being spoken to me, and to you, this morning. As I read them, I strive to be still and to listen for all of that which He desires for me to hear. First, He gives me His peace, which is different from what the world has to offer. It passes my human understanding and can only be grasped and received in my spirit. It is all-encompassing and casts away trouble, despair, anxiety, and fear. These are the very words of my Lord, and they deliver the promise of my Father spoken over me. Hallelujah! But wait, He isn't finished. Next, the Spirit leads me to John 15, where He commands:

> Remain in me, and I will remain in you. No branch can bear fruit by itself; it must remain in the vine…apart from me you can do nothing. This is to my Father's glory, that you bear much fruit, showing yourselves to be my disciples. (John 15:4–5)

I can do all things through Jesus who strengthens me, but apart from Him, I can do nothing. I have to be always conscious and aware of this truth. Holy Spirit, please remind me daily. And Jesus is still not finished speaking to me. He continues by instructing this: "Now remain in my love" (John 15:9). Lord, You know that I love You with all that is in me, what is it that You are saying? "If you obey my commands, you will remain in my love, just as I have obeyed my Father's commands and remain in His love" (John 15:10). Our Father has many commands, but Jesus narrows them to one for us a verse later. "My command is this: Love each other as I have loved you. Greater love has no one than this, that he lay down his life for his friends" (John 15:12–13). So Jesus wants me to remain in His love, and to do so, He is telling me to obey His commands—more specifically, to obey one command, which is to love one another as He loves us.

79

Love that led Him to lay down His life for me, His friend. So I get it! He wants me to lay down my life for my friends, to put them and their needs before myself and my own, and that by doing so, I will remain in Him. And there is something else. He wants me to know this, first, so that His joy will be in me and that my joy will be complete (John 15:11) and, second, so that whatever I ask in His name will be granted unto me by my Father. *Wow!* Messages of peace, abiding, sacrifice, and love—all in one morning. What an amazing Word from my Lord and my God!

December 25, 2019

It is Christmas morning, and for several days now, the Holy Spirit has been impressing this truth upon my heart and into my mind: at the moment of His birth, from the very second that He took His first breath, Jesus was "Immanuel." That small baby was fully God and completely Messiah. He was totally filled with majesty and splendor, with power and authority, directly from the throne of God. He did not have to grow into His position. He did not have to earn His authority, nor was it necessary that He learn how to access the privileges available to Him. He was Immanuel, He was God, and He had been since the beginning of time. And now He had come to be with us for the very specific purpose of saving us. The animals, the shepherds, and the wise men bowed down before this baby because it had been revealed to them that they were in the presence of the Messiah sent from heaven. The King of all kings and God Himself was with them. He always was God, and He will forever be God, and that is why this and every day I too will bow down before Him. Have a blessed Christmas!

December 26, 2019

My complete attention has been drawn of late to Paul's words found in Philippians 3:10 and 11: "I want to know Christ…" Not just to recognize Him or to know what He did or to spend time with Him and His disciples—all of which are necessary and amazing—but in addition, to know all that He is, every single beautiful, life-giving element of who He is.

"And the power of His resurrection…" To know, experientially, here and now, the degree of power that was imparted to raise Jesus from the dead. Power for now, not for when we die and go to be with Him. Evidencing, justifying, consoling and comforting, life-giving power. Resurrection life power.

"And the fellowship of sharing in His sufferings…" Sharing in fellowship with Jesus absent any suffering is beyond-description amazing. But being afforded the honor and the privilege of sharing with Him in His suffering affords a degree of fellowship that is indescribable and prepares us for a level of relationship, service, and discipleship that Paul knew was life changing and that he longed for. So do I. And I am certain that I am being called to this place for a purpose, for His glory.

"Becoming like Him in His death…" Not that I would die as He did, although maybe that will be the case. That is for Him to determine, not me. But that I would become like Him in such obedience, in such forgiveness, and in such love. Completely and fully trusting in my Father, surrendered to His will with His glory, and the love of His children being my sole motivation.

"And so, somehow to attain to the resurrection from the dead." Paul was not doubting his salvation or his eternal destination. He was, however, longing greatly for the completion of his journey, yearning to be with His Lord. That is where my Father desires for me to be, and to live, and it has therefore been placed in my heart, just as it was Paul's, to attain. I am *so greatly blessed*! (Guzik 2015; Phil. 3)

December 28, 2019

Jesus and I are one! I am in Him and more importantly He is in me. "Christ in me the hope of Glory" (Col. 1:27). By faith, I receive the reality and the truth of this covenant relationship that was birthed in the throne room of heaven and then graciously gifted unto me. "The life I live in the body, I live by faith in the Son of God" (Gal. 2:20). The life spoken of here is the life that grace conferred upon me at the moment of my new birth and is unmistakably the life of my Lord, Jesus Christ. This union is all-sustaining and fully sufficient and is freely and lovingly mine by faith. The same faith by which I grasp Jesus with a firm and determined grip and with the heartfelt intention of never letting Him go. And He, filled with delight, never ceases to strengthen and sustain me with His loving embrace and all-sufficient support. It is a place where He and I bask in love and joy unspeakable. A place of sublime spiritual fellowship that affords my heart and my spirit the privilege of residing as near to heaven as they are able here on earth. Blessed am I to be one with Jesus. Greatly blessed! (Spurgeon 1995, 726).

December 29, 2019

Yesterday, during a conversation with several men of God, one of them made this statement that immediately found agreement with the Spirit within me: "Identity changes everything." For months, maybe years, God has been walking out this truth in my life without me being able to describe what was happening. Then yesterday, the Holy Spirit did so for me. For two years, the revelation of my God-declared identity, of who I am in Christ, of who my Father says I am, has radically changed my life. For some reason, I believe mostly of my own doing, I did not grasp my God-spoken identity during the first thirty-two years of my walk with Jesus. Because of that, I struggled and floundered and was unproductive in my relationship with my Father. Then, upon receiving this revelation of truth, my relationship with Jesus was so changed that it caused me to question whether I was ever actually saved prior to receiving it. I am convinced, by faith, that I was in fact a child of God; but I now know that without this identity revelation, I was missing out completely on the fullness of God's promises, His presence, and His favor in and over my life. Receiving the gift of full knowledge of who God says that I am has radically changed my spiritual perspective. I no longer view myself through human eyes, including my own, but through my Father's. I am not the sin-filled, self-obsessed, unproductive, fearful, angry person that the world wants me to be. What I am is holy, blessed, blameless, forgiven, Holy Spirit filled, redeemed, saved, an adored child of God, and a greatly loved citizen of heaven. I am near to God because I am His. I am raised up with Jesus and seated with Him; and as such, I am granted each and every honor, benefit, and privilege afforded unto Him. Hallelujah! While this knowledge has given me so very much (peace, joy, love, trust, boldness, and a heart to serve), maybe the most significant gift is the desire and the passion to impart it to others, who like the old me, are living unaware of their true identity. Father, allow me the opportunity to pass the gift of this revelation on to those that You are pleased to bring my way.

December 31, 2019

The year 2019 comes to an end today, and as such I was led to contemplate what the last 365 days have revealed to me. Almost immediately, it was brought to my mind that I have found real hope and true identity in Jesus and the immense need for each in our lives. I would be less than honest if I said that during this last year, I was not confronted with many negatives. I was. Many of which involved my health, some of which persist. Enter hope. Hope from heaven. Hope in the form of God's presence, God's favor and His promises. Hope in the knowledge and the assurance that He adores me, that He is always with me, and that my sufficiency is in His hands. Hope in the certainty that He has never failed me and never will. Hope in knowing that He works all things together for my good. That every negative is designed to upgrade me, to conform me more to His image, and to allow His nature to rise up in me. So I thank you, Father, for 2019 and all that it introduced into my life because through it, I have discovered hope and identity in Your Son, Jesus.

January 2, 2020

My attention this morning is being drawn to the subject of prayer. Prayer in its simplest sense is communicating with God. It is a means by which He can hear from and speak to His children. We were created to be in relationship with our Father. Relationship requires interaction, a primary tool for which is prayer. Through Adam, sin entered the world and, because God cannot be in the presence of darkness, inhibited our interaction with Him. Through atonement, sin is cancelled and relationship restored. Until Jesus arrived, that atonement came by way of the blood sacrifices of animals. At Calvary, our Lord sacrificed His life and shed His blood one time for all sin, thus completely removing the sin barrier that separated us from God and restoring His relationship with His children. In essence, Jesus reopened the lines of communication between heaven and earth and instilled in each of us the freedom to approach our Father with confidence through prayer. As a result of our Lord's work on the cross, we can be assured that not only does God hear us when we reach out to Him but that He answers us as well. He even knows what we want before we want or ask for it. Knowing this, I sometimes am confronted with the notion that if God knows my requests before I present them to Him, then why is it necessary to do so? Immediately, the Spirit prompts me with this answer: Do you love your children? Do you often know what they need without the necessity of them asking? Do you not long to hear from and commune with them nonetheless? Your heavenly Father is no different. In addition, our prayers are not purposed solely for communication. They also establish and foster relationship, which builds faith, trust, and surrender. All of which are necessary to both please God and to help us to grow in our effective service of Him. Prayer is also a means by which to praise and worship our Father. He inhabits the praises of His people. Want to experience the presence of God? Then communicate with Him, interact with and be in relationship with your Father. Pray in all manner. It is what you were created to do. He is waiting patiently to hear from you. And should you find yourself at a loss for what to pray, then simply ask the Holy Spirit to help you. He always knows exactly what to say.

January 3, 2020

Jesus Christ is the sum and substance of the New Covenant entered into between God and His people, and as such, He belongs to each and every one of us who believe. In Him, all the fullness of the Deity lived in bodily form and now lives forever in God's kingdom. All that Jesus, as God or man, ever had or can have is ours, out of pure, free love and kindness, to be our inheritance forever. Each and every one of His magnificent and glorious attributes have been bequeathed to us by our Father. Jesus is all-powerful, and that power is yours to support and strengthen you, to overcome your enemies, and to preserve you. Jesus is love to its maximum degree, and every drop of that love is poured out on you. He is justice, and as such, He will see to it that every last thing to which you were promised will be secured for you. He is accepted by the Father, who delights in Him, and His acceptance is ours as well. God's delight in His Son belongs equally to each of us. Lastly, that perfect righteousness that our Lord worked out at Calvary is ours, assigned to us. All that He did was for us and all that He has is ours. That is who we are and how our Father views us. Receive and walk accordingly (Spurgeon 1995, 6).

January 4, 2020

Three years ago this month, God began a new thing in my life. I had no idea what lay ahead, but I did have a sense that it was real and that He was in the center of it. I have come to realize that Jesus was rescuing me from myself, from the world that had captured my heart and from the enemy who was destroying me. He was leading me on a journey of truth; of identity; of restoration, sanctification, and preparation. He was preparing me to serve Him and to fulfill His purpose established long ago for me, and He did and continues to do so by simply revealing who He is to me and who I am to Him. From that place, all truth follows. I have also come to realize that every step along this sojourn has had a very specific purpose and has been ordained by Him. As such, I am thankful for each, whether difficult or easy. Each person whom I have encountered was brought by Him with the assignment of fulfilling His purpose over me. Along the way, I was being restored to right relationship with my Father and being set apart and consecrated for His service. It is certain that who He calls, He equips. That He provides everything that we need to bring glory and honor and praise to Him, to His Son, and to the kingdom that He has established. I am a living, breathing testimony of the greatness of His love and goodness. You are, or you can be, as well.

January 6, 2020

Today I find myself in day nine of a sickness that has incapacitated me and that is beginning to wear on my mind and my spirit. It would seem that since moving to North Carolina two years ago, I have struggled greatly with my health and attacks on my body. Just when one malady subsides, another rises up. At first, I questioned the reason for this trend inasmuch as I have rarely battled with sickness up to this point in my life. Had I done something to offend God? Were these consequences for years of turning a blind eye to Him? Was He instructing me? Or was it just as Megan surmised that the years were catching up with me? Whatever the reason, my health conditions were coming at the exact same time that God was rescuing me, capturing my heart, and restoring my relationship with Him. I love Him passionately, and I am certain that He likewise adores me. While I am yet uncertain of His plan and His purpose for the remainder of my life, I know for sure that He has me squarely in the palm of His hand, that He knows exactly where I am and what it is that I am going through. That He cares greatly for me, and He is compassionate over me each and every day. That His hand of providence will yet heal my every wound. I trust Him with my soul, and I can do the same with my body. He is at work in me to His glory, to His honor, and to His praise. Be still and be patient, my soul and my body. Victory is on the horizon, and it is ours.

January 8, 2020

How great is the love that the Father has bestowed upon us that we can be called His sons and daughters. The adoration that our God has for us is indescribable, and the revelation and acceptance thereof is the key to the realization of our identity and the foundation of our hope. Praise be to His name for He has done great things for me. He has placed my feet upon a solid rock. He withholds no good thing from me. And yet beware, oh my soul, that His great goodness does not become unappreciated. That I do not take this amazing gift for granted, and most importantly, that I do not allow the presence of it to cultivate pride and self-aggrandizement within me. That I would never lose sight of the truth that every good and perfect gift comes from Him and is given to me for His glory and not for my own. Never forget the deep, dark hole of sin and despair that my own auspices led me to, nor the depths of His mercy, grace, and love that pursued me there and rescued me. Holy Spirit, please make me aware of any pride that attempts to rise up within me and give me the courage and the strength to smack it down if and when it does. Never cease to remind me that "He must increase; I must decrease." Father, that I could be the least of Your servants that You would be glorified.

January 9, 2020

Our Father's desire, His intention, His plan, and His purpose is that each of His children would view their existence through an eternal, heavenly lens. That they would no longer think with a mind concentrated upon the flesh but, instead, reason from above, focused on the Spirit; and that by doing so, they would develop a mindset that connects with all that He is for us. God's majesty is far greater than our humanity, and the new person created within each of us in Christ Jesus has direct access to all that splendor. Every benefit, every privilege, every gift, and every promise that God has bestowed upon His Son is likewise ours through the gift of the cross. What He longs for is that we receive this truth and then live our lives according to it. That we would no longer readily accept fear, doubt, anxiety, and stress as the world dictates; but that practicing and abiding in our Father and His unconditional, ever-present love would become our new normal. That we would embrace each of our life situations, regardless of how they present themselves, as a means by which we may increase in the knowledge of who we truly are and of what that means eternally. That we may develop a heightened awareness of our God declared identity along with the all-sufficient privileges and benefits that are freely ours as a result thereof. That we would be transformed as our kingdom mindset develops (Cooke 2017, 93–102).

January 11, 2020

In years gone by, I observed so many references to John 3:16 on placards at sporting events and elsewhere that I became almost oblivious to its message. Since that time, I have come to understand that it was seemingly everywhere for good reason. Its message forms the very basis of our faith. "For God so loved the world that He gave His only Son that whoever shall believe in Him shall not perish, but shall have eternal life." It is the bedrock of our hope. It is the foundation of our peace. It is the truth of God's great love for His children and the pathway to eternal life with Him. It is of the utmost importance and never to be neglected or forgotten. The same can be said for the Twenty-third Psalm. It seems as though every open Bible in many churches as well as those found on a coffee or end table in a faithful relative's home is turned to this passage of scripture. Yet for that very reason, I, and I can only assume many others, give it nothing more than a passing glance with no meaningful comprehension of the life-changing truth spoken therein. As I have been led by the Holy Spirit on a deeper, more Christ-centered journey, He has shown me the richness of the assurances and the promises written by David in a cave so long ago, and of their impact still today.

"The Lord is my shepherd, I shall not want..." A shepherd guides, leads, and takes great care of his sheep. He provides for their every need. They want for nothing. This is exactly what our Lord promises for us.

"He makes me to lie down in green pastures, He leads me beside still waters..." This depicts the most peaceful of surroundings with no anxiety, no stress, and no strife or turmoil. This is what God provided for David and what He will do for us, His children.

"He restores my soul..." We all like sheep have gone astray, and we need to be restored to right relationship with our Father. God does that for us through Jesus and by the Holy Spirit.

"He guides me in paths of righteousness for His name's sake…" Our Father leads us down paths and in ways that reflect right relationship and right standing with Him. He does so that we might be a living testimony and witness to His goodness and mercy and that He should receive glory, honor, and praise. That His kingdom, and not ours, will be advanced.

"Even though I walk through the valley of the shadow of death, I will fear no evil for You are with me, Your rod and Your staff they comfort me…" A valley is not depicted as a pleasant place; and David speaks of one where death, a scary concept, dwells. He may be alluding to real, actual death or just the thought of it. In either case, I believe it to appear real to the child of God who is walking through it. God, through His servant David, chooses to refer to the shadow of death as opposed to death itself. Why is that? I believe it is because we have no reason to fear shadows. They cannot harm us. Our Lord will not allow actual death and its darkness to touch us, only its shadow. Therefore, we shall not fear. But there is more reason for our encouragement. He is with us throughout the entire journey, with His rod and His staff comforting us. David was experiencing this presence and its accompanying comfort at the most difficult of times, a time when he felt the sentence of death upon him. Both the feeling of death and the comforting of God were real to him, but he had come to understand that the comfort had power over the affliction. We too have access to the benefits that David experienced.

"You prepare a table for me in the presence of my enemies…" David and His Lord were in the midst of a battle with much at stake; and right there in the center of the struggle, in clear view of David's enemies, God chose to bless him with a table of good things. And not only that, but He chose to sit and commune with him there. To do so right before those whose purpose it was to do him harm, to show David that He had power over everything that plotted his demise and that He loved him enough to take time to sit with David at this critical time in his life. David was very important to God, and so are we!

"You anoint my head with oil; my cup overflows…" Anointing with oil was a sign of blessing and of healing. David felt the blessing of God as well as His healing hand upon him. Our Father offers the same to us today. If we fill our cup with our own righteousness, little will be found there. For it to run over, only God could have filled it. God did so for David; He will do so for us.

"Surely goodness and mercy will follow me all the days of my life…" God was David's shepherd, out in front of him to lead his way, and now he describes a double blessing of goodness and mercy following behind him, loving and caring for him. This is amazing and beautiful! Picture the same for you, all the days of your life!

"And I will dwell in the house of the Lord forever." David concludes with the realization that everything that he was experiencing was God's gift to him, not only at that moment but forever. He was encountering the rapturous joy of knowing, not only that his Lord loved him enough to see him through this difficult time in his life but that He wanted David to live with Him in His house, *forever*! And at the risk of being redundant, He wants the exact same thing for you and for me. There is a reason why so many of those Bibles in homes and in churches are open to the book of Psalms. It is because the message that is written there from God to His children, through David, is one of the most significant ones ever sent. It is one of love and adoration, one of peace, one of great hope, one of assurance, and one of identity, not only for David but for each and every one of us. Thanks be to God our Father!

January 13, 2020

Recently, my mind has been filled with the concept of abiding—abiding in Jesus and in His love, in His presence, and His favor; to take up residence in Him and to constantly remain there. Abide is biblically defined as to rest or dwell, to continue permanently, to be firm and immovable, to remain or to continue, to wait for, to endure or sustain patiently. Digging deeper, I learned that abiding contains three interwoven aspects. First, connection, having a life-giving union with Jesus. This aspect is mutual in nature. We abide in Him and He in us. Without this connection, there is no life, no fruit. The second aspect of abiding is dependence, which is not reciprocal. The branch (us) is dependent on the vine but not vice versa. Without the vine, the branch is useless, powerless, lifeless. We are completely dependent upon Jesus for everything that counts as spiritual fruit. Apart from Him, we can do nothing. The final aspect of abiding is continuance. Abide actually means to remain or to stay or continue. We are not only to connect with Jesus and to depend upon Him, but to go on trusting, depending, and believing in Him; to continue to persevere in Jesus and His teachings. So to abide in Jesus is to be united, to rely, and to remain in Him. In John chapter 15, Jesus speaks to the vine and the branches and specifically states that we are to abide in Him and He will abide in us. That absent such abiding, we can bear no fruit. That we are to abide in His love, the result of which will be complete joy and free access to His grace and mercy. So how exactly do we abide? What it does not require is advancement beyond the gospel to some mystical experience. It simply means keeping the words of Jesus in our hearts and minds so that they are renewing and reviving us, shaping and sanctifying us, filling and forming us. It means keeping ourselves in His infinite, enduring, sin-bearing, heart-filling, life-giving love. That is what it means to abide, and that is what we are called to do—to abide in Jesus (Hedges 2014).

January 15, 2020

Jesus and His disciples, along with a large crowd, were walking out of the city of Jericho when they passed a blind man sitting by the side of the road begging. His name was Bartimaeus. It was about to become a life changing-day for Bartimaeus, although up until that moment it seemed no different from any other. I am certain that he had sat there countless times before, but on none of those occasions had the Son of God passed his way. I wondered how this man with no sight even knew who it was that he was divinely encountering. Then I read that he heard that it was Jesus. Who did he hear from? We do not know, but we can be certain that the God of heaven wanted Bartimaeus to know who was passing his way and that He had purposed this moment in order that He would be glorified. We can wake up each day either thinking that it will be the same as all the others, or we can arise and proceed with the hope and the expectation that God will divinely choose to interact with us and touch our lives in the precise manner necessary, right where we are. Bartimaeus was expectant and intentional. How do we know this? Because he immediately cried out to Jesus. And why did he do so? Because he knew who Jesus was and believed in His compassion and His love. So much so that when others without such faith or knowledge rebuked him, he shouted all the louder. Many will make every effort to quiet you and to discourage your faith. Do not listen to them. Instead, hear the still, small voice of the One who adores you and desires an encounter with you. Jesus loves you and has compassion for you, just as He did Bartimaeus. He will ask you, "What do you want Me to do for you?" When He does, be certain that you are ready, like Bartimaeus, to say, "Rabbi, I want _____." Then trust that His response will be, "Go, your faith has healed you." Do you doubt that your faith is strong enough? Don't! Bartimaeus simply showed up and cried out; and that degree of faith, combined with the love and power of Jesus, was more than enough to meet his need. Your Lord is ready, willing, and able to meet your needs as well. Just cry out to Him and believe. When He does, do not neglect to respond as Bartimaeus did. He immediately followed Jesus, and so must we.

January 16, 2020

Are you in need of help this morning? If so, you are not alone. Each of us, left to rely on our own strength, will fall woefully short of the goal. But be encouraged for God promises: "I myself will help you declares the Lord" (Isa. 41:14). It is a small thing (to Him) for your Father to help you. Just consider what He has done for you already. He sent His Son to die for you and bought you with His blood. Before the world was spoken into being, He chose you. He made a covenant with you by laying aside His glory and becoming as you. He provided you with a Helper to guide you and teach you and to reveal the riches of Himself and His promises to you. He endowed you with an identity and with the privileges and honors that accompany being His child. So if He has done all this, then surely, He will help you now. If you were in need of a thousand times more help, He would be able, and He would give it to you. It is much for us to need but nothing for Him to give. Bring your empty pitcher to your God. His river is full for your supply, and He longs to fill it for you. He is your Helper both now and forevermore (Spurgeon 1995, 32).

January 17, 2020

At the time when a lost sinner is drawn by the Holy Spirit to call upon the name of Jesus to rescue them and save their soul, he or she is made keenly aware of two realities. First, that they are lost and destined for eternal separation from God, and second, that He has provided a reprieve from this death sentence by way of the crucifixion and resurrection of His Son Jesus. At that moment in time, such revelations are more than sufficient to draw us into a relationship with Him and launch us on our journey to eternal fellowship and residence with our Father. Nothing more is required for our salvation. However, God, because of His great love, desires so much more for us. He wants us to be captured by His immeasurable love. He wants us to embrace our true identity as He declares it, and He wants us to receive the benefits and the privileges that flow to us therefrom. He desires that we not just know who Jesus was in human form, but that we intimately know who He is as God. That we know all of Him along with the power of His resurrection and the fellowship of sharing in His sufferings. That we become like Him in His death and by so doing, we attain to the resurrection from the dead. The treasure chest of riches that our Father has for His children is limitless, and it is freely available to each of us, but only through Jesus. Without salvation, we are eternally lost. With it, we are in Jesus and entitled to receive so very much more from God.

January 19, 2020

Most mornings when I am led to write by the Spirit of God, I do so with a sense of speaking a word of truth for others who may be given the opportunity to read it. Amazingly, when I later return and read what God has spoken, I find that the Word speaks directly to me, and I am greatly encouraged. This particular morning I am sensing that God wants to speak to me in particular, and that He is doing so through His Word found in 2 Timothy 4:1–5. This is what He is saying:

> In the presence of God and of Christ Jesus, who will judge the living and the dead, and in view of His appearing and His Kingdom, I give you this charge: Preach the Word; be prepared in season and out of season; correct, rebuke and encourage with great patience and careful instruction. For the time will come when men will not put up with sound doctrine. Instead, to suit their own desires, they will gather around them a great number of teachers to say what their itching ears want to hear. They will turn their ears away from the truth and turn aside to myths. But you, keep your head in all situations, endure hardship, do the work of an evangelist, discharge all of the duties of your ministry.

This Word confirms another spoken over me through a brother in Christ several months ago. I receive it humbly and with a sense of great excitement and anticipation. Praise be to God!

January 21, 2020

While searching the Scripture this morning, I was led to Romans 12:9–21. This portion of God's Word is simply entitled "Love." I was reminded that God is love and that His most important commands to us are to love Him and to love one another. With that in mind, I concluded that the wisdom and instruction imparted in this section of the book of Romans must be significant, and after reading and absorbing it, I concluded that it most certainly is. Therein, our

Father provides us with clear, simple, and concise instructions for living a life that honors and pleases Him, all of which begin and end with His love for us and ours for Him. Let's examine this Word together.

"Love must be sincere." The world is filled with fake love, which is unacceptable to God. The love that we receive from Him is real and that which we give must be the same, genuine and from the heart.

"Hate what is evil." The Holy Spirit clearly exposes evil to us, and it is not enough that we simply avoid it; we must abhor it.

"Cling to what is good." Likewise, He shows us what is good and commands that we hold on to it desperately, like our lives depend upon it, because they do.

"Be devoted to one another in brotherly love." Devoted means with all that is within you, loyal, faithful, above everything else. Brotherly love exceeds regular, average love. God wants us to give our all to one another, with love, like brothers.

"Honor one another above yourselves." To honor is to hold high, to esteem. It is usually reserved for kings and leaders. Our Father is instructing us to hold each other high, even higher than we do our own selves.

"Never be lacking in zeal, but keep your spiritual fervor, serving the Lord." If you are like me, you began your spiritual journey with great zeal and much fervor, desiring to serve Jesus with all your heart, with all your mind, and with all your soul. But unfortunately, somewhere along the way, your spiritual flame began to weaken. Maybe it was the distraction of the flesh or the cares of the world or simply complacency and laziness setting in. Whatever the cause, our God is aware of this waning, and His instruction is to do everything in our power to maintain the zeal and fervor of our first love. We will need it.

"Be joyful in hope…" I believe that hope is essential to our existence. Without it, we wither and eventually perish. The good news is that in Jesus we have eternal hope. We are never without the life-giving and life-sustaining gift of hope, and as a result thereof, we have cause for joy. God is telling us to live and to walk in the joy of hope.

"Patient in affliction..." There is another whole message here, but suffice it to say that trials and troubles will come, and with them, the opportunity to build trust and faith and surrender. All of which are necessary to equip us for the calling that has been placed upon our lives. Like most good and important works, this requires time, so be patient. It will be worth the wait.

"Faithful in prayer." We can do nothing on our own, but we can do all things through Christ who strengthens us. Our Father desires to commune with us and to give us good things. Do not neglect to go to Him, often, with all of your cares. You will not be disappointed.

"Share with God's people who are in need." This command is of great importance and often neglected. God gives to each of us as He chooses, and He does so for the purpose that we pass the gift on to others. Regardless of what we think we have, or do not have, we all have been given something to share. It is not just about money. Seek God's wisdom, and then follow it by imparting what has been gifted unto you.

"Practice hospitality." Hospitality simply means caring, being kind, and helping others—all of which are accomplished by being considerate and meeting their needs. Open your heart, your home, and your wallet.

"Bless those who persecute you." This is a hard one, but it is exactly what Jesus did, and He conquered the world. Jesus told us that certain things require prayer and fasting and the power of God that flows from each. This is most likely one of those things, so do not hesitate to pray, to fast, and to ask your Father to help you. The results will be far reaching.

"Bless and do not curse." Again, bless them, but then go one step further and refrain from speaking ill of them. Do not speak harm over anyone.

"Rejoice with those who rejoice; mourn with those who mourn." Be all things to all people that they may see the love of God in you and give praise to His name. When you encounter those who are joyful or thankful, rejoice with them, and do not hesitate to share your reason for hope and for joy. And when you are with those who are hurting or sorrowful, mourn with them. Stand with them, and again, share the hope and the love that you have found in Jesus with them.

"Live in harmony with one another." The little foxes spoil the vine. Do not allow them to do so. Refuse to be easily offended. Be patient, loving, peaceful, gentle, kind, and good with one another. God wants His children to get along with each other because it presents a powerful testimony to the world that exists outside of the church.

"Do not be proud, but be willing to associate with people of low position. Do not be conceited." We are not to think too highly of ourselves. Just remember where you were when your Father rescued you as well as how you got there, and that should be sufficiently humbling. God opposes the proud and gives grace to the humble. From that truth alone, find your motivation. Out of such humility, strive to live lovingly and caringly with everyone. They are each God's creation, and He adores them one and all. So should we.

"Do not repay anyone evil for evil." Many hated Jesus, and yet He responded by loving them all. We are called to reflect and emulate everything that He said and did. At times, He instructed to simply walk away, but not once did He advocate paying back evil for evil, so neither should we.

"Be careful to do what is right in the eyes of everybody." This is interesting to me. Why not command to do what is right in the eyes of God instead of the eyes of everyone? It is because He desires that the unsaved world can find no fault with us and, more importantly, with our God. And why is that important? It is because He desires that they be drawn unto Himself, just as we were.

"If it is possible, as far as it depends on you, live at peace with everyone." Jesus said, "My peace I leave you, my peace I give unto you…" He was the greatest example of peace that ever existed, and He has given us His peace. Sometimes peace is beyond our control, but to the extent that it is, we are to exercise the peace Jesus gave us to everyone who we come into contact with.

"Do not take revenge…" "Vengeance is mine sayeth the Lord." Leave to Him what is His; He is able. The command is simply to not take revenge, so do not.

"If your enemy is hungry, feed him; if he is thirsty, give him something to drink…" This may not be easy, but neither is it complicated. Be obedient. Do what your Father says because He said so.

"Do not be overcome by evil, but overcome evil with good." This one we need help with. We are no match, standing alone, for evil. But Jesus is. Good is in us because He is there. So lean on Jesus to defeat and overcome evil for you. Allow His goodness in you to show forth.

There it is, the instruction manual from God on how to love Him with all your heart, with all your mind, and with all your soul and then to love your neighbor as yourself.

January 22, 2020

Last evening, while at church, I was blessed to have the opportunity to spend time with my very dear brother in Christ, Filipe. We prayed, worshiped, and received communion together. As we were leaving, Filipe placed his hand upon me and told me that the Lord had given him a Word for me. Filipe is a Spirit-filled man of God, so my Father had my attention. The Word was this: "Rejoice, Rejoice, for the day of your salvation is near." Filipe told me that he was not given its meaning, only the Word. I received it by faith and with much thankfulness. I know that my Father adores me and is fully aware of where I am at this season of my life. Filipe loves me greatly, and God knows that I trust him completely, which assures me that it is He that is speaking to me. While I do not know exactly what it is that my future holds, I am certain that my Father is declaring blessing, goodness, love, favor, presence, grace, and mercy over me. This morning I was taken to Philippians 4:4–7, which states:

> Rejoice in the Lord always. I will say it again: Rejoice! Let your gentleness be evident to all. The Lord is near. Do not be anxious about anything, but in everything, by prayer and petition, with thanksgiving, present your requests to God. And the peace of God, which transcends all under-

standing, will guard your hearts and your minds
in Christ Jesus.

Tomorrow an event will occur in my life that the enemy has
attempted to use to instill fear and anxiety within me. He will not
and cannot succeed. What Satan has intended for evil Jesus has
turned to good. During this season, my Father has never left me. He
has poured out His love and compassion over me every day. He has
forgiven me of my anxiety and taken it away, replacing it with trust.
He has helped my unbelief and increased my faith. So when He tells
me to rejoice, rejoice because the day of my salvation is near, all I
need to do is celebrate and wait to see His goodness revealed.

January 23, 2020

As each day turns into another and each week passes by, they
form a season in the life of a child of God. I have come to understand
that while each of those seasons may have different outward appear-
ances, inwardly the work that God is completing is cumulative and
ordained with the same ultimate purpose. Regardless of whether life's
circumstances bring adversity and affliction or success and prosperity,
our Father's desire is that our response be the same, and that it rises
from our heart and from our spirit. A heart filled with love, peace, joy,
patience, goodness, kindness, gentleness, faithfulness, and self-control that can only come from God Himself through the presence of
His Holy Spirit that is within us. Through each season, no matter its
appearance, His purpose, His will, and His reflection become more
visible in each of us: our faith increases, our trust grows, we become
more joyful, we pray more frequently, we give thanks regardless, and
we love everyone unconditionally. Our mind shifts to eternal things,
and we long to worship and adore Jesus. Circumstances change, our
God does not, and neither should our response to Him.

January 24, 2020

When young men and women enlist to serve and fight for their country, those in leadership do not simply hand them a weapon and some rations and send them to the battlefield. That would certainly result in the loss of both battle and war, not to mention the life of the soldier. Instead, they first train them in the skills necessary to effectively and successfully fight the battle. Such training most assuredly includes first clearing their minds of any preconceived thoughts and ideas that would hinder their ability to respond and think as an effective soldier must. Next, they must be thoroughly instructed in and given the tools and skills necessary to complete the mission to which they will be assigned: to win the battle, to take ground for the cause, to defend that which they care so greatly for. We, the children of God, are not unlike these young men and women. As a matter-of-fact, we are often referred to as soldiers of the cross. We too sign up to defend and to take ground for a cause that we care passionately for. The problem is that we, like the soldiers described earlier, have no idea what the battle entails and/or what will be required of us. We desire to fight for our Lord, but we have no clue how to do so. Therefore, we must be trained. If simply given a Bible and sent into the battlefield, the world, we will most certainly bear no fruit. So we, like the young soldier, must first be equipped for our calling. Our minds and hearts must be cleared of the flesh-driven, world-influenced ideals that were leading us down a path of destruction. Then those notions must be replaced with an eternal mindset fueled by the truth and promises of God's Word. Only then will we be fully prepared to engage in and complete the mission to which we have been assigned. Charles Spurgeon penned this prayer that captures completely what God is speaking this morning: "Oh Heavenly Sower, plow me first, and then cast the truth into me, and let me yield a bounteous harvest for you." (Note: The timing and duration of the training and of the mission to which we are called is different for each of us and directed by God's hand.)

January 26, 2020

God never intended for us to become physically comfortable. He will always take us out of our bodily comfort zone because He knows that in that place, our focus upon and need for Him wanes, our passion for His presence diminishes, and our desire to serve Him fades. All one need do is examine the lives of His powerful saints to learn that physical comfort and effectiveness did not go hand in hand. Paul, Peter, John, Moses, Noah, Elijah, Steven, David, and many others lived lives marked by trial, tribulation, persecution, and isolation. Because of their faithfulness and commitment to their Father, they were misunderstood, ridiculed, cast aside, and even killed. And yet through all such discomfort, they were greatly encouraged in their spirits and used mightily by God to advance His kingdom and point people to His Son. The deeper and the farther we are led down the path of relationship, knowledge and understanding, the more physically uncomfortable we shall become. But do not be discouraged, for such bodily discomfort is accompanied by unspeakable peace and joy. It is a great privilege and honor to be called to God's service, and the reward that awaits those of us who are, is beyond amazing.

January 28, 2020

Child of God, when you look upon and ponder your beloved Savior, what do you see? Do you behold a sacrificial lamb soaked in blood hanging on a cross? If you do, your vision would reflect the truth. Do you see a friend who is closer than a brother listening to and caring for you? Again, your eyes would not be deceiving you. Do you envision an advocate interceding for you at the throne of grace? What you see is accurate. In whatever manner you view your adored Jesus, it is only a glimpse of who He truly is. His splendor and majesty no one can fathom. They are always before Him. He is robed and clothed in each. We can speak of His glorious splendor and His overwhelming majesty, and we may even from time to time be afforded glimpses of the same, but until we see Him as He is, face-to-face, we can only ponder His greatness and His beauty. For now we can only imagine what it will be like to stand in His presence and to walk by His side. Just know that "no eye has seen, no ear has heard, no mind has conceived what God has prepared for those who love Him" (1 Cor. 2:9). That promise includes the splendor and the majesty of our Lord and Savior. However you envision Jesus, be certain that He is more, so much more, than we can ever imagine. And then worship Him.

January 29, 2020

For twenty-nine years, between 727 and 698 BC, Hezekiah reigned as king of Judah, which was the southern kingdom of what is now Israel. He was known as a good king because he mostly did what was right before God. During his reign, the powerful Assyrian king and his huge army defeated and seized all of Judah with the exception of the fortified city of Jerusalem where Hezekiah ruled. Eventually, the Assyrians arrived at Jerusalem, and from outside of the city, the king's general delivered a letter demanding their surrender and boasting that God could not save them. Upon receiving the correspondence, Hezekiah, who had not always made good decisions before the Lord, went to the Temple. Once there, he decided on a course of action that should not amaze me, although it nonetheless does. He laid the letter out before his God on the floor of the Temple and then earnestly prayed that the Lord would avenge Sennacherib's mocking of Him and deliver Jerusalem and its people from the king. God heard Hezekiah's prayer, and through the prophet Isaiah, spoke to him, assuring the king of two things: first, that not one Assyrian soldier would enter Jerusalem and, second, that He would send Sennacherib back to from where he came, defeated. That very evening the angel of the Lord put to death 185,000 men in the Assyrian camp, forcing King Sennacherib to break camp and withdraw to Nineveh, where he remained until he was killed by two of his own sons while worshiping his false god.

Several thoughts come to my mind. First, at a time when most of the kings of Israel and Judah encouraged idol worship and did not do what was right before the Lord, Hezekiah was the exception, and as a result, God took care of and rewarded him. Next, although Hezekiah made some bad decisions, God searched his heart and knew that he was faithful; and therefore, when Hezekiah humbled himself and cried out in desperation, God heard him and answered his prayer. Lastly, there were over three hundred thousand soldiers in the Assyrian army, and God wiped out over half of them in one night. Nothing is too large or too imposing for our God! But wait, the story doesn't end there. Sometime after this great victory, Hezekiah became ill, and Isaiah told him that he was going to die. Did Hezekiah respond by getting his affairs in order? No, once again he cried out to his God in prayer, asking and believing that He would spare him. The passage says, "Hezekiah wept bitterly" before the Lord. Before Isaiah could even leave the king's court, the Word of the Lord came to him, saying, "Go back and tell Hezekiah that I have heard his prayer and seen his tears and I will heal him." Hezekiah wasn't perfect, but he knew from where his help came from, and to Him he went in his time of need, believing that His God was able and would answer his prayers. Hezekiah's God is our God, and He has not changed. We too can cast our cares upon our Lord. Will you trust Him and do so?

January 30, 2020

Chapters 4 and 5 of the book of Revelation provide a portion of that which was revealed to John upon being taken up into heaven, in the Spirit, from the island of Patmos. By way of a song and a dream, I am led this morning to verses 11 through 13 of chapter 5, which state:

> Then I looked and heard the voice of many angels, numbering thousands upon thousands, and ten thousand times ten thousand. They encircled the throne and the living creatures and the elders. In a loud voice they sang: "Worthy is the Lamb, who was slain, to receive power and

wealth and wisdom and strength and honor and
glory and praise!"

What an awe-inspiring vision John was given of what it is that
awaits each of God's children. A picture painted for us of ten thousand times ten thousand glorifying, praising, and honoring Jesus in
a loud voice. (I did the math, and that's ten million angels/saints.)
And there is more.

Every creature in Heaven and on earth and under
the earth and on the sea, and all of them, singing, "To Him who sits on the throne and to the
Lamb be praise and honor and glory and power,
for ever and ever!" (vs. 13)

All creatures praising and glorifying, in one voice, He that sits
on the throne of heaven along with His precious Son. It is a difficult
picture to wrap one's human mind around, and yet one that is visible
enough to inspire a desire to be present at and to bask in its awe and
splendor. A longing that will be fulfilled and an eternal event that
will be experienced by each of us who have been chosen to be His
child. How incredible is our God, and how greatly blessed are we to
be called His children! As I slept, I was given a dream in which I was
leading a large throng of worshipers who were passionately singing
a song entitled "Hallelujah Here Below." It is an amazing anthem
by Elevation Worship that, in part, speaks to the scene from heaven
described by John.

Ten thousand angels surround Your throne; To
bring You praise that will never cease; But hallelujah from here below; Is still Your favorite mel-
ody. We sing Hallelujah, Hallelujah, Hallelujah;
We sing Hallelujah, Hallelujah, Hallelujah...
Jesus Christ our King enthroned; All the praise
is Yours forevermore. Hallelujah here below; All

the praise is Yours forevermore. (Repeat) We sin
Hallelujah, Hallelujah, Hallelujah. (Repeat)

In my dream and in the song's video from Elevation Church, I was overwhelmed by the multitude of people praising their God in one loud voice. Even more so, I was captured by the indescribable joy and deep love for their Lord that shined forth from each face. Then the Spirit of God spoke these words into my heart: "As amazing as what you have witnessed in your dream is, it is momentary and only a glimpse of that which John described that your Father has waiting for you. Remain in my love that my joy may be in you and that when you see me face-to-face, your joy may be complete." Hallelujah!

January 31, 2020

My mind is filled this morning with thoughts of the Holy Spirit. It is clear to me that this equally majestic and all-important member of the Holy Trinity is, in truth, God and, therefore, fully worthy of all glory and honor and praise. And yet He is much misunderstood, often shunned, and even at times feared. Why is this? How could this be? The answer being revealed to me revolves around knowledge, or the lack thereof. Hosea 4:6 says, "My people perish for lack of knowledge." The Holy Spirit is God's gift to His children; and as such, it is necessary for us to not only know Him, but to understand who He is and the purpose behind God sending Him. He is our personal guide, delivery specialist, interpreter, trainer, and comforter all wrapped up in one. He guides us into all truth. He takes what belongs to Jesus and gives it to us. He reveals the promises of heaven and then trains us to receive and walk in them. He empowers us to respond and to ask. He authorizes us to receive and enables us to live in the new space created for us by Jesus. He commissions us to serve and then shows us how and where to do so. And finally, He brings us comfort when we feel inconsolable. What He will never do is harm us or lead us astray. He is God, and therefore, we can be certain that He adores us and works all things out for our good. That is who the Holy Spirit is. Walk with Him and in Him (Cooke 2017, 108–120).

February 2, 2020

Last night, as I slept and then throughout this morning, the Holy Spirit flooded my mind and my spirit with the chorus from yet another song. God often speaks to His children in such a manner. The chorus is taken directly from Psalm 121:1–2: "Where does my help come from? My help comes from the Lord…" I am uncertain of the exact reason that He brings this particular Word to me today, so I will speak of it here and then wait expectantly. In a more general and instructive sense, the Holy Spirit is revealing to us our Father's will and desire that we come to Him for our every need and that we know and never forget His great love for us and accept that the only meaningful, lasting help that is available to us flows from Him. Not from family or friends or possessions or money or status or appearance—all of which serve some purpose—but not one which is lasting or fail proof or completely reliable. Isaiah 41:10 declares, "I will strengthen you and help you; I will uphold you with my righteous right hand." Where does our help come from? It comes from heaven, from the Lord, and all other help is merely sinking sand.

February 4, 2020

The United States would appear to be dangerously divided philosophically, politically, and spiritually at this point in time. Most of those who call this country their home seem to be aligned, to some degree, with one of two factions: conservative or liberal, with the remaining persons attempting to exist somewhere in the middle. Our Founders envisioned such a scenario as good, fostering a level of debate, cooperation, and partnership that would produce resolutions benefiting everyone. And for a period, or periods of time, their hopes were actually realized. Unfortunately, not all seasons in our history have resulted in such successful outcomes, with the current climate reflecting just the opposite. Not only does a great and clearly delineable divide exist in the United States at this time, but it is accompanied by a depth of negative sentiments and intentions that have rarely before been witnessed in our storied history. All of which leads to where God has directed me this morning, His Word. In Romans chapter 13, He says:

> Everyone must submit himself to the governing authorities, for there is no authority except that which God has established. The authorities that exist have been established by God. Consequently, he who rebels against the authority is rebelling against what God has instituted, and those who do so will bring judgment on themselves...

It is easy, in the flesh, to not only harbor anger, and even hatred, for those who do not share our opinions and beliefs, but in addition, and maybe worse, to justify those emotions under some misplaced theory of self-righteousness and privilege. Last I checked, neither anger, nor hatred, nor self-righteousness, nor pride were found among the fruits of God's Spirit. We are God's children, His ambassadors and His representatives to the world around us, and as such, we are to live our lives as He directs. That includes putting our personal philosophies and biases aside and loving our neighbors—all of them, regardless of on which side of the political aisle they sit.

February 5, 2020

For several days now, I have had the chorus from the song "King of Kings" by Hillsong Worship in my heart and upon my lips. I awake to it most every day and believe it to be from my Father. Therefore, it has significant meaning to me and for anyone who I am afforded the opportunity to share it with.

> Praise the Father, praise the Son, praise the Spirit, three in One. God of glory, majesty; Praise forever to the King of Kings.

We were created to praise our God. "From the lips of children and infants You have ordained praise" (Ps. 8:2). "Let everything that has breath praise the Lord." (Ps. 150:6). Jesus told the Pharisees when they demanded that He rebuke those who were praising Him upon His entry into Jerusalem, "If they keep quiet, the stones will cry out." Praise invites and maintains the presence of God in our lives. We are promised that He inhabits the praises of His people (Ps. 22:3). Ponder that for a while. Our heavenly Father, the Creator of all things, who is everywhere at every moment; He who sits on a throne and rules and reigns over all of creation; He who inhabits everything that is good declares that His presence is to be found in our praise. Want to experience the splendor and the majesty of your Almighty God? Praise Him. Want to be wrapped in the blanket of His immeasurable love? Praise Him. Want to be drenched in His life-changing grace and mercy? Praise Him. In need of His peace, His joy, the touch of His healing hand? Praise Him. We were created to commune with Him, and to do so, we must know who He is and where to find Him. Praise is the GPS to His presence. It takes us directly to where He is and affords us the privilege of relationship with Him. How, you ask, do we do this?

> Praise God in the sanctuary; Praise Him in His mighty heavens. Praise Him for His acts of power; Praise Him for His surpassing greatness. Praise Him with the sounding of the trumpet; Praise Him with the harp and the lyre; Praise Him with the tambourine and dancing; Praise Him with the strings and flute; Praise Him with the clash of cymbals; Praise Him with resounding cymbals. Let everything that has breath praise the Lord. (Ps. 150)

Are you receiving what our Father is declaring to us this day? It could not be more clear. *Praise him!* It is there that He resides. It is there where He longs for us to be.

February 6, 2020

Many years ago, after I received the gift of salvation and eternal life, I was introduced to the doctrine of sanctification while attending a particular church. As presented, it was an intimidating and scary concept that involved pain and sacrifice and hardship at the hands of a judgmental and uncompassionate God. While I am not certain whether my perception rose out of my own lack of knowledge or that of those attempting to disciple me, I know without a doubt that what I felt was real. Fast-forward to three years ago when God, through the Holy Spirit, divinely rescued me from the self-centered life that I had been deceived by the enemy into choosing to pursue. During the time that has followed, Christ has taken His rightful place at the center of my life and the Holy Spirit has revealed who God is to me and for me and how He adores me and has a plan and a purpose for my life, one that glorifies Him and advances His kingdom. Part of that work in my life has been to once again address the process of sanctification, only this time from a truth-based, Holy Spirit-inspired perspective. It has been a completely different, amazingly exciting, and life-altering experience. I now know that my Father loves me beyond measure and that He will do nothing to harm me. That whatever path He chooses to lead me down it will be for my good and for His glory. Sanctification is the process of making one holy, and it can only be accomplished by God. Through it, He sets us apart for a sacred, holy purpose for His use. It frees us from the bondage of sin and prepares us for His service. It sets us apart from the corruption of the world. God does not leave us to accomplish sanctification on our own. He completes it in us and through us. The key to being sanctified is found in truth. The Word of God read, heard, understood, and applied. In John 17, Jesus, while praying for His disciples, says, "Sanctify them by the truth. Your Word is truth." The more truth we receive and believe, the more sanctified we become. The operation of truth, and its role in sanctification, is to separate a person from the world and unto service for God. The sanctification that Jesus had in mind when He prayed for His disciples was not primarily one of holiness but was more so for being set apart for God's service and mission. Jesus sanctified Himself because He is God and for the work of service that He was about to complete upon the cross. He set Himself apart for the cross; and through that work, the Word of God, Jesus, became fully effective in the lives of His disciples—a group in which we have the privilege of being included. In closing, let me say that sanctification no longer scares or intimidates me. To the contrary, it is exciting, invigorating, and empowering. It is a gift from and a work of my Father, and therefore, I now embrace it (Guzik 2015; John 17).

February 8, 2020

Recently I was taken to the seventeenth chapter of John for the purpose of considering Jesus's prayerful instruction regarding sanctification. While there, I immediately noticed that each and every word written was in red letters. All of them, without exception, spoken directly from the lips of our Lord. This fact alone peaked my desire to not only read them but to ask the Holy Spirit to implant them permanently into my heart, my soul, and my mind and to grant me a better understanding of each one. Since that time, those words, spoken in prayer by Jesus, have not strayed far from my thoughts; and last evening, I believe that my Father directed me to rise this morning and begin to write that which the Holy Spirit provides regarding the matter.

The first thing that my attention is drawn to is the timing of Jesus's supplication. He has just finished partaking in the Passover feast (the Last Supper) with washing the feet of and teaching and comforting His disciples. He is about to travel to the garden of Gethsemane, where He will be arrested and taken away to be crucified. It is about to be a very painful and troubling time for our Lord, and yet He never loses sight of Who He is, Whose He is, His purpose for being there: those that He so greatly loves and from where His help comes from. With all of that clearly in focus, He looked toward heaven and prayed earnestly to His Father, first for Himself, then for His disciples, and, finally, for all believers. The words of Jesus always stir my heart and capture my attention. However, these particular ones, when taken in the context of the moment and with the knowledge of to whom they were spoken, are of enormous importance to each and every one of us, His children. Not only do they speak rich truth into our hearts, minds, and souls but, in addition, provide us with a template for the manner in which we should approach our Father, both regularly and at times when we are in need of an enhanced portion of His presence and favor. Jesus's words are always beautiful and will forever pierce the hearts of those of us that love and adore Him. These in particular have captured my attention so much so that I am compelled to write of them over the coming days. I invite you who are reading here to travel this journey of knowledge, insight, and revelation along with me. I am very excited to see what it is that the Holy Spirit has for us.

February 9, 2020

Many great prayers are recorded in Scripture. The book of Psalms is filled with them. However, Jesus's prayer chronicled in John 17 is considered by many Bible scholars to be the greatest of all supplications. It is the longest, most continuous prayer lifted up by Jesus to His Father to be recorded in the Gospels. While the words and sentences are not complicated, the concepts are profound and filled with much wisdom and compassion. The true nature and real heart of our Lord are clearly revealed in John's recording of Jesus's petitions to His Father. In Matthew 6:9–13, Jesus teaches His disciples, and all of His followers, how they should pray. While that instruction and His John 17 prayer have much in common, in the latter, we witness devotion on a different level. Jesus is not inferior to His Father, as we are, and His words reflect their oneness. No attempt is made to convince God of anything. Instead, we witness Jesus speaking the purpose and protection of His Father over those that He had been given. Jesus was, and is, in constant intercession for His church and never was that more evident than at this place in time. John affords us a clear look into the mind of Christ, one that reveals His adoration for His Father's children, one that is continually advocating and interceding for them, one that even in the face of a brutal death can think only of and for them. The public portion of Jesus's ministry was ended, and He was nearing the completion of His mission on earth. There was nothing seemingly left but the cross, and in the face of the pain and the brutality that it would inflict, our Savior gave Himself wholly to prayer. Prayer for Himself, yes, but only that He would be allowed the privilege of glorifying His Father. More notably, it was prayer dominated by His desire that those that He had been given and that He loved so greatly would be cared for and protected. Any doubt or question why John 17 so captures our hearts? Simply put, it is because it reveals the true heart of Jesus, our Lord and our Savior, for each and every one of us. Glory be to His name! (Guzik 2015; John 17).

February 10, 2020

Jesus begins praying in John 17 by looking toward heaven. Out of a sense of surrender and respect, we most often bow down before our Father as we pray, believing, as is the case, that we are not able or worthy to stand in His actual presence. But I believe that in this instance, we are being shown specifically how Jesus prayed for a purpose. Didn't Jesus say that "all of these things that I have done you shall likewise do"? And have not all of the benefits and privileges bestowed upon Him been likewise afforded to each of us? The answers are yes and yes. In Luke 21:28, Jesus, speaking of the end of the age, states, "When these things begin to take place, stand and lift up your heads, because your redemption is drawing near." Surely, if our God was standing before us, our human bodies could not withstand or survive gazing upon Him. However, such is not the case here. Jesus is petitioning His Father by lifting His eyes to heaven where He can be found. He is looking to where His help comes from, and so should we. "I lift my eyes to the hills—where my help comes from? My help comes from the Lord, the Maker of Heaven and earth" (Ps. 121:1–2). Jesus knew exactly where help resided, and He looked there before beginning to pray. Let's follow His lead.

February 11, 2020

Back to John 17. Jesus first prays for Himself: "Father, the hour has come. Glorify Your Son that Your Son also may glorify You." Jesus knows exactly who He is. He is fully aware that He is the Son of God, and He declares it to His Father. We too are children of God. That is who we are, and we should not hesitate to proclaim it to our Father when we commune with Him, especially during difficult and painful times when our relationship with Jesus affords us His particular favor. Jesus also knew where He was on His journey: "The hour has come..." Gethsemane, His beating, and the crucifixion would require more than an hour; but Jesus knew that they represented only a short period of time in light of eternity. Agony and anguish awaited Him, and yet out of great love, He speaks of it as but a moment in time. Even though Jesus was praying for Himself, His petition was not narcissistic: "Glorify Your Son, that Your Son may glorify You." He knew that in order to glorify His Father, His Father had to first glorify Him. He was asking God to make it clear to those around Him that Jesus, the man, was also God and that, as a result, death could not hold Him, that He would be resurrected and ascend to His rightful place. Jesus proceeded to give reasons for His request to be glorified:

> Because the hour has come; Because the Father would be glorified; Because He had already been granted authority; Because He was the only way to life; Because it would finish the work for which He had been sent.

We too should not hesitate to give reasons for our requests before the throne of God:

> I tell you the truth, my Father will give you whatever you ask in my name. (John 16:23)

> Let us approach the throne of grace with confidence, so that we may receive mercy and find grace to help us in our time of need. (Heb. 4:16)

> The Spirit himself testifies with our spirit that we are God's children. Now if we are children then we are heirs—heirs of God and co-heirs with Christ... (Rom. 8:16)

We too ask our Father to exalt us. Unfortunately, the motives behind our requests are in no manner as pure as those of our Lord. We may not specifically say so, but our desire is that God will increase us as opposed to Him. Jesus's one and only purpose in everything that He did was to bring glory to His Father. So when He asked to be glorified, it was only to bring attention to the immeasurable love, grace, wisdom, and power that God was pouring out over His creation. Our motive should be the same as Jesus's! Next, Jesus claimed His rightful authority over all mankind, out loud, directly to God who had given it to Him in the first place. Everything that Jesus was given was bestowed upon Him by His Father, including the authority to grant eternal life to as many as God would give Him. We may not have been granted such immense responsibility, but we are otherwise no different. All that we are and all that we have comes from our Father. Jesus declared who God spoke Him to be, and we must do likewise. Our Father knows exactly who we are, and by our declaration of the same, we affirm our faith in not only Him but also in His promises over us. Lastly, Jesus restated what filled His heart at this covenant-changing moment of His earthly assignment: "And now, Father, glorify me in Your presence with the glory I had with You before the world began." Only Jesus can and could make this request. It was His main petition: that His Father would receive Him back to the glory that He had relinquished in order to complete His assignment. We will not be received back to a relinquished glory when we finish our calling; however, we absolutely can be received into eternal life with the One whose blood paved our way. Do not hesitate to ask your Father for that which is already yours (Guzik 2015; John 17).

February 12, 2020

God has taught me to become keenly aware of when He, through His Holy Spirit, is speaking a specific truth into my heart and over my life, one that He desires that I write down in this place to be passed on to whomever He chooses. I am sensing His voice, and therefore, I will break, momentarily, from John 17, surely to return as soon as He leads. Today, this is what I believe it is that my Father wishes for me to pass on: a comfort-filled heart has no room for Him. We find no need for His compassion when the sky is clear and the sun is bright. When the wallet is bursting and the cupboard full, we neglect to call upon His providence and favor or to crave His presence. Shame on us! But do not lose heart, for your Father is filled with grace and mercy and love. For in these pride-filled seasons enter trials and difficult circumstances, each of which He uses to break our comfort-driven heart and, in turn, create room for His compassion, His grace, and His presence. "A broken and contrite heart, O God, you will not despise" (Ps. 51:17). It is in these places that we desire our God and have the most intimate dealings with Him, thus experiencing our greatest joy. These difficult places are the spaces where God is upgrading His relationship with you and with me. "I live in a high and holy place, but also with him who is contrite and lowly in spirit, to revive the spirit of the lowly and to revive the heart of the contrite" (Isa. 57:15). Therefore, do not despise or spurn such seasons. Instead, relish and bask in them, not neglecting to ask your Father to reveal to you exactly what it is that He is purposing to write on your heart and create in you in such a place. What a good Word that God has chosen to impart to us this morning (Spurgeon 1995, 86).

February 13, 2020

I was all set to return to John 17 this morning when, as I turned the page, I felt the Holy Spirit leading me to a different place. The scripture verses addressed by Charles Spurgeon in my *Morning and Evening* devotional this morning are 1 John 3:1–2. Immediately after reading them, I felt a compulsion to address the same here. Then as

I began to write, I found the exact same passage below. Okay, Father, You have my attention. Most importantly, Your still, small voice is telling me to write, "How great is the love the Father has lavished on us, that we should be called children of God! And that is what we are!… Dear friends, now we are children of God…"

Do you have children of your own? If so, can you even describe the depth of your love for each of them? Does your heart not burst at the seams at the very thought of them? Is there anything that you would not do for them, any place to which you would not travel to protect or rescue them? To be a child is to reside in the most privileged of all relationships, to exist in the most favored of all places. It affords one the peace and assurance of knowing that they are taken care of and protected. That they can live free from fear and filled with joy. That their mother and/or their father will be with them wherever they go, whenever they go there. That they will never be forsaken. That they can rest on and trust in each and every word that comes from the mouth of their parent(s). What amazing love a parent has for their child and that the child experiences in return. That measure of love, and much more, is how our Father chooses to describe His love for each of us. He declares that we are His children and then follows by emphatically proclaiming, "And that is what we are!" (He even uses exclamation marks, twice!) It is no small thing for your parents to call you their child. How much more incredible, awesome, and amazing is it for the God of all things to announce that you are His. Start getting used to it because that is "what you are!" Hallelujah!

February 14, 2020

Last evening I began a twelve-week journey with seven other men in a small group entitled "Freedom." We will follow a curriculum birthed by God and delivered from the Church of the Highlands in Birmingham, Alabama. From time to time, I will share my experiences and revelations from this study. Let me start by sharing that I was presented with the opportunity to join one of two Freedom groups. The first had several men that I am friends with already and who would appear to be at a similar place in their relationship with Jesus as am I. This group would have been my first choice. The second group had only one person that I knew and was made up of six others who are at different stages of their faith journey than I am. This group was God's choice, made abundantly clear to me by the Holy Spirit. Any question which group I am a part of? I am very excited to see how God will impact my journey and my life through these incredible men of God. There are two things that my Father revealed to me during the hour and a half that I spent with my group last night.

First, as we each shared a condensed version of our stories, I learned that these brothers of mine do, in fact, face certain struggles and have particular questions that are different from mine and most likely from those of the men in the group that I did not join. However, all struggles are and every question is important to God, regardless of the form that they take or the manner in which they are presented. And to the one who is encountering or presenting it, the trial or the inquiry always is and will forever be of great significance to God. What captured my attention and my heart last evening was the openness and honesty of my new brothers, along with their vulnerability to and their desire for Jesus and His help. God is going to do something amazing here. What an honor and a privilege to be allowed to be a part of it. I will only address the second revelation briefly with more to come. The lesson spoke of two approaches to our relationship with God. Each one from the book of Genesis and the Garden of Eden. One is a tree-of-the-knowledge-of-good-and-evil approach and is driven by a desire to earn God's favor and approval. This is the approach that I had lived my life under for over thirty years. One that resulted in a lack of truth, favor, presence, identity, purpose, relationship, fulfillment, and many other of the privileges, benefits, and promises that my Father had for me. The second is a tree-of-life approach that declares that Jesus has already made a way, that God adores His children, and that we do not have to earn any of the gifts set out above. They are already ours. This is the path upon which God has been taking me for the last three years. The eyes of my heart, mind, and spirit have been opened; and the focus of my journey has become crystal clear. I told you that God had something incredible in store for me and my new brothers. It is just beginning.

February 16, 2020

I am reminded that this pilgrimage of the highest honor that I have been called upon by and for my Father is wrought with hardships and troubles. While the incredible joy that fills my heart from serving my Lord is ever-present, so too is the steady wave of thorns in my flesh. Uncertain of whether they originate from heaven and are purposed to instruct, strengthen, and mature me or if they are sent from the enemy in a feeble attempt to discourage and defeat me, in either case, my heart will always guide my response. For that is where my Lord resides. There is the ground that He has fully captured. It is there that only His love and the truth of His promises reign victorious. So if difficulty's purpose is for good, then He who dwells there will accomplish the same and confirm it within me. And if the opposite be the case, then no success will be found because I know in my heart that He has me and that no weapon formed against me shall prosper. Praise be to God!

February 17, 2020

Today I am led back to John 17 and the second of Jesus's recorded prayers. In this instance, Jesus is praying for His disciples. While His prayer is lifted up specifically for those whom God chose to travel at His side during His earthly ministry, it certainly must continue to be His plea to the Father for each of the many disciples who have answered His call from that time forward. Jesus begins by speaking of His mission among the disciples and their reception of it. He declares His manifestation (living out) of God's name (His nature of love, goodness, and holiness) before them as well as their faithful acceptance of the same. Many witnessed Jesus's reflection of His Father without accepting the truth of its meaning. Our Lord was proclaiming His disciples' openness to receive and willingness to accept and believe His message. Next, Jesus leaves no question for whom specifically He is praying: "I pray for them. I do not pray for the world…" His focus was on those that He had intimately shared the truth with and to whom He would soon call to spread that revelation to all the world. It was not that He had no care for the rest of the world; we know that He did, as He would unquestionably reveal in a few short days. In verse 11, we find Jesus's first actual request for the disciples: "Holy Father, protect them by the power of Your name…so that they may be one as we are one." While He was with the disciples He protected them and kept them safe. They, like all of us, need to be kept and protected. Our opposition, the world, our flesh, Satan are too strong, too alluring, and too much to overcome without the power, cover, and protection that comes from the nature and authority of God. The mere mention of His name keeps and protects us. Jesus also asked that the disciples be one as He and the Father are. He knew that unity of spirit, unity of heart, and unity of purpose would be essential to the completion of the calling that had been placed upon their lives. The same rings true for God's chosen people today. Next, Jesus asks His Father to give them His joy and to keep them away from the evil one. He cared deeply for these men just as He cares deeply for each of us, and as a result, He desired that they experience the full measure of the abundant joy that He possesses. Joy that is rooted in and derives from His relationship and fellowship with His Father. Jesus could have asked that God allow His disciples to come with Him to heaven. He did not. His assignment was complete; theirs was not. What He did request was that they remain in the world and experience the amazing blessings that accompany trusting and serving the kingdom of God. In so doing, He knew that they would come under the attack of the enemy, so He specifically asks that His Father protect them from Satan. Finally, Jesus requests that God would sanctify the disciples by the word of truth. As discussed in this journal earlier, to sanctify means to set apart for God's special calling and purpose. It implies holiness and being kept from the corruption of the world. Jesus was sending the disciples, and us, into the world for a specific purpose (to make disciples of all nations, to point people to Him and the cross, to preach the gospel, to heal the sick, and to cast out demons). One that could not be accomplished without being set apart by God for the assignment, just as Jesus had been. Sanctification is essential for effective ministry. Fully aware of the same, Jesus asked His Father to complete it in these men, and in us. What an incredible supplication. And there is still one prayer in John 17 left to examine (Guzik 2015; John 17).

February 19, 2020

Throughout the Bible, we are told the stories of many amazing men and women of God. Saints who were called by Him to serve as kings, ark builders, nation leaders, prophets, musicians, psalmists, disciples, evangelists, preachers, teachers, and martyrs among others. Their names are too numerous to mention here. While a different story is told through each, collectively the Word of God that instructs and guides us today is formed by way of their journeys. The lives they lived, the difficulties they encountered, the lessons they learned and taught, and their victories won are recorded to serve as a road map for our pilgrimage for the kingdom. While all their stories have at some point in time profoundly impacted my life, there is one through which the Holy Spirit particularly ministers to my spirit. That would be Peter, or the Disciple, as I like to refer to him. Peter was a simple man whose priorities in life were his family, his work, and his friends. God does not appear to have played a significant role in Peter's life when we first hear of him. He was not searching for God, even though God had his eye on him. God had a plan for Peter, one that would impact the world. To those who fancied themselves to be religious leaders and men of God, Peter did not present as the picture of someone who God would choose to walk with His Son. In fact, he was the exact opposite. However, what the leaders could not see was in clear focus to our Father. As is always the case, God did not regard the outward look of a man or woman when selecting them to serve Him. He only viewed the heart. As we come to learn through Peter's story, the outer man needed some work. Work that his Father was all too able and willing to undertake in return for the passion, obedience, and faithfulness that He had stored up in Peter's heart. Our Father always sees beyond what the world views in a person and then takes what He finds deep within and uses it to His glory, to His honor, and to His praise. I suppose what draws me to Peter in particular is his infectious commitment to, his exceeding passion for, and his unfettered zealousness toward Jesus. All qualities that God would use in Peter to advance His kingdom after the resurrection, but which would result in difficult lessons beforehand. And doesn't that directly reflect the path that God has many of His children travel on their journey to fulfilling His purpose in their lives? Our Father chooses each of us and places within our hearts a gift. One that only He can see at the beginning, one that will grow and mature until in the perfection of time, He will call upon us to use it for the advancement of His kingdom. Along his journey, Peter encountered trials, disappointments, corrections, even feelings of separation from his Lord. We will and we do experience the same. But at that incredible moment when he heard the words, "Peter do you truly love me?... Feed my sheep," Peter's identity, his purpose, and his calling became crystal clear. The season of preparation was complete, and now the gifts that only God could see would become abundantly visible to the world. God's plan and purpose for Peter was about to be put into action. The pain and heartache that accompanied his mistakes and denials would be replaced by the joy and fulfillment of serving his God and completing his calling. Peter's journey is our journey. How exciting is that!

February 20, 2020

Approximately three years ago, God gave me four scriptures through which He will lead and guide me on my journey through the remainder of my life. One of those passages is Joshua 1:8–9, which finishes with this assurance: "For the Lord your God will be with you wherever you go." Never have I needed those words from my Father more than this morning. Facing a stressful medical test involving a difficult health trial, I find myself being bombarded by the enemy with feelings of anxiety. So much so that it is manifesting itself with physical symptoms. Being fully convinced of where my help comes from, I cried out to God. Almost immediately, He answered me, several times over. First, as He often does, He placed a song in my heart: "See a Victory" by Elevation Worship. The chorus goes like this: "I'm gonna see a victory, I'm gonna see a victory, For the battle belongs to You Lord." Completely aware that the battle has already been won and victory is mine, my Father nonetheless sent the perfect reminder to comfort and encourage me at my time of need. He heard my cry and provided an answer. But wait, there's more. ("Our God will provide exceedingly and abundantly beyond that which we may ask or think.") Next, the Holy Spirit had me turn to yesterday's entry and reread it, all three pages of it. What He wanted to say to me was not to be found in the text of the entry but in the scripture passages at the bottom of each page. First, Isaiah 43:1–2: "Do not be afraid, for I have ransomed you. I have called you by name; you are Mine. When you go through deep waters, I will be with you." Next, Psalm 46:10: "Be still and know that I am God." And finally, Jeremiah 29:11: "I know the plans I have for you, says the Lord. They are plans for good and not for disaster, to give you a future and a hope." Not one but three promises. *Wow!* What an amazingly good God and Father we have. Even more amazingly, He was not finished answering my petition. In the midst of my struggle, in the heat of the battle, His still, small voice spoke to me and assured me that He would send someone to be with me during the procedure, someone who would be there on His behalf to comfort me and bring me peace. I immediately wondered who that would be and what form they would come in. Would they appear in the flesh or in the Spirit? Then, as I often do, I let it slip from my mind. That is, until the nurse/tech who was administering my test said this to me several minutes after we met, "You are an usher at my church." Immediately, I was reminded of my Father's promise, and I instantly felt at ease and overwhelmed with His love. This was God's ambassador sent to fulfill His promise(s) to be with me wherever I go, to answer me when I call on Him, and to be my ever-present help in times of trouble. She was so kind as we talked of our families, our faith, and God's promises.

I share this as a testimony to God's incredible goodness to His children and because written on my desk are these words: "Seek after a vital experience of the Lord's loving-kindness and when you have it, speak positively of it, sing gratefully, shout triumphantly" (Spurgeon). Glory to God!

(Note: It is now the morning of February 22, 2020, and as I was rereading this message from God, I noticed, for the first time, that the scripture passage on the bottom of the page that I was writing on yesterday was Joshua 1:9. *Wow!* Any doubt that our Father has us exactly where He purposes us to be?)

February 23, 2020

Some mornings God speaks to me through a devotional written by Charles Spurgeon entitled *Morning and Evening*. Charles was an amazing man of God, and the Holy Spirit has encouraged and instructed me greatly through his writings. His thoughts from this morning's entry are directed to the book of Hebrews. In chapter 13, the writer, quoting Deuteronomy 31:6, states, "Because God has said, 'Never will I leave you; never will I forsake you.'" Mr. Spurgeon, with that passage guiding him, begins by declaring, "Whatever God has said to any one saint, He has said to all. Whether He said it to Abraham or Moses doesn't matter, O believer; He has given it to you as one of the covenanted seed." Lift your eyes to the east and to the west, to the north and to the south, for all of it is yours. Take in every last one of His life-giving promises and stand upon them, for they are yours. God gives to His people everything. Not one thing good does He withhold. Therefore, be bold and believe. "Whatever attributes may compose the character of the Deity, every one of them to its fullest extent shall be engaged on our side." There is nothing that you can need or ask for, nothing in this world or the next that is not fulfilled in these words: "Never will I leave you; never will I forsake you." Thank you, Father, for Your word of truth and for Your servant Charles Spurgeon, through whom You speak it into my heart, my mind, and my spirit daily.

February 24, 2020

Jesus told a crowd of His followers along with His disciples: "If anyone would come after me, he must deny himself and take up his cross and follow me" (Mark 8:34). So what is your cross, you might ask? Before gaining an answer to that question one must have a clear understanding of the purpose and function of this simplistically constructed object. During biblical times, it was fully understood that the cross was a ruthless apparatus of death. It served no other purpose. The cross was created to execute people, and that is the only reason that it was used. It resulted in death every time that it was utilized. Those to whom Jesus was speaking knew exactly what the cross was and what it represented. To their knowledge, He may as well have said grab your cross and follow me down death row, although that is not what He wanted them to hear or to comprehend. What He was doing was painting for them, and for us, a picture. One that would come clearly into focus in a few short days. One of a man condemned to die and required to carry His cross to the place of His execution. A Man who was denying Himself for a greater purpose, the salvation of others. Jesus, being fully aware that He could not save Himself, took up His cross, put aside His personal desires, and followed His Father's leading. And that is exactly what He was teaching in Mark 8:34. Jesus was not saying build a wooden cross and carry it around. Instead, He was referring to the way of the cross—a self-denying, sacrificial, often difficult, others-centered yet eternally rewarding existence. Jesus completed the assignment perfectly; we will not. But we are to follow in His steps all the same. Why? The answer is found in verse 35: "But whoever loses his life for My sake and the gospel's will save it." We will never truly live until we walk down death row, in a spiritual sense, with Jesus. To gain resurrection life, you must first die to yourself. "What does your cross look like?" The answer is that I cannot give you an answer. What I can tell you is that your cross is appointed for you alone by your Father, out of His divine love. You are not allowed to choose it. You are to accept and carry it but not judge or run away from it. Amazingly, I have discovered that the more I carry it, the more God's Spirit teaches me to love it. So much so that I do not want to exchange it, knowing that someday it will be followed by a crown. Take up your cross! Follow Jesus! (Guzik 2015; Mark 8).

February 26, 2020

I am led this morning to write regarding a matter that most, even the saints of God, consistently avoid. One that raises fears and doubts and generates a level of discomfort that is discernible. One that, for all of its mystery, is as much a part of our journey as any of the other staples of our faith. The topic of which I speak is death. It has been my experience that children of God, myself included, often speak of death in a casual, matter-of-fact manner. That is, until they find themselves face-to-face with it. The reality of dying, combined with its uncertainty, is both overwhelming and scary. I have found it, at times, to even be debilitating, both physically and mentally. Why is this? It is understandable that the unredeemed would be terrified at and by the concept of death; but blood-washed, blameless, adored saints? That should not be, and yet it is. Again, I ask, why? The Holy Spirit is showing me that this, like so many other struggles that we encounter, is the product of our lack of knowledge and understanding. Proverbs 4:5 says, "Get wisdom, get understanding," and verse 7 commands, "Though it costs all you have, get understanding." The enemy of our souls is fully aware of these passages and will do everything in his power to keep us from the wisdom and truth that can only be found in God's Word. Wisdom and truth regarding every aspect of our earthly sojourn, including death. With that in mind, let's examine the scriptures to uncover exactly what God has to say.

Death is real and is as every bit a part of our existence as life itself. Ecclesiastes 3:2 declares that there is a time for everything, "A time to be born and a time to die." Ecclesiastes 7:2 pronounces, "For death is the destiny of every man; the living should take this to heart." Accepting the reality of dying is necessary, but only the first step in receiving the truth regarding death. It does not necessarily render it less daunting. Next, God wants us to know that death is not unique to us individually, but is common to all of His children.

"In this way death came to all men, because all sinned" (Rom. 5:12). "Just as man is destined to die once…" (Heb. 9:27). The question may arise: "Why me? Why now?" Know that you are not being singled out and you are not alone. To be fully aware of and to accept the reality of death is necessary to uncover the truth regarding it. The truth that Jesus conquered death and the grave once and for all at Calvary.

> The last enemy to be defeated is death. For He has put everything under His feet. (1 Cor. 15:26–27)

> Death has been swallowed up in victory? (Isa. 25:8)

> Where O death, is your victory? Where O death is your sting? (Hos. 13:14)

The sting of death has been taken away from us by a loving Savior. One who will greet us at that moment when our earthly journey is over and usher us into His glorious kingdom. A voice from heaven told John, "Write: Blessed are the dead who die in the Lord from now on" (Rev. 14:3). Our eternal destination is certain if we invite Jesus to save and redeem us. "If we died with Him, we will also live with Him" (2 Tim. 2:11). Jesus said, "I am the resurrection and the life. He who believes in me will live, even though he dies" (John 11:25). Children of God, not one of us will die alone.

> For not one of us lives to himself alone and none of us dies to himself alone. If we live we live to the Lord; and if we die we die to the Lord. So whether we live or die, we belong to the Lord. (Rom. 14:8)

> Even though I walk through the valley of the shadow of death, I will fear no evil, for You are

with me, Your rod and Your staff they comfort
me. (Ps. 23:4)

Satan will use every weapon at his disposal to attempt to convince us that death is a terrifying event to be greatly feared. For
us who are God's children, it is not! His Word declares otherwise.
Decide today which voice you will choose to listen to. Armed with
the knowledge and understanding gained through God's Word, that
decision should be an easy one. It certainly has become so for me.
Then being fully convinced of the truth we can declare, sincerely,
with Paul:

> I eagerly expect and hope that I will in no way be
> ashamed, but will have sufficient courage so that
> now as always Christ will be exalted in my body,
> whether by life or by death. For to me, to live is
> Christ and to die is gain. (Phil. 1:21)

When the enemy knocks on your door with the fear of death in
his hand, arm yourself with the truth of God's Word and send him
packing in Jesus's name.

February 27, 2020

For most of my life as a Christian, I read Ephesians 6:10–18
("The Armor of God") and struggled to receive anything beneficial
or enlightening from it. I read the words written and found them to
be only that, words. Neither their meaning nor the power that they
imparted was ever received into my spirit or my heart, and thus, I was
blinded from the huge benefits which my Father was affording me.
So that there be no misunderstanding, this condition was in every
sense a result of my neglect of my relationship with Jesus. During this
time, I willingly allowed sin to separate me from my God who adores
me, His Son who died for me, and His Holy Spirit who was pursuing
me. As a result, the privileges, benefits, and promises contained in
His Word escaped me. I opened myself to the dangerous ploys and

schemes of the enemy and, in so doing, was unable to receive the very thing (Armor) that my Father had provided to ward off the same. Praise be to Him that such is no longer my story. A little over three years ago, the Holy Spirit, who was pursuing me, completely caught and rescued me from the state of separation that I had allowed to occur. Since that time God, through His Son Jesus, has restored our right relationship and completely captured my heart. He has cultivated the soil contained there, as well as that found in my spirit, in order to prepare both to receive the truth that He reveals daily. Today, that truth came by way of Ephesians 6:10–18. As I read it, my spirit jumped with excitement. The words sprung off the page and into my heart. What an amazing gift from my Father! Spiritual armor to ward off the schemes of the enemy of my soul and with which to fight the battle. And make no mistake there is a war being fought over us. If you have any doubts, simply resolve to deepen your walk with Jesus, and you will know otherwise. As I read this morning, the significance of each piece of armor was crystal clear.

First, the belt of truth. Jesus declared that He was the truth. In addition, our Father proclaims His Word to be truth and His Son to be the Word. Want to fend off Satan? Profess Jesus as yours and speak God's Word directly to him.

Next, the breastplate of righteousness (right standing with God). Before we can put this piece on, we must accept that it is ours. For many years, I had little idea that through Jesus, I am righteous. I am fully convinced now! Right relationship with my Father that provides me with powerful protection in the battle with Satan. *Wow!* All those years unprotected, but not anymore.

Next, my feet fitted with the gospel of peace. In the past, my focus here was on "gospel" when I am now being shown that it should have been on "peace." Jesus said, "My peace I leave you, my peace I give you." He fully knew how very important peace was going to be in our everyday battle with the enemy. The peace that comes from knowing both who and whose we are provides the strength necessary to stand and not give in. Again, *wow!*

The shield of faith is next. Faith is the substance of things hoped for and the evidence of things not seen. We are to walk by faith and not by sight. At times it will appear to our human eyes that we are losing the battle. Rest assured we are not. During such seasons, we will need faith to shield us from Satan's lies (flaming arrows). Walk by faith, child of God. He is with you always. He will never forsake you.

Two more pieces of armor. First, the helmet of salvation. We are fully saved, blood-bought, redeemed children of God. That cannot be taken away. Satan will try to convince us that it can. Be certain to remind him otherwise at every turn. And while you are at it, refresh his memory regarding the protection and privileges that are yours through Jesus. He cannot have you. Next, is the sword of the Spirit, which is the Word of God. When Satan tempted Jesus in the desert, He refuted him with the words of His Father. Satan fled. He will do likewise when you do the same. Finally, we are to pray in the Spirit on all occasions, with all kinds of prayers and requests. God has given us no greater weapon than prayer. It is our direct avenue to His power, His presence, and His favor—all of which provide us with the utmost protection from the one who comes to kill, steal from, and destroy us. Ephesians 6:10–18, don't go anywhere without it.

February 28, 2020

Do you, like me, often feel as though the enemy has set up camp in your front yard with a pod filled with temptation by his side? And are you also of the mind that he has chosen you to the exclusion of every other person on the earth to serve as the target of his fiery arrows? In my case, the answers are yes and yes. In reality, the responses are no and no. The truth is that, "our enemy prowls around like a roaring lion looking for someone to devour" (1 Pet. 5:8). Take heart, child of God, and be assured that he cannot succeed. Jesus has proclaimed that He would not lose one that our Father has given Him and that each would be with Him and see Him in His glory (John 17:24–26). And while it may seem as though Satan is singling you out, God's Word declares otherwise:

> No temptation has seized you except what is common to man. (1 Cor. 10:13)

Because you know that your brothers throughout the world are undergoing the same kind of sufferings. (1 Pet. 5:9)

So know for certain that you are not being singled out when the enemy arrives with his bag full of schemes and ploys designed to discourage you and render you ineffective in your service for your Father. And be every bit as certain that when he does come, you have a great high priest, Jesus Christ our Lord, who is able to sympathize with your weaknesses having been tempted in every way (Heb. 4:15). Jesus was not only tempted but, in fact, suffered when He was; and therefore, He is able to help those who are being tempted (Heb. 2:18). Temptation will come in many forms: some obvious, others not so much. It is a common misconception that temptation signifies allurement or seduction to sin. While temptation can present in that form, it primarily denotes a circumstance in which we are given a choice to be faithful or unfaithful to our Father. Therefore, be alert for anything that's purpose is to lure you away from your God, and be certain to draw near unto God. For when you do, He will draw near unto you (James 4:8). And the Holy Spirit, who is within you, will provide you with a way out. What Satan intends to harm you, God will turn for your good. When the enemy shows up, rest assured that you are not alone and be confident that He who is with you is far greater than the one trying to establish residency in your yard.

March 1, 2020

In the eighth chapter of the book of Acts, from verse 26 through verse 40, we are told of Philip's encounter with an Ethiopian eunuch, an important official. What an amazing story of God's great love, revealed from two divergent perspectives. First, the eunuch. This was a man of high status, a treasurer. Yet that was not what God saw in him, nor was it what stirred God's attention. We read that he was seeking God in the only way that he knew, through the scriptures (Isaiah). The problem was that he had no understanding of that which he was reading. The good news is that such did not matter to

God. "Draw near unto God and He will draw near unto you" (James 4:8). The eunuch was making an effort to draw near to His God, and so His Father revealed His great love by doing just what He said He would do, drawing near unto him. He did so by sending His Holy Spirit to Philip for the purpose of assigning him to minister that great love. The incredible truth is that by doing so, He was likewise pouring out that love on Philip by affording him the privilege and the honor of being His hands and feet in the fulfillment of this divine purpose. We read that an angel of the Lord spoke to Philip and told him to simply, "Go south on the road that goes from Jerusalem to Garza." Philip did not hesitate; he just obeyed God's Spirit. What amazing faith! Then, when he encountered the eunuch, the Spirit of God again gave Philip the simplest of instructions: "Go to the chariot and stay near it." Again, Philip was obedient. After that, the Holy Spirit's preparation of Philip (which occurred well before this day) kicked into action. Philip explained the scripture that the eunuch could not discern, including "the good news about Jesus," and then at his request, he baptized the important official in a ditch. Immediately, we are told that the Lord took Philip away, and the eunuch did not see him again. Finally, we are told that the eunuch went on his way rejoicing and that Philip continued to preach the gospel in all the towns. As far as we know, the two men did not encounter each other again here on earth. What a powerful story of God's great love for us viewed from two different perspectives. The story of two of God's children divinely encountering each other, however briefly, for the purpose of advancing His kingdom. One that reveals the measures to which God will go to rescue one child and use another. He continues, even today, to rescue and call to service each of His children. Be prepared and on the lookout for either or both. They could appear anywhere at any time.

March 2, 2020

Today I will write the final entry directed at Jesus's prayers found in John chapter 17. You will recall that John details our Lord's pleas to His Father, first for Himself, then for His disciples, and, finally, for all believers. Jesus's last prayer begins by asking God to have all of those who believe in Him through the message of His death and resurrection be one. This is the second instance where Jesus pleas for unity among His followers. He fully knew that their faith would result in them being attacked on all sides by the enemy and that together they would be better equipped to stand firm, just as He was able to do with His Father. In addition, He asks that they be allowed to live in the presence and under the influence of the Holy Trinity in order that they may fulfill their purpose of pointing people to Himself. Two more times Jesus pleads with His Father for complete unity among those who believe, declaring that the glory given to Him from heaven has been passed on to each of us. Think about that for a second. The glory of God was given to Jesus, who in turn has given it to all believers. *Wow!* What would compel God to do such a thing? Two reasons, both found in verse 23. Because He loves us beyond measure, just as He loved Jesus, and because He also loved this lost world to such a degree that He longed for them to know and understand the amazing gift (His Son) that He had sent. Ever question the depth of God's love for all of His creation? Let what you just read sink in, and any such doubt will disappear. Next, Jesus further evidences His immeasurable love by requesting that each of those that His Father had given to Him be allowed to be with Him in heaven and view His glory. You remember, the same glory that God had given Him and that He then passed on to us. Jesus longs to spend eternity with each of those who believe in His name. So much so that on the night before He was to carry the sins of the world to a horrific death, His undeterred focus was on securing our eternal destination. Never allow yourself to underestimate or take for granted the enormity of His love for you. It is unimaginable to my human mind. Glory to God that the Holy Spirit allows my spirit to receive and fathom it. Finally, Jesus asks His righteous Father to instill His love for His Son into the hearts of all believers. He declares that even though we do not know the Father, He does, and that He will never cease to reveal Him to each of us. How important and necessary is it that we have Jesus inside of us and that we receive and grasp the love of our God? So important that forsaking His own self on the night before He was to die, Jesus pleaded for nothing else. That is love! Love for all believers, which includes you and me.

March 3, 2020

Last night as I slept, the Holy Spirit again placed a song in my heart. As we have spoken of previously, it is in this manner that our Father often speaks truth into our spirits and our hearts. ("Where is God our Maker, who gives songs in the night" [Job 35:10].) Truth that I am then led to declare in this place. Truth that this morning proclaims the greatness, the majesty, and the power of the name of Jesus. The song is by Rend Collective and is titled "Your Name Is Power." I have heard it played many times on the radio and not paid particular attention to the message conveyed therein. Then last night, through the guidance of the Holy Spirit, God divinely chose to change that and have the truth of these lyrics explode into and minister to my spirit. I pray that they will do likewise for whomever He has chosen to receive them from this place.

> You're the only answer to the darkness, You're the only right among the wrong, You're the only hope among the chaos, You are the voice that calls me on. Louder than every lie, Our sword in every fight, The truth will chase away the night. (Chorus) Your Name is Power over darkness, Freedom for the captives, Mercy for the broken and the hopeless. Your Name is faithful in the battle, Glory in the struggle, Mighty it won't let us down or fail us. Your Name is power, Your Name is power. When You speak You scatter darkness, Light arrives and Heaven opens, Holy Spirit, Let us hear it, When You speak the church awakens, We believe the change is coming, Holy Spirit, Let us see it. Your Name is power over darkness... (Repeat chorus)

I cannot speak for anyone else, but far too often, I lose sight of the enormous power that is released by the mere mention of Jesus's name: power over darkness, power to save, power to heal, power that is faithful, power that is with us in our struggles, power that will never fail us, power that comes only from our Father. "Therefore God exalted Him to the highest place and gave Him the Name that is above every name" (Phil. 2:9). And incredibly, it is power to which we have free access. Jesus said, "I tell you the truth, My Father will give you whatever you ask in My Name" (John 16:23). There is power in the name of Jesus, and it is for us to claim. Power that is unmatched and only comes from heaven. God's message is clear: "His name is power." Avail yourself of it.

March 4, 2020

Most days I arrive at this place with simply a scripture or a teaching or a thought given to me by the Holy Spirit, along with the desire to write it down and to receive it into my spirit. Where I go from there is definitely not of my doing nor do I ever want it to be. Should the words I pen at any point become my own, may this pencil be taken from my hand. Father, search my heart and, should You find one bit of selfish ambition there, reveal it to me that I can repent immediately thereof. My prayer is that by every step I take, by every thought I have, and every word I speak, that by every breath I breathe, You would be increased and I would be decreased. That should there come a time when I choose to step outside of the guidance and wisdom of Your Holy Spirit, You would intervene by whatever means You choose and redirect me to the peace and safety of Your bosom. Please remind and caution me to always be still and to wait and listen for You to speak before moving. Oh, my Lord and my God, that I would never bring shame or disgrace to Your name or to Your kingdom, but that all I do and all I say would bring You glory and honor. Today, that is what You have placed upon my heart.

HE MUST INCREASE; I MUST DECREASE

March 5, 2020

My heart, my mind, and my spirit are flooded this morning and overwhelmed with the faithfulness of God. Like so many other of the benevolences of my Father, His unrelenting devotion and fidelity to His children are clear to me. But have I taken the time to allow the depth and magnitude of His loyalty to absorb into my spirit? I have not. Today, through the ministering of the Holy Spirit, that will change. The truth can be found in God's Holy Word. Over and over again the Scriptures testify of His unceasing and passionate commitment to His saints.

He is faithful in all He does. (Ps. 33:4)

The Lord is faithful to all His promises. (Ps. 145:13)

The Lord who remains faithful forever. (Ps. 146:6)

And God is faithful; He will not let you be. (1 Cor. 10:13)

He will remain faithful... (2 Tim. 2:13)

For He who promised is faithful... (Heb. 10:23)

Your faithfulness reaches the skies. (Ps. 57:10)

Love and faithfulness go before You... (Ps. 89:14)

The faithfulness of the Lord endures forever. (Ps. 117:2)

Great is Your faithfulness. (Lam. 3:23)

Is there any doubting our God's faithfulness to and over us? His Word declares it repeatedly. He is by His very nature passionately devoted and committed to us. Take time to consider and ponder this truth. Let it absorb into your inner being. In order to fully receive the overwhelming greatness of God's faithfulness, we need look no further than Calvary. It was there that our Father displayed a depth of love and devotion to His children that has never been witnessed before or since. A degree of commitment to each one of us whom He adores that is beyond the comprehension of our human minds. Is His faithfulness great? Absolutely, it is! Its greatness shone for all to see over two thousand years ago outside of the city of Jerusalem, and it continues to do so in the lives of the saints of God each and every day. You can count on it, and because of it, you can be assured that He will be with you always, that He will never leave you, that He adores you, that you can stand upon His promises, and that which He says He will do. Last night as I slept another song rang out in my spirit: "Better" by Pat Barrett.

> Your love is better than life, You are the well that won't run dry, I have tasted and I have seen, You are better than all these things.

God once again being greatly faithful in my life and in the lives of all His children. Glory be to His name!

March 8, 2020

In three of the four gospels, we are told of Jesus taking Peter, James, and John up on a high mountain and of how He was transfigured before their eyes there. We are also told of a voice from heaven, saying, "This is My Son, whom I love; with whom I am well pleased. Listen to Him." Later, Peter, in his second letter to the church, declares, "We were eyewitnesses to His majesty. For He received honor and glory from God the Father when the voice came to Him from the Majestic Glory…" (2 Pet. 1:17). Highly blessed were Peter, James, and John; but how much more greatly rewarded will be those who have not seen or heard directly from God and still believe. And in actuality, have we not been given at least an equal portion of the presence and the favor of our Father by way of His Holy Word, taught and explained to us by the incredible gift of His Holy Spirit. Yes, God spoke directly to the three disciples on that mountain, but never lose sight of the fact that He continues to do the very same thing to each of His children every day through His Word and by His Spirit.

March 10, 2020

Time and time again in God's Word we are instructed to not be afraid. We are repeatedly reminded to be strong and courageous and to not fear or be discouraged. Why so many times? Because it is very important. Our Father knows full well that fear is a potent tool in the hands of our enemy. One that we are particularly susceptible to. Satan is completely aware that fear can never separate God's children from His great love that is theirs in Christ Jesus. Nothing can accomplish that result (Rom. 8:39). Nonetheless, the enemy will not stop attempting to render us ineffective and unsuccessful in completing our God-directed assignment of advancing His kingdom. Can fear negate our heaven-declared identity or redirect our eternal destination? No, it cannot. Can it steal our joy and impede our focus upon the truth that is declared over us in the Word of God? Yes, it can. Can it get in the way of our communication with, our worship of, and our service for our heavenly Father? Yes, it can, if we allow it to. One need look no further than the story of Peter to understand the reason behind this great attention to fear. Peter spent three years walking with, learning from, and serving Jesus. No one loved Him more or more zealously defended our Lord. Peter swore that he would never deny Jesus, and yet at His greatest time of need, that is exactly what he did. How could that happen? One word: *fear.* I believe that we have all at some point or another fallen prey to Satan's use of fear: fear of death, fear of illness, fear of suffering, fear of lack, fear of failure, fear of loss. It presents itself in many forms; all of which are directed at God's children with the same purpose. But wait, as always, there is good news. We serve a God who is greater than all our fears. Over and over again He reminds us to not be afraid, to fear not. One of my favorites is found in Mark 5:36 where Jesus, speaking to Jairus, says, "Do not be afraid, only believe." Simple? Yes! Laden with truth and reassurance? Absolutely! Our Father provides us with an infallible defense to the weapon of fear. His name is Jesus. Through His Son, God established His perfect love for each of us and then declared, through John (1 John 4:18), "But perfect love drives out fear…" Fear is a liar. Perfect love is the truth that casts it away. Jesus is perfect love. Lean on Him, and watch fear flee.

March 11, 2020

God instructs that my role and responsibility as a husband is a most sacred calling and one of the utmost importance. One that I have all too often neglected. One that I allowed to be driven by emotions, desires, and ambitions that originated far outside of the plan of God. A mindset that allowed the enemy to gain a stronghold into and come within a breath of destroying my marriage, a marriage that God had ordained and purposed. How could that happen? Isn't our Father greater than Satan? Didn't Jesus destroy the works of the enemy once and for all at Calvary? Yes, He is, and absolutely He did. The problem was not with God or with His authority and power. The issue was with me. My willingness to allow sin to enter into my life and to separate me from God's love, God's Word, and God's promises to and over me. Separation that deprived my marriage of the love, the blessing, and the protection that my Father intended for it and which it needed to thrive. Just to be clear, I have always loved my wife, just not in the manner that God intended. That is, not until the last three years. Not coincidentally, during the time which my Father has been performing an amazing work of sanctification in my life, He has simultaneously opened my eyes to the incredible gift that is my wife and shown me, through His Word and by His Spirit, how to love and honor her in the manner in which He has purposed. "Husbands, love your wives, just as Christ loved the church and gave Himself up for her…" (Eph. 5:25). For thirty-three years, I had no idea how to love Megan to that degree. For the last three years, I cannot imagine loving her any other way. Jesus died for the church, so great was His love for her. Husbands, that is the degree to which He calls us to love our wives. If it seems like a tall order, it is not. Draw near to God, press into His Word, and lean upon His Spirit; and you will be amazed at how easy and how rewarding it is to love your wife the way God desires you to.

March 12, 2020

God's Word is filled with both His commands for His children as well as the promises that He assures are ours through His Son Jesus. At no place in Scripture are each more revealed than in the Thirty-seventh Psalm. David's writing serves as a treasure trove of directives and promises from heaven and provides us with invaluable guidance regarding both the manner in which we are to live our lives along with the privileges and benefits that flow therefrom. This morning we will examine what our Father has to say through His servant David.

"Trust in the Lord and do good…and enjoy safe pasture" (vs. 3). I have come to understand that what God wants most is our love and our trust. When we give Him both, He promises to protect us.

"Delight in the Lord and He will give you the desires of your heart" (vs. 4). Does your relationship with your Father bring you great joy? Do you long for Him and His presence? If not, you can. He wants you to. Draw near to Him and watch your joy explode, and at the same time, prepare to see the desires that are deep within you fulfilled.

"Commit your way to the Lord…and He will do this: He will make your righteousness shine…" (vs. 5 and 6). Surrender to God, get off the fence, go all in; for that is what He longs for from His children. Obey this command, and your right relationship with Him will be evident to all.

Next, we receive three directives with one promise flowing from them collectively:

> Be still before the Lord and wait patiently for
> Him… (vs. 7)

Refrain from anger and turn from wrath… (vs. 8)

Do not fret; hope in the Lord… (vs. 8 and 9)

You will inherit the land and enjoy great peace.
(vs. 9 and 11)

God demands our attention, and we need His. To accomplish both, we *must* be still and wait patiently. Nothing else can be allowed to get in the way. Our Father will not be second fiddle to anyone or anything. He is also a gentle Father who demands the same from His children with no room for anger or wrath. And finally, fear must be replaced with hope. We are repeatedly told to not be afraid. "Perfect love casts out all fear." So do not fret, just place your hope in your Lord. Do these things, and the promise of having your every need met (inheriting the land) will be yours, along with the immeasurable gift of "great peace." And there is more.

Verses 12–19 do not proclaim a command so much as they declare a truth, one that is for all God's children and one that is only ours through Jesus. "You are righteous and blameless" (vs. 12–18). Only by way of Calvary do we find right standing with our God and only by the cross is our guilt removed. Declare Jesus your Lord and receive the gifts of forgiveness, salvation, and righteousness, along with eternal life ("Your inheritance will endure forever") and strength in times of trouble ("In times of disaster you will not wither").

Next, "Give generously and lend freely and your children will be blessed" (vs. 26). God's plan always includes our service to others. Whatever you have is His, not yours. Use it to His honor and to do His will, and when you do, He promises to bless those most important to you, your children. *Awesome!*

"Turn from evil and do good, be just and wise…" (vs. 27–31), and you "will be protected forever" (vs. 28). God is good and just and wise. There is no darkness within Him. It cannot stand in His presence. As He is, so we must be. Therefore, we are called to do good, to be fair, and to embrace the wisdom that comes from heaven.

Do these things, and God's hand of protection will be over you and follow you all the days of your life.

Finally, "Wait for the Lord and keep His way" (vs. 34), for when you do, "He is your stronghold in time of trouble. The Lord helps them and delivers them" (vs. 39–40). Again, we must wait and be patient, always being mindful to live as He instructs ("keep His way"). This command is not always easy to accomplish; however, the reward for doing so is great. You will receive strength and deliverance.

There you have it, a virtual guidebook for living a life that honors God, along with the promises, privileges, and benefits that flow therefrom. Let's strive to walk accordingly all the days of our lives.

March 14, 2020

The last three verses of the last chapter of Matthew's gospel (chapter 28) record the final words spoken by Jesus before He ascended to His rightful place with His Father in heaven. The actual last statement that He made was this: "And surely I am with you always, to the very end of the age" (vs. 20). One of what I refer to as my life scriptures is found at Joshua 1:9. It states: "For the Lord your God will be with you wherever you go." Both reassuring and comforting promises from our Lord, without a doubt. But do we ever take the time to consider the impact of each upon our daily walk with Jesus? If not, we most certainly should. Our Father adores each of His children, and from that great love flows a desire to be with and to walk through life with us. His presence is by no means gifted to us out of some sense of obligation or duty but arises naturally from His amazing love that has always existed and will continue to live on forever. Love that is spoken of 316 times in my Bible. Love that led Him to send His only Son to be sacrificed upon a cross in order that right relationship may be restored between He and His children. Love that drives His passion to live and walk with us not only in His kingdom, but also here on our earthly journey. Take a moment to absorb the real meaning of "I am with you always..." and the love that motivated it. It should overwhelm us, reassure us, and comfort us. It does me. In addition, it should inspire and prompt us to more vigilantly follow and obey the instructions found in 1 Peter chapter 4. Being fully convinced that He is with us always, should we not "live the rest of our earthly lives…for the will of God" (vs. 2)? And should we not also be "clear minded and self-controlled so that we can pray" (vs. 7), "love each other deeply" (vs. 8), "offer hospitality to one another without grumbling" (vs. 9), "use the gift we have received to serve others" (vs. 10), "speak as one speaking the very words of God" (vs. 11), "serve with the strength provided by our Father in order that He may be praised" (vs. 11)? Jesus promised that He would be with us always, wherever we go. Those words declare a powerful truth, one that is overflowing with assurance, comfort, and awareness of responsibility. Let's resolve to be ever mindful of His presence and His favor and to reflect and walk in each for the remainder of our heaven-ordained pilgrimage.

March 15, 2020

Not long ago I was led to write of God's plan and purpose for men in their calling to be good husbands. Today the Holy Spirit is desirous of doing likewise to women regarding their divinely appointed role as wives. This is not a topic with which I am either familiar or comfortable. Having obviously never been a woman or a wife, I am unable to draw from experience or speak directly from my heart in this regard. However, what I am able to do is trust God's Spirit to fill my mind with the truth that He purposes to impart and then to guide my hand in writing it, as is often the case that begins with His Word. The scripture to which I am led to is not Ephesians 5:22–24, as one might expect, but is instead found at 1 Peter 3:1–6. Immediately upon reading these six verses, I am taken by how profoundly different God's perspective is from that of the world, and I am reminded of Isaiah 55:8, which declares, "For my thoughts are not your thoughts, neither are your ways my ways…" Peter begins by writing this:

> Wives, in the same way, be submissive to your
> husbands, so that, if any of them do not believe

the Word, they may be won over without words
by the behavior of their wives, when they see the
purity and reverence of your lives. (vs. 1 and 2)

In the world in which we live, the word "submission" gives rise
to negative emotions, especially among women, who are continuously challenged to attain equality with and even superiority over
men. However, the submission of which our Father speaks shares
little in common with the one of the world. It is characterized by
respect, trust, and love and results in glory, honor, and praise being
lavished upon our Father. It does not subrogate, enslave, or indebt.
Do we believe for even one second that each and every one of God's
children, whether man or woman, are not viewed equally in His eyes?
Of course, we do not. Peter continues at verse 3:

Your beauty should not come from outward
adornment, such as braided hair and the wear-
ing of gold jewelry and fine clothes. Instead, it
should be that of your inner self, the unfading
beauty of a gentle and quiet spirit, which is of
great worth in God's sight. (vs. 3 and 4)

Again we are provided a perspective of God that is diametrically
opposed to that of the world. The society in which we live propounds
that the more makeup, the more jewelry, the smaller the waist, the
larger the other parts, the more appealing the woman. A view from
the outside in. Our Father defines beauty directly opposite, from the
inside out, and declares the same to be of great worth in His sight.
Wives, do you long to be beautiful in the eyes of your God and of
your husband? If so, then heed His Word.

For this is the way the holy women of the past
who put their hope in God used to make themselves beautiful. They were submissive to their
own husbands, like Sarah, who obeyed Abraham
and called him her master. You are her daughters

143

if you do what is right and do not give way to
fear. (vs. 5 and 6)

Sarah was submissive, not as the world defined but as her God
described. She was beautiful, not by worldly standards but in the
sight of her Father. That is God's formula for every woman (wife)
who is a part of His family. Live according to God's plan, and not
only will you be pleasing in His sight but in the eyes of your husband
as well. I can personally testify to the same.

March 16, 2020

Recently, the Holy Spirit had me write His thoughts regarding
fear and how the perfect love that flows from heaven overcomes all
such trepidation. Perfect love, whose name on earth was Jesus and
who from the beginning was the Word and who was with God and
who was God (John 1:1–2). Throughout my journey, that perfect
love, which can only be found in and through Jesus, has been poured
over me by way of the Word and has served to cast fear from me.
Frequently, such love is presented by way of God's amazing promises
spoken to me by the Holy Spirit, most often through scripture. At
His direction, I will share several of those promises with each of you
who have been led to read this, believing that our Father purposes to
deliver you from fear(s) just as He is accomplishing in my life. In no
specific order, here they are:

> Yet this I call to mind and therefore I have hope.
> Because of the Lord's great love we are not con-
> sumed, for His compassions never fail. They are
> new every morning; great is Your faithfulness. I
> say to myself, "The Lord is my portion; therefore
> I will wait for Him." The Lord is good to those
> whose hope is in Him, to the one who seeks Him.
> (Lam. 3:21–25)

Have I not commanded you? Be strong and courageous. Do not be terrified, do not be discouraged. For the Lord your God will be with you wherever you go. (Josh. 1:9)

He will have no fear of bad news; his heart is steadfast, trusting in the Lord. His heart is secure, he will have no fear; in the end he will look in triumph on his foes. (Ps. 112:7–8)

I will lead the blind by ways they have not known, along unfamiliar paths I will guide them; I will turn the darkness into light before them and make the rough places smooth. These are the things I will do; I will not forsake them." ("Who is blind but my servant...? Who is blind but the one committed to me?") (Isa. 42:16 and 19)

All the days ordained for me were written in Your book before one of them came to be. (Ps. 139:1)

God is our refuge and our strength, He is our ever-present help in times of trouble. Therefore we will not fear... (Ps. 46:1–2)

Be still and know that I am God; I will be exalted among the nations, I will be exalted in the earth. The Lord Almighty is with us; the God of Jacob is our fortress. (Ps. 46:10–11)

So do not fear, for I am with you; do not be dismayed for I am your God. I will strengthen you and help you; I will uphold you with My righteous right hand. (Isa. 41:10)

Because he loves me, says the Lord, I will rescue him; I will protect him, for he acknowledges my Name. He will call upon me, and I will answer him; I will be with him in trouble, I will deliver him and honor him. With long life I will satisfy him and show him my salvation. (Ps. 91:14–16)

The Lord is my shepherd I shall not want; He makes me to lie down in green pastures; He leadeth me beside still waters, He restores my soul. He guides me in paths of righteousness for His Name's sake. Even though I walk through the valley of the shadow of death, I will fear no evil, for You are with me; Your rod and Your staff they comfort me. You prepare a table before me in the presence of my enemies. You anoint my head with oil; my cup overflows. Surely goodness and mercy shall follow me all the days of my life, and I will dwell in the House of the Lord forever. (Ps. 23)

There it is, the perfect love of God spoken over you by way of promises found in His Word. Receive them and fear not.

March 18, 2020

During this season of my journey, the Holy Spirit is leading me down a path toward freedom—freedom from sin as well as from the guilt and shame that accompanies it, freedom from worry and fear, freedom from control and unforgiveness, freedom to walk and live in the fullness of God's presence and favor. One of the means by which He is revealing this truth to me is a curriculum entitled "Freedom," which originates from heaven and is administered through the Church of the Highlands in Birmingham, Alabama. Week 6 is entitled "A Life of Surrender," and for the next couple of mornings, I will share some thoughts regarding surrender and offense found therein.

First, surrender. Typically, surrender is associated with defeat, waving a white flag or hands in the air on a battlefield. But when it is applied to our lives in Jesus, the act of giving control to Him actually leads to our freedom. In order to live a life of surrender, we must first have unwavering faith in the One to whom we are yielding. This is a level of trust that can only be gained through relationship. Trust is earned. Until you know and understand someone, you cannot trust them with something of value. Therefore, in order to surrender our lives to God, we must first know and have confidence that He is good and worthy of our affections. That is not always easy or painlessly accomplished. Grasping the reality of what Jesus did for me was both the first and a giant step toward fostering trust and building relationship. A huge element of trust is love; and never has greater, deeper, more unconditional love been exhibited than at Calvary. In order to build relationship and acquire the trust, surrender, and freedom that accompany it, it is necessary that you get to know your Father better. That doesn't have to take a particular form, although it always begins with spending time together. Feed your spirit with His Spirit through prayer, the Word, service, and time spent with fellow believers. Your relationship with Him will blossom, and your life will flourish. You will find that your Father's ways are different from yours in many situations. That is where trust and surrender become essential, because His ways are higher than ours and His thoughts are better than ours (Isa. 55:9). We must give up control of our lives to the One who writes better stories than we do. Jesus, take the wheel. Know that your God wants to make the dark places of our life light and the rough places smooth (Isa. 42:16). He will do so when we surrender control of every part of our journey over to Him. Spiritual order comes when He has complete control. Whatever we hold on to becomes our responsibility to maintain. How's that been working for you? Yeah, that's what I thought! Same here! We were created to worship, and we will worship what we value most. If we desire to walk in spiritual order, God must be first. He must be the subject of our worship, of our affection, of control in our lives, and of our trust. Want to experience true freedom? Then surrender everything to Him that is worthy, to Him that is able ("Freedom," Church of the Highlands 2001–2021).

March 19, 2020

In yesterday's entry, I was led to pass on some of God's thoughts regarding surrender. Today, He wishes to speak to the concept of offense. The first thought that comes to my mind when I consider this subject is that my brother, who is a pastor and a man who loves God deeply, has been led by God's Spirit to speak on offense many times over (seemingly once or twice a year) during his ministry. Why would that be? It is because offended people are spiritually unhealthy people. When asked which is the greatest commandment, Jesus responded, "Love the Lord your God with all your heart and with all your soul and with all your mind. This is the first and greatest commandment. And the second is like it: Love your neighbor as yourself..." (Matt. 22:38–39). When we harbor offense toward our neighbor and, yes, even toward our Father, we render ourselves unable to fulfill either of these two most significant directives proclaimed by Jesus. When we are unyielding of our own principles and unwilling to give up our "right to be right," we fail to honor our Father, and we inhibit His presence in and His favor over our lives. However, if we instead choose to be unoffended, no matter the situation, we glorify our God and open the floodgates of His blessings and promises over us (Prov. 19:11). But is making the choice to overlook an offense levied at us as simple as saying that we will do so? In most cases, it is not. Like the majority of adjustments that the Holy Spirit purposes in our character, some effort on our part is required. Here are six ways to stay unoffended that I found in the Church of the Highlands' "Freedom" curriculum. I trust our Father that each is divinely purposed to assist us in living an offense-free life for Him.

First, "Take the lowest seat." Consider everyone more important than yourself. Put the needs of others before your own. Honor and please God by being a servant.

Number two, "Always remain grateful." Gratitude keeps us aware of God's provision and blessing.

Number three, "Give others their freedom." Do not try to control people. Their decisions are theirs not yours, let them make them.

Number four, "Make decisions that promote life in others." When someone offends you maintain a positive attitude toward them. Choose to speak words of life over them and to build them up.

Number five, "Trust God to bring justice when an offense comes." Vengeance belongs to the Lord. None of us wants what we really deserve; and thankfully, as a result of Calvary, we will not receive it.

And lastly, number six, "Dedicate time to the lord." Refresh your spirit in prayer, Bible study, and fellowship with Jesus. God's presence brings change. There is a reason why the Holy Spirit led my brother to so often caution versus offense. It separates God's children from each other, from a world that needs Him, and, worst of all, from Him. Strive to live a life free from offense because unoffended people are, generally speaking, spiritually healthy people; and those are the ones who glorify God ("Freedom," Church of the Highlands 2001–2021)

March 20, 2020

We are all familiar with the story of Jesus taking five loaves of bread and two fish and miraculously feeding five thousand plus followers on the shore of the Sea of Galilee (Matt. 14 and John 6). It is Matthew's account of what transpired next that I will speak to this morning. We are told that Jesus immediately made the disciples get into the boat and go on ahead of Him (Matt. 14:22). He was intentional and clear in His directive. As was always the case, there was a plan and a purpose behind His actions, one that we learn in verse 23: "He went up to the mountainside to pray. When evening came, He was there alone..." Jesus desired and needed to be with His Father. He still does, and so should we. The troubling element of the story, at least to the human eye, is found in verse 24: "But the boat was already a considerable distance from land, buffeted by the waves because the wind was against it." Storms were prone to be severe and to arise suddenly and without warning in this region. The disciples had to have been greatly fearful of perishing, not to mention exhausted from rowing three plus miles. Their minds must have been racing with flesh-driven questions. How could Jesus have sent us to die in such a manner? Why did He demand so strongly that we go ahead without Him? Did He save Himself at our expense? Didn't He just feed five thousand people in a miraculous manner? Where is He? Were we wrong about Him? Oftentimes, we find ourselves in similar life circumstances as did the disciples. Our boat may not be buffeted by wind and rain in the middle of a lake near Capernaum, but it is filled and paralyzed by fear and doubt nonetheless. Instead of being threatened by wind, we face health, financial, family or relationship crises that propel us on a downward spiral laced with angst and panic. A freefall that leads us to ask many of the same questions that surely flooded the disciples' minds at this overwhelming moment. One that causes us to abandon all semblance of faith, trust, and surrender. Oh, we of little faith, why do we doubt? (Matt. 14:31). Almost immediately, the disciples' doubts and questions were resolved. "Jesus went out to them, walking on the lake...and they were terrified... (vs. 25–26), and He said to them, "Take courage! It is I. Don't be afraid" (vs. 27). Jesus had never lost sight of them, just as He never does us. He knew right where they were and exactly what their need was, and we are no different. Did He come and rescue them when they desired? No, He did not, but His eye was always on them. Though it may have appeared otherwise, He never left them, and at the perfect time, He walked across the water to save them. Know this, dear saint of God, His eye is directly upon you. He knows where you are and what you are going through, and He is walking across your sea of despair to deliver you at just the perfect time. Trust and believe in Him. And when He arrives, do not neglect to respond as the disciples did by bowing down and worshiping Him.

March 21, 2020

As I write, we find ourselves in the middle of a pandemic. A virus called COVID-19, or coronavirus, is spreading throughout the world and causing sickness, fear, and death. People everywhere, including

God's children, are restricted to their homes and burdened with concern that this scourge of sickness will land on their doorstep. Here are a couple of things to never forget. Our Father remains on His throne. He is far superior to Satan and greater than any virus! Jesus defeated the devil at Calvary once and for all. No weapon formed against us will prosper. God was not surprised nor caught off guard by COVID-19! He is in control. He always has been, and He always will be. He adores us, each and every one of us, especially those who are His children. So what are we to do in the midst of this pandemic? We pray, and we seek His presence and His favor. We trust Him and stand upon His promises. Then when we have done all else, we simply stand (Eph. 6:13). As I was earnestly praying this morning for those that I love dearly and for those whom God has placed under my care, the Holy Spirit spoke gently to me and said, "This is the urgency with which you should pray and seek Me always. This season is no different from any other. Satan is always prowling around to see who he can devour. Seek Me always and do so fervently. This season may appear to be more concerning, but it is not, it is just more visible. Always pray and do so with urgency."

March 22, 2020

During the last month or so I have, on two separate occasions, had friends express their uncertainty regarding their eternal destination. Their doubt would not have surprised me but for the fact that each has welcomed Jesus into their heart and asked Him to be their Savior. In addition, I have witnessed firsthand their desire to draw closer to and to serve Him. At first, I was troubled by their sentiments and wondered how this could be. Then almost immediately the Spirit gently reminded me that I too had lived with the same uncertainty for most of my life. God has shown us that embracing our identity in Him changes everything and is the key to spiritual maturity. Our enemy knows that he cannot have those that God has declared to be His, but that does not stop Him from doing anything that he can to obscure our true identity and the promises that accompany it. Immediately after the first of my conversations described above, I was compelled to put pen to paper and begin writing the thoughts that were flooding my spirit and my mind—thoughts that had freed me from the bondage of doubt and uncertainty. I am led to write those here, believing my Father to use them to do likewise for you. Receive them by the power of the Holy Spirit.

> For those who are in Jesus (have invited Him into their heart and asked Him to save them from their sins) their eternal destination is certain. Regardless of what anyone else says or what we ourselves think, God declares it to be so and therefore it is established. Here is how the story goes. God created man to be in perfect union and relationship with Himself. Then sin entered the world through Adam and that union was severed. Sin separated us from God and broke our fellowship with Him. Through Abraham and by way of Moses God entered into a covenant with man which was based upon many laws and the shedding of blood sacrifices. While this covenant worked, sorta, God had a better plan in mind. A new covenant, one that would once and for all heal the separation that sin had caused and restore the fellowship between Himself and man that He had always desired. That new covenant was Jesus. God sent His perfect, sinless Son to be sacrificed, one time, for all of the sins of the world. And all that He required in return for that amazing gift (forgiveness, redemption, eternity with Him) was that we, by faith, receive Jesus into our hearts, acknowledge that we are hopeless sinners without Him and ask Him to save us from our lost state. When we have that moment of decision, and there needs to be such a moment, then our salvation is secured and He sends the Holy Spirit to lead and guide us through the remainder of

our journey (prayer, the Word, serving, discipleship, witnessing, etc.). From that moment forward our eternal destination is established. The thief on the cross beside Jesus is proof. He simply asked Jesus to remember him when He entered into His glory and Jesus assured the man that it would be so. No more do's and don'ts, no more guilt, no more shame. Jesus died for ALL sins, not just some. The next really important truth to receive into your heart and into your spirit is that your Father ADORES you! You are His child. Good fathers do not cast their children away when they mess up and they never disown them. God is more than a good father, He is the BEST Father and His children can 100% count on His promises. Remember that He sent Jesus to die a horrific death for ALL of your sins, not just the ones that you committed prior to asking Him into your heart. Is the God that we know really going to treat His chosen children otherwise? Read Ephesians, chapters 1 and 2 and you will find a list of who your heavenly Father says that you are. (Blessed, Holy, Blameless, Redeemed, Righteous, Forgiven, Chosen, Included in Christ, Marked with a Seal, the Holy Spirit, Alive in Jesus, Raised and Seated with Him, Saved, His Workmanship, Near to God, A Citizen of Heaven, A Child of God, His and Adored) All God's words, not mine! That is who you are and He desires that you live accordingly. So know that if you are in Jesus your eternal destination is not in doubt. It is CERTAIN! It was bought with a very high price. And if there has never been a moment where you asked Him to be your Savior, then now is the time. Simply pray this prayer or one similar to it and mean it sincerely in your heart: "Jesus I need a Savior. I am a sinner. Please forgive me of my sins and come into my heart and be the Lord of my life. By faith I receive my salvation." If you prayed that prayer all of Heaven is rejoicing and your eternal destination is secured! You will NEVER have made a more important decision in your life. The Holy Spirit is now in you and will guide and direct you on your journey through this life. You are also now a member of an enormous family of believers who want nothing more than to stand with you and help you in whatever way that they are able. All you need to do is ask! My prayer is that the presence and the favor of God be with you and upon you all the days of your life. Be blessed and be well!

Love in Christ!
Jeff

In case you were wondering, I gave a copy of this writing to both of my friends and will do the same to anyone else whom the Spirit leads, trusting God to reveal the depth of His love, the assurance of their identity, and the certainty of their eternal destination through the truth proclaimed therein. Truth declared by our Father through His Holy Word and ministered by His Holy Spirit to and over each and every one of His children. How blessed and honored and privileged are we to be counted among the same!

March 23, 2020

My wife and I rarely watch television together. She records many different shows and movies and watches them on one of our TVs while I view other programs on another. Yesterday, I was nearby when she began, as she has done countless times prior, to watch a movie. Normally, I would simply move on to some other task, paying no attention to what she was viewing. But on this occasion, something was different. My focus was instantly drawn to the television in general and to one actor in particular, Tim McGraw. I really like Tim as an actor and know that of late he has mostly played roles in inspirational and/or faith-based movies. The Holy Spirit had my attention. I sat on the couch and asked Megan for the name of the movie.

"*The Shack*," she responded.

"What's it about?" I asked.

"I am not sure, but I have wanted to see it for some time," she said.

That was enough for me. I was all in, and it did not take long for the Spirit to reveal His purpose for bringing me to that place at that time. *The Shack* is an interesting movie with a powerful witness and testimony of God's incredible love for, mercy and grace over, and relentless pursuit of His children. While I have no intention of spoiling the film for those of you who are led to see it, I do want to share a couple of thoughts with you. As you are well aware by now, my Father has me on a journey, at the center of which is identity, both His and mine. I have come to realize that the revelation, knowledge, and acceptance of each is essential to the completion and fulfilment of my God-ordained calling and purpose. Without embracing His unconditional love, His endless mercy, His relentless devotion, and His eternal faithfulness for and to me, I will be unable to impart each of the same to those who have been placed under my care and, in turn, share with them the truth that has been poured into my life. While *The Shack* may not exactly present our Father, His Son, and the Holy Spirit in a traditionally accepted manner, it does indisputably convey the attributes, qualities, and character that define and form the identity, which has been revealed to me on my pilgrimage, of Each. One has to be enlightened to and convinced of who God is, and the implications of the same upon their own identity, before being fully able to share that truth with the world around them. Truth of which I have become not only aware but am now completely persuaded. Revelation that I found a rich and moving depiction of in *The Shack*. I am not very often prone to the shedding of tears, although I have recently discovered that when the Holy Spirit is at work and moving in my life, I cry uncontrollably. Yesterday, I wept or fought back tears for three straight hours.

March 24, 2020

Forgiveness is a mandatory requirement for God's children—one that is perceived as doable, until it is not; one that is too often avoided or ignored—that is, until the Holy Spirit deems otherwise; one that is freely received yet begrudgingly withheld; one that Jesus, and then later Paul, spoke of in clear terms on several occasions. "For if you forgive men when they sin against you, your heavenly Father will also forgive you. But if you do not forgive men their sins, your Father will not forgive your sins" (Matt. 6:14–15). Jesus also declared, "And when you stand praying, if you hold anything against anyone, forgive him, so that your Father in Heaven may forgive you your sins" (Mark 11:25). On another occasion, in response to Peter's question regarding the number of times that he should forgive his brother, Jesus replied, "I tell you, not seven times, but seventy times seven" (Matt. 18:21). Later, Paul, writing first to the Ephesians and then to the Colossians, wrote, "Forgiving each other just as in Christ God forgave you" (Eph. 4:32) and "Bear with each other and forgive whatever grievances you may have against one another. Forgive as the Lord forgave you" (Col. 3:13). In my experience, forgiveness is easily granted when the offense is less painful. A harsh word from a friend, a neglectful snub or rejection, or an unintentional mishap to one's person or property are, or should be, readily forgiven. However, the deeper the hurt, the more reluctant we are to pardon. To the one whose spouse has abandoned him or her for someone "better"; or to the person who has been defrauded of their life's savings; or to the heartbroken soul whose child has been stolen, injured, or even worse, forgiveness is a foreign concept that cannot or will not be fathomed. And yet Jesus used the words "anything" against "anyone," and Paul wrote, "Forgive whatever grievances…" Forgiveness is hard! A truth of which our Father is completely aware. Consider the degree of pain that He incurred watching His Son beaten, scourged, ridiculed, and murdered at Calvary. And why did He endure such unspeakable agony? Because of the depth of His love for you and for me. Love that exceeded the pain. Love that led to forgiveness. Forgiveness that was possible only because of love. Forgiveness that was necessary for our redemption. Forgiveness without which we could never see or stand before Him. See now why forgiveness is so important to our Father. His Son gave His life for it. Without it, His sacrifice has no meaning. Is it easy? No, it is not. Is it impossible? Because of love, the answer is again no. We are called to forgive those who sin against us, every one of them, because our Father has forgiven us of all our sins—every last single, filthy, wretched one of them. Forgiveness founded on love. Love that He pours out on us so that we can do likewise on each other. Love that is greater than all our sins. Love that empowers us to *forgive*!

March 25, 2020

Surely we are all familiar with Judas Iscariot. Mark's gospel describes him from the very beginning as the one who betrayed Jesus (Mark 3:19). Let's examine not only who Judas was but the warning that our Father declares to His church by way of his story. Judas was chosen by Jesus, at God's direction, to be one of only twelve who would spend three years walking in the closest of fellowship with Him. Debate exists as to whether or not God chose Judas for the sole purpose of betraying Jesus. It is my conviction that He did not, that He did not cause or purpose Judas's actions but that the allure of sin beguiled him and resulted in the same. Jesus loved Judas greatly, and though He was well aware of what was to come, I believe that He did not purpose it. You decide for yourself. For the purpose of today's writing, that answer is not critical. What is important is that during those three years Judas lived in the most intimate of relationships with our Lord. He sat beside Him, spoke and listened to Him, laughed and cried along with Him. He witnessed firsthand Jesus heal those who were sick, cast out demons from those who were possessed, and raise to life those who had died. He was baptized in Jesus's name, was a visible member of His church, and sat at His communion table. Yet for a mere thirty pieces of silver, he was enticed to betray his Lord, the Son of God, and with a kiss nonetheless. Judas professed to be a follower of Jesus but lived in the world so carelessly that it opened the door for the enemy to seduce him into the unthinkable. Sound familiar? It does to me. It is exactly where and how I chose to live for most of my life. What an incredibly dangerous manner in which to proceed, one in which so many embark. But praise be to our Father that His love is so great that He pursues and rescues His children and restores them, as He has done with me, to right relationship and fellowship with Himself. Let the story of Judas serve as a caution to each of us and then let our cry be, "Oh Lord keep me from being seduced by the things of this world. Preserve me from every false way. Make me sincere and true in my love for and faith in You. Never let me betray You Jesus. I do love You so. Help me to abide faithful to You even to death. Forbid that I would rise to great heights in professing Your name and then betray You with a kiss. Thank you, Lord!" (Spurgeon 1995, 170).

March 26, 2020

"He must increase; I must decrease." Words of John the Baptist chronicled by John the disciple in chapter 3 of his gospel (John 3:30). Some translations state, "He must become greater; I must become less." To set the context in which John the Baptist spoke these truth-laden words, one must recollect that he had been called by God to a highly visible, immensely important ministry—one of preparing the way for the Messiah. Among those who followed and were baptized by him, he was greatly revered. Many even believed him to actually be the Messiah. In the instance chronicled by John (the disciple), John the Baptist is advised that Jesus is also baptizing and that "everyone is going to Him," a fact that would appear to have troubled those relaying the information. But not John. If anyone had reason to be filled with pride, and thus envious of Jesus, it would have been him. God had chosen to greatly advance His kingdom through John. Multitudes followed him and came to repentance having their hearts prepared to receive Jesus. Incredibly, in the midst of such favor and blessing, pride never welled up within John. He not once lost sight of where his help came from. Nor should we! His reply to those relaying the news of Jesus conducting His Father's business:

> A man can receive only what is given him from Heaven... I am not the Christ, but am sent ahead of Him... The friend who attends the bridegroom waits and listens for him, and is full of joy when he hears the bridegroom's voice. That joy is mine and it is now complete. He must increase; I must decrease.

Never has more humility been exhibited by someone conceived by the flesh. Oh, that we would purpose and strive to complete our journey in like manner. That we would proceed forward armed only with that which is gifted from heaven and with the sole purpose of pointing others to our Jesus. That we would commit to waiting and listening and only moving when and in the direction that He commands, being filled with joy upon the sound of His voice. Yes, that He would increase, and we would do the opposite. Let's make that our heart's cry.

March 27, 2020

"Therefore if anyone is in Christ, he is a new creation; the old has gone, the new has come" (2 Cor. 5:17). Take a moment and ponder Paul's words. Consider the truth he declares and the ramifications that flow from it. Now recollect Jesus's words to Nicodemus found in John chapter 3:

> I tell you the truth, no one can see the Kingdom of God unless he is born again...born of water and the Spirit. Flesh gives birth to flesh, but the Spirit gives birth to the spirit. (John 3:3, 5–6)

For those of us who are in Jesus, we who are born again, there exists two separate and very distinct existences: the old man, or woman, as it is often referred, who was born of the flesh with a sinful nature passed down from Adam and the new one who has been born again of the Spirit, a new creation in the lineage of Jesus, the New Covenant, the author and finisher of their faith. Nicodemus struggled to grasp what Jesus was saying and, at first, so do all who are chosen by God to be His children. But then, over time and with the help and guidance of the Holy Spirit, the blinders are removed and the truth revealed. The old person that you were is gone, finished. He or she is no more. They are dead and buried with Jesus. If you are in Him, your sinful, selfish nature died when He did and cannot be resurrected. When your Father looks at and considers you, He cannot see that person because they are no more. All He can see is the new man or woman, the one who was raised from the dead when Jesus was resurrected, the one who is born again, the one who is a new creation. God's heart is fixed upon this new, true you in His Son. His Holy Spirit teaches you, moment by moment, to practice and walk in the righteousness that is yours through Jesus. Every day, in each circumstance that you encounter, you are being trained to live from your new man, not your old. Embracing who you are in Him, your God-declared identity, and who He is in you changes everything. It empowers you to walk in the fullness and richness of His presence, His favor, and His promises. Are you in Jesus? If so, then you are a new creation. The old man is dead and buried, and the new man has been resurrected to life. Your Father longs for you to embrace this truth: "Who the Son sets free is free indeed" (John 8:36). Walk in the freedom and the identity that is afforded those who are in Him (Cooke 2017).

March 28, 2020

On certain days, of which today is one, my mind is blank. Unlike other mornings where the Holy Spirit floods my spirit with particular thoughts or scriptures, on days like this, I sense no specific topic upon which to write. Wondering whether His intention is to tarry briefly or for a longer period of time, I choose to sit in the still quietness of the moment knowing without any doubt that my Lord and my God is near. He always is. It is so sweet to just sit with Him, to feel His presence around me, and to experience His love for me. The peace and joy that abound at times such as these are of greater value than any other thing. He is my Father, my Papa, and simply sitting in His presence makes everything else in life fade away. He is my Lord and my Savior, my brother and my best friend, and nothing can match or surpass merely being with Him. And finally, He is my Comforter and my Guide, the only One whom I can trust enough to surrender my life to in this and every moment. That is who He is, and that is why today just being with Him is all that I need.

March 29, 2020

Oftentimes, I awake early in the morning to rays from the rising sun peeking through the partially opened blinds and to the peaceful solitude that heaven sends to proclaim the presence of my King. It is a glorious time, perfectly prepared for me to commune with my Lord. A time for petition and praise, for confession and assurance, for receiving and returning love and adoration, for listening and for revelation. It is during these moments that the Holy Spirit will many times speak into my spirit the truth that my Father desires for me to write. Luke, in chapter 11 of his gospel, records a moment when one of the disciples approached Jesus after He had just finished praying and said, "Lord, teach us to pray, just as John taught his disciples" (Luke 11:1). What followed was Jesus's teaching of that which most of us have come to know as the Lord's Prayer. It is an incredible supplication. Amazing because it comes from the lips of the Son of God. One that should never be ignored or neglected. One that is all encompassing and, did I mention, one that Jesus instructs that we pray. Several years ago, I heard a teaching that suggested that Jesus was giving us a formula or a guideline for prayer more so than a specific petition always to be strictly adhered to. Which of those two theories is most accurate would not seem to be of as much import as the need that our communication with our Father be sincere and heartfelt. Not just words spoken as a formality out of tradition or obligation, but earnest and fervent expressions and requests that arise from our reliance upon our love for and our trust in our Father. This morning, as I was closing my time spent with my Father by declaring Jesus's words from Luke chapter 11, I sensed a revelation regarding the same. The Holy Spirit gave me eight words each beginning with the letter *P* and each describing a particular portion of the Lord's Prayer. I have come to know, with certainty, that when I receive such a Word I am to share it.

"Our Father, who art in Heaven, hallowed be thy name..." In this opening section, Jesus is teaching us to "praise" our God. First and foremost, worship and glorify Him.

"Thy Kingdom come, Thy will be done on earth as it is in Heaven..." Our Lord is reminding of the need for God's "presence" and His favor (His will) and that we must not neglect to ask for it.

"Give us each day our daily bread..." Our Father longs to "provide" for His children. Ask for His "provision."

"Forgive us our sins as we forgive those who sin against us..." Jesus knew that sin separates us from God and had to be absolved. Therefore, He instructs that we not only ask for "pardon" for our own sins, but that we simultaneously forgive those who have wronged us.

"Lead us not into temptation but deliver us from evil..." He knew that we are no match for the enemy, so Jesus teaches us to ask God for His "protection" from the evil one. Our Father will see us through the battle, just ask!

And finally, "For thine is the Kingdom, thine is the Power and thine is the Glory for ever and ever. *Amen!*" I love this last portion. Jesus did not want us to end our petitions without "proclaiming" the unmatched greatness of our God by "professing" His almighty "power" and by acknowledging that everything in heaven and on earth, including ourselves, belongs to Him.

There it is, a perspective of Jesus's teaching regarding prayer that will hopefully help us to better understand how He desires that we approach the throne of God: praise, presence, provision, pardon, protection, proclamation, profession, and power—all a part of our Lord's guide to communing with our Father.

March 31, 2020

> God is our refuge and our strength, an ever-present help in times of trouble. Therefore we will not fear... The Lord Almighty is with us; the God of Jacob is our fortress... Be still and know that I am God; I will be exalted among the nations, I will be exalted in the earth. (Ps. 46:1–2, 7, 10–11)

As I was reading these words, I was reminded of where our help comes from and of how great our God is. That power is in His one hand and majesty in the other. That no matter the circumstance, He is with us, and He will be exalted. All that we are instructed to do is to be still, to not fear, and to know that He is God. Comforting and reassuring truths to stand upon during any season of our journey, but especially encouraging at this particular time. With the coronavirus everywhere, we are experiencing a different type of normal in our lives. Nothing appears the same as it was just a month ago—that is, except for our God. He never changes. His love for us and His protection over us are forever present. Rest upon those truths. In the midst of fear and uncertainty, I am finding that so much of the noise and busyness that is usually present is being replaced with quiet and peace. And that at a time when we are being told to distance ourselves from each other, I am actually being led to interact, safely, with those whom God has placed closest to me. Wouldn't it be just like Him to turn something that appears so bad into something for our good? Rest in Him; He is your refuge!

April 2, 2020

For most of yesterday, I found that there was an uneasiness in my spirit. A feeling that I do not very often experience. One that troubled me and resulted in my being on edge and struggling to discern God's presence. Finding myself in such an unfamiliar place, I pressed in, waiting and listening, only to experience more unsettledness. At some point, I sensed being directed to the word "ponder" and then to Psalm 64:9, which in my uncertain state, I quickly discarded as being self-contrived and not from my Father. I should have known differently. I have been afforded the privilege of knowing His voice, although I am still learning to act upon it decisively. Instruction can, at times, be uncomfortable. However, it is always profitable and for our good. As the day turned into night, thoughts of my past, not all good ones, flooded my mind. Where were these coming from? This type of experience was not normal for my new man in Christ. I was, and am, fully aware that the old man was crucified and buried with Jesus. That my sins were completely forgiven and are no more. That they are normally only dredged up by Satan in a feeble attempt to distract me from my God-appointed purpose. But this seemed different. I had a sense that the source of what I was encountering was not at all from the enemy but from my Father Himself. I now know that what He wanted me to do was to "ponder," to consider not my past transgressions but instead the overwhelming, all-encompassing, life-changing gift freely given to me on a cross outside of the city of Jerusalem. By contemplating, only for a short time, the darkness and depravity of my sin, I was led to a place of reminder of the depth and magnitude of the unconditional, sacrificial love that was necessary to atone for my sin and to restore me to right relationship with God. Amazing! All of which circles me back to the place of instruction where He began yesterday: Psalm 64:9. David writes, "All mankind will fear; they will proclaim the works of God and ponder what He has done." David also declares at 1 Chronicles 16:12, "Remember the wonders He has done…" God has done such great things in the lives of His children. Things that from time to time should be "pondered" in order to encourage us, to strengthen our faith, to move us to praise and worship Him, and to glorify and exalt His name. While in 1 Chronicles, I was drawn to a prayer of King David that is found in chapter 17 verses 16 through 27. In closing, I would like to pray my own personal version of the same and would encourage anyone who is reading this to do likewise.

> Who am I, O Lord God and what is my family
> that You have brought me this far? And as if this

were not enough in Your sight, O God, You have spoken promises to me over my future. You have looked on me as though I were the most exalted of men, O Lord God. What more can I say to You for honoring me? For You know me Lord! For my sake and according to Your will You have done great things and spoken Your great and amazing promises over me. There is no one like You, O Lord and no God but You. You have redeemed Your people, of which I am one, for Yourself. O, that You would be glorified! You have performed great and awesome wonders over me. You are my God and I am Yours forever. Do as You have promised so that Your name will be exalted, and that all will see that I am Yours. Because of Your presence and Your favor and Your many great promises I have courage to pray to You. Thank You for blessing Your servant up to now and forevermore. I love You!

Take time to ponder what He has done for you, and then thank and praise Him for it.

April 4, 2020

There are six days until Good Friday and eight before the indescribable joy of Easter Sunday. Beginning today, I am to focus upon the time leading up to and then the three days that changed everything in the lives of those who choose to believe in Jesus and the New Covenant that He was sent to deliver. Three years of ministry, teaching, and preparation had all led our precious Lord to this moment in time. No one other than Jesus Himself had any grasp or understanding of the depth and significance of what was about to take place over the coming days. Not even His disciples, to whom He had foretold His fate and purpose, truly conceived the magnitude of what they were about to witness. I will say this time and time again from now until Easter simply because it is of great importance: Jesus, knowing full well the horrific treatment that awaited Him, never wavered in the fulfillment of His God-assigned purpose. Not once did He lose sight of the reason(s) for which He found Himself at this specific place and time. He looked right through the beating, the scourging, the betrayal, the ridicule, the humiliation, the pain, and the separation from His Father that the cross would bring and saw the victory, the joy, the restoration, the adoration, and the eternal security that were awaiting Him, and each of us whom He loves so greatly, on Sunday. His eyes were fixed on you and on me, dear child of God. Over the coming days, as we revisit each of our Savior's steps, let the true meaning and overwhelming magnitude of that love be a reality to you. Allow it to absorb into your spirit so that a day will not pass that it will not be the focus of your thoughts and the passion of your heart. That it will birth a mindset of gratitude and an assurance of identity that will compel you to fulfill your heaven-declared purpose of pointing others to the One who never took or takes His eyes off you. It is going to be a blessed week!

April 5, 2020

Today is known in the church as Palm Sunday, a day that marks the beginning of Holy Week. Approximately seven days during which Jesus shared His final thoughts and goodbyes, told those nearest to Him that He loved them, and then poured that never-before-seen love out upon all of us. Each of the Gospels describes this day under the heading "The Triumphal Entry" (Matt. 21; Mark 11; Luke 19; and John 12), and unlike other events in Jesus's earthly ministry, there appears to be unanimity among the writers.

We join the accounts as Jesus and His followers are headed to Jerusalem. His disciples believed that the sole purpose of their journey was to celebrate the Passover, while Jesus was fully aware that a far greater mission awaited Him. (He attempted to prepare the twelve, but their hearts and their minds were not yet ready to receive the true meaning of what was about to happen.) As they approached the city, Jesus instructed two of His disciples how and where to secure a donkey (a colt in some accounts). He did so in order that He may ride the animal into Jerusalem in fulfillment of Zechariah's prophecy: "Say to the daughters of Zion, see your King comes to you, gentle and riding on a donkey, on a colt, the foal of a donkey" (Zech. 9:9). The time had come for the King of kings, the Son of God, to fulfill His heaven-declared purpose as Savior of the world. The Messiah was among men, and He was about to enter the Holy City, not as a powerful commander as many anticipated but as a servant. And yet even as such, those who believed in Him could not help but worship and honor their Lord, to lavish attention upon Him as He began the process that would lead to His taking His rightful place. So they laid down coats and palm branches along His route to praise Him and to testify to the world that He was King—because He was and He remains the same. They shouted, "Hosanna, blessed is He who comes in the name of the Lord." For most of His ministry, Jesus discouraged people from acknowledging Him openly, but here He was welcoming their praise. He continues to invite us to do likewise today. He went so far as to declare that if necessary the rocks would cry out. Let us do everything possible to ensure that those stones are never heard from. Holy Week has begun. God is about to pour out His great love on the entire world. Jesus will soon change everything. Please do not let the significance of this week pass you by (Guzik 2015; Matt. 21; Mark 11; Luke 19)

April 6, 2020

After His triumphal entry into Jerusalem, Jesus and His disciples left the city to spend the night in Bethany, most likely in the home of Lazarus and his sisters, Mary and Martha, who we know Jesus loved greatly. It is Monday, and everyone is beginning to prepare to celebrate Passover, a time during which God brought the last of the great plagues upon Egypt in order to convince Pharaoh to set the Israelites free. It was a time when there was much death in the land, and fear and despair were everywhere; a time when God, by way of the blood of a spotless lamb, spared the lives of His people (Exodus 12). Currently, the world finds itself in the grips of another horrendous plague. COVID-19 is spreading fear, death, and despair throughout the earth, the worst of which, to date, is projected to occur during this week. The very week that those of the Jewish faith commemorate Passover, while Christians celebrate their salvation by way of the shedding of the blood of the spotless Lamb. Blood that promises eternal life. Blood that provides freedom for all who will receive it. Is it any coincidence that we find ourselves at this place on Monday of Holy Week? I believe that it is not. In only five days, the blood that will usher in the New Covenant between God and man will be poured out on a hill just outside of Jerusalem. Blood shed to take away the sins of the world. Blood freely sacrificed to rescue and deliver those who receive it and to protect them from all harm, including a plague named COVID-19. Our Father adores His children so much so that He would stop at nothing to deliver them from the oppression and bondage inflicted by the Egyptians. To a depth of which He would be moved to spare not His only beloved Son that we might spend eternity with Him and be safe from harm on our journey. On Monday, Jesus again entered Jerusalem and, upon doing so, continued to be about His Father's business. First, teaching about bearing fruit through genuine faith by way of a fig tree and then demonstrating His passion for His Father's house by ridding the temple of money changers. The thing that has always captivated my thoughts and my heart regarding this portion of Jesus's journey is that, knowing full well what awaited Him on Friday, He never neglected to complete what His Father had set before Him on Monday, Tuesday, Wednesday, and Thursday. Oh, what a Savior!

April 7, 2020

Little attention would seem to be given to Tuesday (Day 3) of Holy Week, although to describe it as uneventful would be inaccurate. After spending Monday evening in Bethany—again, most likely with Lazarus, Martha, and Mary—Jesus and His disciples headed back to Jerusalem. Even at this early stage of the week, we are seeing a trend develop of Jesus staring directly into the face of His destiny no matter the cost, no matter the pain, no matter the sacrifice. Certainly, it would have been easier for Him to have simply remained outside of the city in the safety of Bethany until Friday. But Jesus was not called to walk the safe, easy route, and He had His Father's business to attend to. There were lessons to be taught, truths to be dispersed, and followers' needs to be met. Our Lord, with you and me directly in His sightline, fully embraced His God-ordained assignment, every last love drenched detail of it. As they walked to Jerusalem, they passed the withered fig tree that Jesus had cursed the day before. Not allowing an opportunity to pass, He taught of faith and prayer and the power afforded to God's children through each. Upon arriving in the city, Jesus headed directly to the temple where He was most at home, in His Father's house, and where He was fully aware that the chief priests, the elders, and the teachers of the law, those who wanted to kill Him, awaited. Throughout the morning, they attempted to trick Jesus with questions regarding His authority, paying taxes to Caesar, marriage at the resurrection, and the greatest commandment. With never-before-seen wisdom, Jesus answered each ambush-inspired query and, by so doing, dispersed truth and knowledge that would instruct and guide His church from generation to generation, even unto this very moment. Inconceivably, these self-righteous, pompous, pride-filled religious leaders not only refused to receive Jesus's words of wisdom but used them as motivation to plot His demise. Woe to those who refuse the truth of God!

Later in the afternoon, Jesus left the city and went with His disciples to the Mount of Olives. It was there that Jesus spoke what is known as the Olivet Discourse, a detailed teaching regarding the destruction of Jerusalem and end-time events, including His return to earth and God's judgment. While this is not the place to address the truth imparted by our Lord on this Tuesday afternoon just outside of Jerusalem, I would strongly encourage everyone to take the time to ask the Holy Spirit to walk you through and to show you exactly what it is that Jesus wanted each of us to know about the end of the age. After a long day filled with confrontation from the religious leaders and instruction regarding the future, Jesus and His disciples once again headed back to Bethany for the evening. What many would say was an uneventful Tuesday was quite the contrary.

Jesus spent the day fulfilling His assignment, never once taking His eyes off you and me and the joy and the victory that Sunday would bring to each of us (Fairchild 2020).

April 8, 2020

The Bible speaks very little of the events of Wednesday of Holy Week. It is believed by scholars that Jesus and His disciples spent the day in Bethany preparing for the Passover celebration, thus rendering it the only day of the week that He did not enter Jerusalem. The early church referred to this day as Spy Wednesday as it was the time during which Judas decided to betray Jesus and approached the chief priests with his plan. Judas's motivation for turning on Jesus seems to have been purely financial. For a mere thirty pieces of silver, he forfeited the most precious and invaluable gift of all: eternal life. His desire for money exceeded his love for his Lord and cost him everything. This would be a good time for each of us to sincerely examine our hearts and ask what, if anything, sits above Jesus on the throne of our lives. I pray there is nothing to be found there. If there is, then it is time to repent and cast that something, or somethings, down. It is at this point in their gospels that Matthew and Mark choose to recount Mary's (Lazarus's sister) anointing of Jesus with expensive perfume. While we know from John's gospel that this event occurred several days prior to Wednesday, the importance of the exact time is outweighed by the significance of its message. Even before Jesus made His triumphal entry into Jerusalem, Mary understood what was about to come. She got it. She was the only one who did, thus rendering her gesture of anointing Jesus a touching and meaningful gift to her Lord. Mary loved Jesus deeply, and even in her overwhelming despair over what was going to occur in a few short days, she worshipped Him in the only way that she knew. She honored Him in the one way that she was able, which is all that our Father desires. No more or no less. What a valuable lesson we are to take from Mary's gesture. In closing, let me restate the message and the theme that the Holy Spirit has placed upon my heart all week. Jesus may not have entered the city on Wednesday, but His focus did not waver from what was going to occur there beginning tomorrow. His eyes remained fixed on His purpose no matter how horrible it was about to become. He continued to see you and me and you and me only. Praise His name!

April 9, 2020

It is Thursday of Holy Week, referred to in some circles of the church as Maundy Thursday. Maundy is derived from the Latin word for "command" and refers to Jesus's commandment to "Love one another as I have loved you." It is on this day that we observe a distinct, sober pivot from teaching and preparation to betrayal and accusation, in the midst of which we again witness Jesus's amazing love. Love for each and every one of us revealed through His determined focus on fulfilling the purpose for which He was sent. Just as on Wednesday, Jesus spends a majority of this day in Bethany. It is at some point during the day that He sent Peter and John into Jerusalem to prepare the Upper Room for the Passover feast, or what would come to be known as the Last Supper. As He so often did, Jesus gave them specific instructions regarding how they were to carry out their assignment. He could have accomplished the details of this highly important event with a simple spoken word, and yet He chose otherwise. Every single act of our Lord was purposed to testify to His deity and to encourage and build up the faith of all whom He encountered. Here Peter and John were no doubt amazed by Jesus's wisdom and authority and would be bolstered in their future ministry by the same.

After sunset, Jesus arrived in the city with the twelve, and as they partook of the Passover meal, three significant events occurred. First, Jesus washed the feet of His disciples, thus demonstrating by example how believers are to love and serve one another. In my opinion, there is no more unselfish gesture than to wash the feet of another. For that matter, having one's feet washed is pretty humbling as well. In order to impress upon us the manner in which our Father desires that we treat each other, Jesus performed an act commonly designated for a servant and, by so doing, compelled us to do likewise. The second thing that occurred in the Upper Room was Jesus's declaration that one of the disciples would betray Him. Only Judas was not surprised by this revelation. The remaining eleven were deeply saddened, most likely because the reality of what was about to happen was beginning to set in. As an aside, Jesus was saddened as well. He deeply loved Judas, and had there been another path, He would have taken it. There was not. God's plan and purpose had to be completed. Finally, Jesus introduced the right of Communion, or the Lord's Supper, by sharing the elements with His disciples. He was about to give His body to be broken and shed His blood as the last and greatest sacrifice for sin, freeing us from the penalty for it: separation from God and death. By sharing the bread and the wine, Jesus was instructing all of us to continually remember the meaning of His sacrifice by doing the same. After singing a hymn (again instructional), they went to the Mount of Olives, where Jesus informed the disciples that they would all fall away and that Peter in particular would deny Him three times. Peter emphatically rejected Jesus's prophetic words. History would prove our Lord correct. Then they moved to the garden of Gethsemane. For me, what occurred there is deeply impactful. It is there that Jesus's identity as both God and man were on full display. It is there that He asks His Father to spare Him from the cup of which He is about to partake. It is there that He fully and finally surrendered to the will of God. It is there that the pathway to salvation was paved, and the New Covenant initiated. At Gethsemane, our Lord was betrayed. In that place, love was on full display and the Passion of our Lord began. Oh, garden of Gethsemane, what horror began with you and what unspeakable joy arose from within your gates. Without you would come not the necessary heartbreak of Friday or the life-changing victory of Sunday. Thank you, Gethsemane, your garden is most special in my heart. The soldiers then took Jesus away to begin the painful journey that would lead to the indescribable rapture of Sunday. His eyes remained fixed on you, children of God. They always are.

April 10, 2020

Today is referred to almost everywhere as Good Friday, and to those of us who have chosen to accept Jesus as our Lord and Savior and to follow Him, the events of this day are both painful and good. Love, sacrifice, forgiveness, hope, redemption, and so much more were freely given and fully on display both inside and just outside of the city of Jerusalem throughout this Friday of Holy Week. Jesus poured out His passion for His church in an unconditional and sacrificial demonstration of love that has never been nor ever will be again witnessed by mankind. Nonetheless, being fully aware of the immeasurable benefits willingly bestowed does not render what Jesus experienced at Calvary one bit easier to witness. Recently, I watched, for a second time, the movie *Passion of the Christ*. If you have not seen it, I recommend that you do. However, before doing so, I will warn you that it is a most graphic depiction of the unjust and horrific treatment suffered by our Lord, upon the insistence of the Jewish religious leaders, at the hands of the Roman authorities. To say that Jesus was mistreated physically, emotionally, and mentally would be a gross understatement. To declare that He deserved any portion of what was so unjustly imposed upon Him would be an even greater untruth. To view the pain, the suffering, the humiliation, and the ridicule inflicted upon our Lord is completely heart-wrenching. It stretches our human capacities to simply view it. To our mortal eyes, there is nothing good about it. And yet we are to walk by faith and not by sight (2 Cor. 5:7). So by faith, we know that what we see with our eyes on Friday is necessary for us to receive the gift that awaits on Sunday. Forgiveness, atonement, salvation, redemption, and eternal life are awaiting us in two days; but we cannot arrive there without the sacrifice of a spotless Lamb. Sacrifice is not easy. It is painful. It is hard, and it comes at a cost—a price that you and I should have to pay, a debt that Jesus was willing to settle in our stead on Friday, a penalty that each of us deserves. One that He does not! Our sin separates us from the God who adores us. Something or Someone had to bridge that great chasm and restore right relationship between the Father and His children. Such a monumental task was beyond us.

173

The sin of the world was far greater than the number of lambs available to be sacrificed. We were in need of something extraordinary, something unfathomable to our human minds, something from heaven. We needed a Savior! Do you see now why Friday is "Good"? It is because before we could experience the restoration and redemption of Sunday, there had to be atonement. The sacrifice of a Spotless Lamb was necessary. One that occurred on Friday. One that was for you and for me. One that I sadly confess I contributed to. And one that I joyfully receive as my own. Oh, how precious is the cross, for the blood shed there was for me. Its crimson stains washed me white as snow and prepared me for the joy unspeakable that awaits on Sunday. Friday truly was "*Good*"!

April 11, 2020

It is Saturday and as the Jewish community is observing the Sabbath, the horror of Friday resonates in the hearts and minds of those who loved Jesus so deeply. As visions of their Lord's blood-scarred body flash before their eyes, they cannot see the unspeakable joy that awaits them in less than twenty-four hours. Jesus's promise that He would rebuild this Temple in three days is not discernable over their memory of the crowd shouting, "Crucify Him! Crucify Him!" My thoughts turn to Mary and what agony she must have been experiencing. She has just watched not only her beloved son but the One that she knows in her heart to be the Son of God humiliated, ridiculed, and brutally killed. I am certain that Mary believes without any doubt that this is not the end, and yet she is so greatly overwhelmed with a mother's grief that her pain will not allow her to even ponder Sunday and what it will bring. I consider the debilitating guilt and shame that must be paralyzing Peter on this day. Also incapable of grasping what has just happened or what is about to come, he is left to dwell on the fact that when his blessed Lord, his best friend, the One who he himself identified as the Messiah needed him most, he denied Him, publicly before the whole world, three times no less. Peter is alone and defeated. That will all soon change, but not on Saturday. I cannot help but wonder what thoughts also must be running through the minds of the other disciples as well as in those of His throngs of followers. This man who they had seen heal the sick, restore sight to the blind, cast out demons, and raise the dead to life had died before their very eyes. How is it that He could save so many and yet did not save Himself? How could the Son of God, the Messiah, the Savior of the world be allowed to be beaten, scourged, spit on, and hung from a cross by those who hated and denied Him? How could He with His last dying breath plead for His Father to forgive those very same executioners? Oh, Jerusalem, your streets are covered with blood, your air is filled with despair and heartache, your occupants beset with confusion, your hope shattered. The victory that we can see clearly on the horizon is blocked from your view. The immovable stone is about to be rolled away. The young man dressed in a white robe will soon declare from the tomb, "Don't be alarmed. You are looking for Jesus the Nazarene who was crucified. He is risen! He is not here." The Lion of Judah will ask Mary outside of that same tomb, "Woman, why are you crying?" and then simply call her by name, "Mary." Saturday must seem the longest day to have ever passed. Hang on, dear children of God, stir up what little faith remains in you who are greatly loved and blessed. The darkness is about to be turned to light, and the rough place about to be made smooth. The Temple that they thought had been destroyed is about to be restored. Victory is on the horizon! Sunday is coming! *Hallelujah!*

April 12, 2020

"Weeping may last through the night but joy comes in the morning" (Ps. 30:5). It is Sunday morning, and surely, Mary Magdalene has cried endlessly throughout Saturday evening over the loss of her Lord. So overcome with grief and with no sleep to be found, she goes to the only place that her crippled heart would lead her, to Jesus. To be near His lifeless body had to be a better alternative than to simply do nothing. To neglect to pay homage to the One who had changed everything for her was not acceptable to Mary. So while it was still dark, she went to the tomb. She went to her Jesus. Only

175

He was not there. (Hallelujah, He was not there!) Terrified, she ran to Peter and John and told them, "They have taken the Lord out of the tomb, and we don't know where they have put Him!" Still not understanding that Jesus had to rise from the dead, they ran to the tomb, observed that what Mary declared was in fact true, and then returned to their homes. Mary, however, could not leave. So great was her love for Jesus. Her grief had only multiplied. Her world had hit rock bottom. Terrible news had just become worse. In my mind's eye, it remains dark outside the tomb as the morning is about to be revealed. The sun's first light is poised to peak over the horizon as Mary weeps. Through her tear-drenched eyes, she glances into the tomb and beholds the beginning of joy. Two beings (angels) dressed in white are now seated where Jesus should be. Mary's confusion must only have grown, yet all her focus remains on Him. "They have taken my Lord away, and I don't know where they have put Him," she explains. Have you ever felt such deep and all-encompassing love as did Mary at this moment? Love that would drive her to be with Jesus, even a lifeless Jesus, at all costs. What an incredible love! Love that I believe moved Jesus deeply. Love only surpassed by His own love of two days before. Love that now ushered the sun into the eastern sky. Love that wiped away each of Mary's tears and replaced them with the joy of Easter morning. His love that never lost sight of this day and never allowed Him to take His eyes off you and me. Mary turned around and saw a man standing there. Believing Him to be the gardener when He asked, "Woman, why are you crying? Who is it you are looking for?"

She replied, "Sir, if you have carried Him away, tell me where you have put Him, and I will get Him."

Again, we witness her desperation to find her Jesus. (Oh, that we would each experience such urgency to find and to be with Him!) Mary's wait was about to end. Jesus simply said one word to her, and the joy that David wrote of so many years earlier flooded her spirit. "Mary," He said, and with that single declaration, her joy was made complete. All of the horror, the grief, the pain, and the despair disappeared with the uttering of that one word, vanquished in the blink of an eye, and replaced forevermore with the joy that arrives in the morning. Joy that brings with it hope and peace and love and the promise of spending eternity with the One who delivered it. Joy that is available to you and to me. Joy that covers and takes away all of our sin and restores us to right relationship with our Father. Joy that was there all of the time, waiting for us through all of the pain and heartache of Friday and the loneliness and despair of Saturday, only to rise with the sun on Sunday morning. Joy whose name is Jesus. The night has disappeared; the morning has come. Weeping has passed, and joy is upon us. The tomb is empty. He is *risen*. Death has been defeated. Victory is ours. He *never* took His eyes off Sunday nor off you and me. *Happy Easter!* (Lucado 2018, 117–126).

April 13, 2020

I was recently afforded the privilege of beginning a relationship with a brother in the Lord named Stephen. It did not take long for the Holy Spirit to show me two important things about my new friend. Stephen had been given a deep passion and hunger for the things of God coupled with the fact that his faith was both new and fragile. Not long into our friendship, I was afforded the honor of sharing God's word of encouragement with Stephen. What an incredible privilege and blessing it is to be used by our Father as a messenger of His truth. Within a couple of weeks of our connection, I learned that a great tragedy had befallen a member of Stephen's family, causing him immense pain and heartache. As so often occurs, the enemy had come knocking on my new friend's door at a time when his heart and his spirit were vulnerably susceptible to attack. While I have not had the opportunity to speak with him since the accident, I am certain that he is experiencing much pain and confusion. While praying this morning, I was unable to move on from Stephen. I felt a heavy burden for him, sensing that his heart is severely injured, maybe to the point of being broken. A place where so many of us find ourselves on this journey upon which we have been placed. Immediately, God's Spirit reminded me that our Father is the Healer of broken hearts, all of them. Psalm 147:3 promises that "He heals the brokenhearted and binds up their wounds." Our Father adores each and every one of His children, and just like an earthly father, He draws especially near to those who are suffering through great pain. "The Lord is close to the brokenhearted and saves those who are crushed in spirit" (Ps. 34:18). So much so that He sent His Son personally to heal their wounded and hurting hearts. "He sent me to bind up the brokenhearted..." (Isa. 61:1). The "me" that Isaiah prophesied of was Jesus. Is your heart hurting? Is it broken? Then know for certain what I fully intend to tell my new friend Stephen when I speak with him next. Your pain has not escaped your Father's eye, and He is the One, the only One, who heals broken hearts—every one of them!

April 14, 2020

During this season of my journey my heart has been opened to our Father's deep and endless love for His children. In addition, the truth regarding identity and purpose have been clearly revealed to my spirit. Along with these revelations, I have been divinely given an overwhelming passion to pass on the same to anyone who will receive them. These are messages of love, hope, peace, deliverance, and protection, along with the assurances—sent from heaven by way of the Holy Spirit—that accompany them. I am captivated by God's goodness, grace, mercy, and adoration over and for His children; and I am highly honored and privileged to be His messenger thereof. Most often, the words that I am given are purposed, I believe, to inspire, to foster, and to encourage our faith.

This morning the Holy Spirit is leading in another direction, one of warning. Without any doubt, our Father is a God of great and immeasurable love—love that He pours out upon His children without limit, love that was never more on display than at Calvary and the days preceding and following it. But we must never lose sight of the fact that God is God. He is sovereign, and as such, He gets to set the rules and establish the way and the truth. Both of which are found in His Son. Jesus declared, "I am the way and the truth and the life. No man comes to the Father except through me" (John 14:6). For three years Jesus walked the earth and imparted the truth given to Him by His Father. Every word that was spoken from His mouth came from heaven and was of equal importance. All too often I am afraid that we pick and choose to follow the ones that are easy or that suit our purpose and to ignore or reject the others. On two occasions, Jesus spoke of the passageway to eternal life, once portraying it as a gate and a second time as a door, each time clearly describing it as narrow. In Matthew chapter 7, the Son of God cautions us that wide is the gate and broad the road that leads to destruction while narrow is the one leading to life. Then He further warned that many will choose the wide route and only few the narrow. In Luke chapter 13, we find Jesus providing a similar prompt, only on this occasion adding that when those who choose the broader road plead their case to be let in, God will deny even knowing them. Difficult and troubling words spoken directly by God, but only discouraging to those who are traveling the wrong path. Is that you? Are you uncertain of which route you are on? Regardless of your responses, the solution is right before you. It is Jesus! He is the Way, He is the Truth, and He is the Life! He is the narrow gate and the specified road to eternal life. He Himself declared it to be so. If you have chosen a route or a gate that does not pass through Him, then you must recalibrate and change direction. Your eternal destination is dependent upon it. Please don't wait!

April 15, 2020

For so many years of my life, I professed to be a child of God and a follower of His Son. In fact, I had experienced a moment when my need for a Savior was revealed (divinely) to my mind and when I responded affirmatively. Yet, as I reflect upon the days, weeks, months, and years that followed, it is clear that, although saved, I walked neither as a child would with his Father or as a follower would with his Lord. For to do so would require and involve an intimate personal knowledge of the heart and character of Each. A knowledge and understanding that I did not pursue or receive until recently. An enlightenment that I have observed to have escaped many, just as it did me. An absence of truth that results in frustration and confusion and stymies growth and development in the lives of believers. So many with whom I have spoken express a desire for a deeper, more intimate relationship with and knowledge of God. They even seem to be aware that the Bible contains the answers to their longings. Still they, as did I for so long, cannot discover the truth necessary to fill the void within them simply upon reading God's Word. Why is that? The answer is found in the gospel of John: "The Spirit gives life; the flesh counts for nothing. The words I have spoken to you are spirit and they are life" (John 6:63). The Bible is not just a collection of words in a book; instead, it is a powerful body of truth spoken by God. The Word is literally Spirit and life. In order to receive the truth and the life contained within it, we need the leading of God's Spirit. For the longest time, I read the Bible out of a sense of obligation and tried to understand it only with my mind. It was dry and without power. Only when I allowed the Holy Spirit to show me His willingness to open God's Word and reveal its riches did I begin to grasp who my Father and His Son are to me, along with my identity and purpose in Them. All I had to do was ask. You simply need to do likewise. By following a few easy yet powerful guidelines, each of us can experience the Word of God explode off the page and into our lives.

First, make it a priority. We make time for what is important to us. Our spirits need interaction with our Father and with His Son. Each can be found in scripture. Next, believe what you read. Exercise your faith and accept that God's Word is true, not because I say so but because it is. Then watch as it meets your every need and answers all your questions. Finally, meditate on it. Psalm 1:2 states, "A righteous man delights in the law of the Lord and meditates on it day and night." Contemplate and recall God's Word by speaking it out loud, memorizing and declaring it. Make it practical in your life by pondering it frequently and by doing what it says. James 1:22 directs us to not merely listen to the Word and be deceived but to do what it says. To not be like the man who forgets what he looks like after having just looked at himself in the mirror. I have read through the Bible on several different occasions; and yet it wasn't until much later, with the Spirit's help, that the specific truth contained therein began to sink into my heart and leap into my spirit. I now find myself reciting it, sharing it with friends, writing it in my journal, and posting it everywhere. In essence, allowing it to change my life and become a part of who I am. It will do the same for you. All you have to do is ask ("Freedom," Church of the Highlands 2001–2021).

April 16, 2020

Have you ever taken time or been afforded the opportunity to be witness to and then to consider the awe-inspiring power and greatness of God? Such a revelation may present in any number of ways. The birth of a child, a sunrise or sunset, a rainbow or a simple butterfly—all come to mind. Recently, the magnitude of God's enormity and majesty have become more clear and real to me by way of several movies, each depicting a moment in biblical history. These are stories that I have read or heard many times before and to which I have given little or no consideration, accounts that have now opened my mind and my spirit to the mighty power and greatness of my God. Whether it was His angels doing battle at Sodom and Gomorrah, His guiding Moses in leading the Israelites from Egypt, the construction of the Ark, the destruction of the city of Jericho or the life, death and resurrection of His Son—all have led to one extremely impactful conclusion: our God is greater, stronger, more majestic, and more powerful than my mind ever could, ever can, or ever will be able to fathom. He is God, and He is Mighty. So why in all His greatness He would choose to give consideration to me escapes my understanding. But He does. By faith, I am certain of it. How amazing and awesome is that. All glory and honor be to His name, for He is great and greatly to be praised!

April 17, 2020

The words found in chapter 12 verses 18–25 of the book of Hebrews have captivated my mind and my spirit this morning. I sense something from God, so I am attentive to receive what that is. He has taught me to be still, to wait, and to listen for Him; and that is what I have purposed to do. While its author is generally thought to be unknown, scholars believe that the book of Hebrews was written to and for Jewish Christians in Jerusalem. These particular followers of Jesus were greatly persecuted. Oppression that did not escape the loving eyes of their heavenly Father. Through this particular writing, He sends them His words of encouragement to persevere in the face of mistreatment by the nonbelievers in the city. Words that serve the same purpose for those who have read them ever since, which leads to chapter 12 verses 18–25. The Jewish people knew God as the God of Abraham, the God of Jacob, and the God of Moses—the God of the old covenant. Through the death and resurrection of Jesus, God had entered into a New Covenant with His people. One that the Jewish community, even those who had chosen to follow His Son, no doubt struggled to comprehend, especially in the midst of great persecution. In the passage addressed, God reveals the benefits and privileges bestowed upon His children by way of Jesus and the New Covenant that He ushered in and, by so doing, speaks hope and promise to all who are His. He accomplishes this by contrasting two mountains: Mount Sinai, where the Israelites came to meet God but were sternly cautioned to keep their distance, and Mount Zion, where the city of the living God sits and the cross that represents the New Covenant between God and His people was raised. God wanted, and still wants, His children to know that the fear and distance of Sinai have been replaced with the peace and relationship that Zion offers. That through Jesus, the old had passed and the new has come. That they consider and receive the contrasts that He speaks to in chapter 12. Mount Sinai was marked by angst and uneasiness while Mount Zion is a place of mercy and grace. Sinai is a wasteland while Zion is the city of the living God. At Mount Sinai, only Moses could draw near to God while at Mount Zion, all are invited into relationship with Him. Sinai was about exclusion while Zion offers an invitation to all. Sinai represents the law and the blood of animals while Zion is all about the blood of Jesus and the grace that it offers. Our Father has a message of hope and encouragement for His people both then and now. One that is plain and clear. We need not approach Mount Zion as early believers did Mount Sinai. The blood of Jesus speaks better things (redemption, mercy, and righteousness) than the blood of Abel (vengeance, justice, and judgment). So put aside your doubts and your fears and come to Mount Zion. Come to your Father and do so with great hope and high expectation. You will not be disappointed. (Guzik 2015; Hebrews 12).

April 19, 2020

As I write this, my mother is eighty-three years old. She is active and vibrant physically, mentally, and spiritually. If you ask her what the secret is to her sharpness and vigor, she will without hesitation tell you that it is rest. She is the national spokesperson for daily naps. Several years ago, she began, without exception, to set aside a portion of each day to lie down and rest. Rarely do we engage in a conversation that she does not take a moment to encourage me to rest. I should take heed of her advice. Not just because it works for her, but because God had something to say regarding the matter as well. Most, if not all, are familiar with God's creation account that is chronicled in the book of Genesis chapter 1. If so, then it should be of no surprise to you that Genesis 2:2 states, "By the seventh day God had finished the work He had been doing; so on the seventh day He rested from all His work." The thought that immediately filled my mind upon reading this passage was why did He rest? He is God. He doesn't grow tired or weary. He simply spoke; and the world, and everything in it, existed. Just as quickly, I received the answer to my question. (Our Father was having a teaching moment.) You see, God created us, every part of us, physical, mental, emotional, and spiritual. The Bible teaches that He made us in His image. But we are not Him. We exist in earthen vessels that grow tired and weak. Mortal bodies that are unable to fulfill their heaven-purposed assignments without being replenished. Creations that need to be recharged, that require what God has ordained and my mother has discovered—rest. In addition, God's word speaks to a more specific type of rest: rest for the soul. Until recently, this whole concept of one's soul perplexed me. What exactly is a soul and how is it different from your spirit, your mind, and your heart? Now I am faced with the additional question of why it needs rest. As always, God provides the answer. We are made up of three separate and distinct parts: spirit, soul, and body. Our spirit is the part that is made in God's image, and therefore relates to God, while our body is the vessel in which we exist while on earth. The soul, on the other hand, is a bit more complex, being made up of three separate components: our mind, our will, and our emotions. It supplies us with the capacity to think and reason; the freedom to make choices; and the capacity to believe, feel, and remember. It is an incredible gift given to us from heaven. One that requires continued guidance and direction from the One who gave it. One that is constantly in action and continuously at work. One that quickly and easily grows overburdened and heavy laden. One that needs rest. All of which Jesus was and is fully aware of. Matthew recorded our Lord's words on the matter in chapter 11 verses 28 and 29 of his gospel:

> Come to me all you who are weary and burdened,
> and I will give you rest. Take my yoke upon you
> and learn from me, for I am gentle and humble
> in heart, and you will find rest for your souls.

Many years prior, God declared the same promise through the prophet Jeremiah: "Stand at the crossroads and look…ask where the good way is, and walk in it, and you will find rest for your souls" (Jer. 6:16). Our amazing Father knew that we would encounter much on our journey, most of which would tire our spirits, our souls, and our bodies. As always, He provided the answer. It is rest. Rest that takes the form of naps. Rest that comes from relationship and surrender. Rest that is always in Him. Make sure that you never neglect to rest. It is God's plan that you do so ("Freedom," Church of the Highlands 2001–2021).

April 20, 2020

Today I will address the concept of grace. As I begin, my thoughts are jumbled and disorganized, which frustrates my compelling need for order and direction. At the same time, I am presented with a perfect opportunity to exercise my faith and to trust God. Grace is one of those concepts that everyone, at least those in the church, is convinced they understand, until they are asked to define it. Then the task presents more of a challenge. I chose to begin where I often do, in the concordance of my Bible. There I found that the word "grace" appears thirty times in my New International Version, twenty-nine of which, interestingly, are located in the New Testament. Since that portion of God's Word speaks primarily to Jesus and the New Covenant that He ushered in, I believe Him to be the key to grasping this concept of grace. What I did not find in any of those thirty passages of scripture was a concrete definition. So I continued looking elsewhere, discovering that I am not the first to struggle with pinning down the meaning of this thing called grace. The most common definition and the one that first came to my mind is "the unmerited favor of God." I really like this particular description. My second favorite explanation is provided by an anointed Christian author named Graham Cooke who states that grace is "the empowering presence of God." The fact that grace is not easy to wrap into a nice, neat definition can probably be attributed to both the many means by which it is revealed and the place from where it comes. First, its source. Grace originates with God and is about Him. While we desperately need it, grace is not about us. It is our Father's to give, and He does so freely and by many different means. We experience the unmerited favor and the empowering presence of God through the unconditional love that He pours over us, the peace with which He guards us, the mercy and forgiveness that He freely bestows upon us, the justification that is ours, the death from which we have been spared, the sin and separation that He took away, and the salvation that He willingly affords. None of which we deserve; all of which He offers. Each of which is ours by and through His Son Jesus. I mentioned that "grace" was found in my concordance almost exclusively in the New Testament. No coincidence there. That is where Jesus can mostly be found. "How much more did God's grace and the gift that came by the grace of the one man, Jesus Christ, overflow to the many!" (Rom. 5:15). Grace may be difficult to define, but it is not hard to find. The Word of God is filled with it. Jesus, who is the Word, poured it out through His life and death; the writers of the gospels chronicled it throughout; and Paul wrote of it time and time again. It is the foundation upon which believers live each day of their lives. It forms the basis for our identity, our behavior, our holiness, our strength, our service, our sufficiency, our protection, our witness and testimony, our hope and our future, our purpose and our destiny. It can be found in every aspect of a believer's existence. It allows us to experience goodness, safety, and security no matter the circumstance. Grace is powerful, enabling God to transform His children into who He sees them to be. J. Gresham Machen wrote, "The very center and core of the whole Bible is the doctrine of the grace of God." Since the Bible is the Word of God and the Word is Jesus and since Jesus is grace in its fullest sense, then if you want to experience God's grace, you know exactly where to find it. It truly is "*Amazing*"! (Holcomb 2013).

April 21, 2020

"God is not a man, that He should lie, nor a son of man, that He should change His mind. Does He speak and then not act? Does He promise and not fulfill?" (Num. 23:19). I suppose that I have always been aware of the fact that God cannot lie. I remember my mother instilling the words stated in Hebrews 6:18, "It is impossible for God to lie…," into me as a child. While I carried that truth in my mind for years to come, it wasn't until Jesus captured my heart that the Holy Spirit transferred the real meaning and impact of those seven words twelve inches downward into my heart. What came next changed me forever! My spirit, my mind, my heart, and my soul were now open to the life-giving richness and immeasurable vastness of God's promises. The reality of His unchangeable truthfulness provided the key that unlocked the treasure trove of His assurances to be spoken into my spirit and over my life. It seems as though every day a new one of my Father's many great and precious promises is being revealed to me by the Holy Spirit. Guarantees that I can count on to serve as an anchor for my soul (Heb. 6:19). Vows that bring peace, joy, rest, and, most importantly, a certainty of His immeasurable love for me, along with the privileges, benefits, and honors that I am afforded as a result thereof. Words from the very mouth of God that establish my identity and equip me to fulfill His plan and purpose for my life. Great and precious promises through which I may participate in the divine nature and escape the corruption of the world caused by evil desires (2 Pet. 1:4). Promises that are certain and unchanging (Heb. 6). Assurances that you can hold Him to and plead before Him (Gen. 32:12). Promises that will transform you into the minister, the warrior, the ambassador, and the servant that He has purposed you to be. Promises that are freely yours. Never forget that when God speaks, He will do what He says.

April 22, 2020

For most of the day yesterday and then throughout last night, my mind has been flooded with many thoughts, resulting in a feeling of restlessness that I did not understand. Meditations involving matters that I will address during the coming days. For today, however, I am to speak to a related but somewhat different matter. Dr. Charles Stanley has authored a book entitled *How to Listen to God*. My men's group is using it as a guide during our current small group semester. Last evening, I read chapter 3 ("How God Gets Our Attention"). Dr. Stanley expounds upon six means by which our Father gains our total, absolute attention in order that we may receive that which He desires to speak to us. The very first of which is, wait a second, hold on, you will never guess it, okay no surprise, "a restless spirit." The very emotions of unsettledness and uneasiness that I began to experience less than twenty-four hours prior were being described on paper right before me. Dr. Stanley explains that God will make us restless in order to get our attention. Consideration that is necessary for us to receive the guidance and truth that He is desirous of speaking to and over us. Right in the midst of normalcy, this restlessness will begin to rise up in our spirit. You cannot explain it, nor do you understand it. You just know that it is real and that you have no idea what to do about it. My first inclination was that I had to do something, anything, and that I had to do it right away. Through Dr. Stanley, God instructed that I do the exact opposite. "When such a time comes, the wise thing to do is to stop and ask the Lord what He is trying to say" (Stanley 1985, 27). I don't know about you, but being still and listening is an area entitled "Work in Progress" in my life. I am more wired to be a doer. But I am trying to improve in the being still and listening area of my life, and yesterday, I gave it my best effort. I wanted to run to my desk, grab a pencil, and start writing. God had and has something for me to hear first. After reading chapter 3, I headed to bed and fell asleep only to be awakened at 1:30 a.m. with that same restlessness of spirit enveloping me all over again. My mind was filled with ideas and thoughts for a vision that God is birthing in and revealing to my spirit more and more clearly each day. Once again, I wanted to run to my desk and start writing. Then the Holy Spirit spoke to my mind the story of Elijah, the prophet who, after telling King Ahab that rain was coming, had to send his servant seven times to go and look toward the sea before finally seeing a cloud the size of a man's hand rising in the distance. God definitely sent rain, but Elijah had to wait upon Him for it. I have no doubt that at some point during those seven inquiries, Elijah grew restless in his spirit. Later, God instructed Elijah to go and stand on Mount Horeb, for He was about to pass by. Elijah obeyed; and as he did, first, a powerful wind passed, then an earthquake, and next fire, with the Lord being in neither. Elijah waited and listened and finally came a gentle whisper to which he responded. It was God. How did Elijah know that? Because he had come to know God's voice by waiting upon Him and by listening for Him. That is exactly what our Father wants us to do: to not run at the first thing we hear and thus get ahead of Him, but instead, to simply stop and listen for His voice and to only move when we hear it, regardless of how much we may want to do otherwise or of how restless we may become. He has my attention. I am waiting, and I am listening. Father, show me a cloud as small as a man's hand rising from the sea of your promise to me and then make it pour the rain of your plan and purpose over my life (Stanley 1985).

April 23, 2020

David wrote, "My soul clings to you" (Ps. 63:8). Paul penned, "Hate what is evil; cling to what is good" (Rom. 12:9), "Hold on to the good" (1 Thess. 5:21), "Take hold of the eternal life to which you were called…" (1 Tim. 6:12), and "But I press on to take hold of that for which Christ Jesus took hold of me" (Phil. 3:12). Joshua stated, "Be very careful to keep the commandment and the law that Moses the servant of the Lord gave you…to hold fast to Him…" (Josh. 22:5). Finally, the writer of Hebrews declared, "Let us hold unswervingly to the hope we profess, for He who promised is faithful" (Heb. 10:23). Starting to sense a common theme? *Webster's* dictionary defines "cling" this way: "To hold onto something or someone very tightly or tenaciously; to stay very close to someone for emotional support and/or protection; to adhere to; to clutch; to grip or grasp." I was curious, so I researched the meaning of "tenacious" and learned that it is "to keep a firm hold of something; clinging or adhering closely to; not readily relinquishing; determined." It would appear to be clear that what our Father wants us to hear through the words written by David, Paul, Joshua, and the writer of Hebrews is that we are to be clingers and tenacious holders. His instruction is that we stay very close, adhere, clutch, and hold firmly to Him for guidance and protection and to do so with tenacious determination so as to never let go. To lay hold with unswerving resolve to the hope and immeasurable good that are ours through Jesus.

I remember my parents taking my siblings and me to a Wild West theme park near our home. While there, we went on a stagecoach ride where I was given the responsibility of keeping and securing a bag of money. At some point during the ride, we were stopped by a band of bad guys on horses with masks and guns. I was young and very terrified. I clung tenaciously to my dad. When they demanded the loot, I held on even tighter and bravely refused. As long as I had my father there to hold on to, I was brave and determined. Our relationship with our heavenly Father is very much the same. He is there for us to hold on to and to cling to tenaciously. The world is filled with trouble. It lurks around every corner and approaches us in waves. We, of our own accord, are incapable of overcoming it. We need help, someone to see danger coming and to protect us from it each and every time it approaches. A truth of which God is well aware. A responsibility for which He is fully prepared and highly capable. Notice that He does not instruct us to protect ourselves, to find our own hope and peace, or to provide the goodness that we crave. Our Father does not need our help with any of the hard stuff; He's got that. What He does require of us is the exact thing that we need from Him: to cling to and hold on tenaciously to His hand, trusting completely that He will protect us from that which threatens harm. Amazingly, as we do so, our faith in Him increases, His presence becomes more real, His goodness and favor are poured over us, and our identity and purpose made more clear. With the world, clinging is not always well appreciated; with God, it is mandatory.

April 24, 2020

Have you ever been afforded the privilege of a vision of Jesus? I am not speaking of seeing Him in actual flesh as He walked on the earth, but a viewing through the eyes of your spirit. A realization that is imparted from heaven and is life altering, one that cannot be called upon or conjured up as we may desire; a revelation the full impact of which overwhelms one's human nature while simultaneously invigorating and captivating the spirit that exists within. The experience of which I speak is difficult to describe with words, and therefore, I find myself struggling with doing so. The songwriter wrote, "I once was lost but now I am found, was blind but now I see" ("Amazing Grace," Newton 1779). The apostle Paul spent a large part of his life unwilling and unable to see Jesus through the eyes of his spirit. Then on the road to Damascus, the Lord appeared to him; and the magnitude of the encounter took away Paul's physical sight, opened the eyes of his spirit, and changed the course of his life and those of all God's children thereafter. From that point forward, the revelation of the Son of God fueled Paul's every breath. Just a brief glimpse of the Lion of Judah captured his heart, his mind, and, most importantly, his spirit and empowered him to stare into the face of trials, heartaches, and eventually death while fulfilling the purpose to which he had been divinely called. That is the experience that I am led to speak to and share with you. For most of my existence, I could have shown you an image of Jesus or written you a word description of what I believed

His appearance to be. What I could not have done was to portray for you what my spirit now perceives in Him. That very thing that Paul was gifted with discerning and passing on to others of God's children, I can now. Not because I am more special or of greater importance than any other of the saints of God, but for the reasons explained in the prior 180 plus entries herein: I can now. When I am bestowed the privilege of a glimpse of the splendor and magnificence of my Lord, my spirit jumps, my breath seems to leave my body, and my heart appears to both stop and race at the same time. Sorrow for my contribution to His great sacrifice is immediately replaced with the joy that accompanies His presence. The love that emanates from His smile envelopes me. Peace like a river flows through my soul. His beauty renders me awestruck. What used to have little or no effect on me now wrecks me in the most amazing of ways. Unlike Paul, my physical eyesight is not taken; but just like Paul, my heart, my mind, and my spirit are captured by His presence. I am empowered to worship Him, to give my all for Him, and to fulfill the purpose for Him to which I have been called. In a word, I, like Paul, am changed. You too can experience the same. Just earnestly and desperately seek Him, and never forget that He adores you.

April 25, 2020

Several entries ago I was led to write of the power and the greatness of our God. Today I am overwhelmed with thoughts of His goodness and moved by His Spirit, by way of a song in the night, "The Goodness of God" by Jenn Johnson and Bethel Music. My first thought is that very few would disagree with the fact that God is good. After all, we sing about it from the time we are little children. Many pray of it before each meal, and the Bible speaks of it over and over. Yet I fear that the true depth and magnitude of our Father's goodness, just as with His greatness, escapes many. During my late teenage years, I was driving to Baltimore with three friends to see an Orioles game. Along the way, we talked of many subjects. At some point during the trip, our discussion shifted to the topic of spiritual gifts, and I found myself struggling to explain the existence and reality of the same. Suddenly, out of nowhere and with much wisdom, one of my buddies declared, "The gifts are from God, and they become real when you receive and experience them for yourself and not before." That moment has stuck with me for forty years, and it comes to mind this morning. Make no mistake, God is good. It is not just what He does; it is who He is. And who He is never changes. The question is, do we receive and experience that goodness in the manner that my friend described? I mean, really receive it. The kind of acceptance that crawls inside of you, moves you, and changes you. The psalmist did. "Taste and see that the Lord is good" (Ps. 34:8) and "You are good, and what you do is good" (Ps. 119:68). Paul most certainly experienced the true goodness of God. It radically changed his life as he wrote in each of his letters. The disciples got it, having lived and walked with the epitome of it for three years and having heard He Himself proclaim it: "There is only One who is good" (Matt. 19:17). Jesus understood it above all others. He was it! The goodness of God in living, breathing form. Have you experienced and received it? If so, I celebrate it with you. If not, it is yours to encounter and to walk in. My prayer is that it will envelope you and overwhelm you; that you will bask in the joy, the peace, and the love that accompany it. Just for the record, I have experienced and received it. It is amazing and incredible! Just how much so? I will let the lyrics of my song in the night convey that for me. God bless you!

> (Verse 1) I love you Lord; Oh Your mercy never fails me. All my days; I've been held in Your hands. From the moment that I wake up; until I lay my head; I will sing of the goodness of God.

> (Chorus) All my life You have been faithful; All my life You have been so good. With every breath I am able, I will sing of the goodness of God.

> (Verse 2) I love Your voice; You have led me through the fire. In darkest nights, You are close like no other. I've known You as a Father; I've

known You as a friend. I have lived in the goodness of God.

(Chorus: repeat)

(Bridge) Your goodness is running after, it's running after me; Your goodness is running after, it's running after me. With my life laid down, I'm surrendered now. I give You everything. Your goodness is running after, it's running after me.

April 26, 2020

One of the first people that God brought into my life when we moved to North Carolina was a Spirit-filled man named Filipe. I am certain that I have spoken of him before. He is one of my dearest of brothers. Our relationship was initiated and ordained by God beyond any doubt. Filipe has a love for Jesus that is genuine and pure, which makes it infectious and contagious. If asked what makes him that way, my answer would have to be that he opens himself completely to the Holy Spirit and, that by doing so, allows God to reflect His Son through him. Filipe is a walking bundle of each and every one of the fruits of the Spirit woven together to form a powerful resource for the kingdom of God. He often reminds me of our need to be open to and listening for God's voice each and every minute of each and every day and then to be ready, willing, and able to respond when He speaks. That we are to be "intentional." Filipe is intentional on steroids. No time that we are together passes without his relating an instance where the Holy Spirit led him to approach someone in need and serve as God's ambassador by meeting whatever lack was presented. Sometimes it is food, sometimes money, other times a ride or a place to stay. Always it includes prayer and Jesus. Likewise, it is almost exclusively one on one and outside of the spotlight of public attention. Simply, Filipe is loving Jesus by caring for someone in need. That is exactly how our Father relates and ministers to us—quietly, passionately, one on one, out of the spotlight. As if no other person except you or I was in existence. His capacity and desire to do so convinces me of His great love and captures my heart. In a conversation with Megan last night, we agreed and then marveled at the truth that when we get to heaven, we will be showered with the exact same love, attention, honor, and privilege as anyone else that is there. That includes Abraham, Noah, Moses, David, Isaiah, Peter, James, John (both of them), Paul, Lazarus, Mary (all three of them), Martha, Jairus, Bartimaeus, and/or many, many others. That is how God loves us—greatly, individually, and unconditionally. And that is how we are to love one another. For several months now, Filipe has been called to be Jesus to a homeless gentleman. He meets with him at least once a week and feeds him, puts him up in a motel if the weather is bad, and always shares the bread of God's Word with him. God adores this man greatly, individually, and unconditionally. He feels exactly the same about you, Filipe, and me—about all His children. So much so that He affords us the honor and the privilege of passing that love onto others, people that He places directly in our path, right where He has planted us. Let's be open and listen for His call.

April 27, 2020

Led to chapter 3 of Paul's letter to the Ephesians, my eyes have been opened to a powerful revelation. There Paul speaks to a great mystery that was hidden in God until after the finished work of Jesus on the cross. A truth that was revealed to him that he would be equipped "to preach to the Gentiles the unsearchable riches of Christ, and to make plain the administration of this mystery, which for ages past was kept hidden in God..." (Eph. 3:8–9). What is that mystery? It can be found in Ephesians 3:6: "This mystery is that through the gospel the Gentiles are heirs together with Israel, members together of one body, and sharers together in the promise in Christ Jesus." Just to clarify, if you are not a Jew, then you are a Gentile, which makes most of us Gentiles and includes a whole lot of people. God revealed to Paul, and desired for the whole world to know, that in Jesus and through faith in Him, we all may approach the Father with freedom and confidence. This truth is cause for joyous celebration. It is what Paul writes in verses 10–11 that caught me by surprise.

> His intent was that now, through the church, the manifold wisdom of God should be made known to the rulers and authorities in the heavenly realms, according to His eternal purpose which He accomplished in Christ Jesus our Lord.

Did that really say what I believed it to say? I read it again and then again. The words did not change. How could that be? It seemed to say that our Father's intent is that through the church, which is us, He is now going to make known His manifold wisdom to rulers and authorities in the heavenly realms. I was confused. Did that just say to those in heavenly places? I looked it up in my go-to commentary, and sure enough, I was reading it correctly. It still wouldn't quite sink in. I could see serving as a witness to fellow humans, but to angelic beings? Shouldn't that mystery already have been revealed to them? The answer is no. God always has a better plan. What more effective means by which to instruct angels and demons regarding the New Covenant ushered in by Jesus than through His works of salvation and sanctification within His church? Who has a better view of or looks more intently upon us than angelic beings, both faithful and fallen? They observe, up close, this community of redeemed, blood-washed saints, not only standing and serving their God here on earth but also sitting with Him in the Holy Place above. They watch in wonder as the mystery that Paul wrote of is carried out, being either greatly encouraged or discouraged depending upon which side they war for. God uses His church—He uses us—to play a part in the graduate training of the principalities and powers that roam in heavenly places. What an awesome privilege. So be aware that school is in session and the students' eyes are on us (Guzik 2015; Eph. 3).

April 28, 2020

God's promises are many. They are filled with peace and love and assurance and are purposed to serve as a guide and to equip for the journey set before us. Sometimes spoken singularly, while in other instances in a group, they never fail to strengthen, undergird, and encourage God's children for the challenges before them. This morning I will share two separate experiences, along with the promises that accompany them, trusting that our Father will use each to strengthen your faith and encourage you as you continue your journey for and to Him. I have previously only shared this first story with Megan. I am not certain why such is the case, but it leaves me feeling a bit vulnerable doing so here. Nonetheless, I am convinced that I am supposed to do so.

At some point during my college years (eighteen to twenty-five), I was home in Maryland for the summer and living with my parents in our hometown of Bishopville. One evening, at just about sunset, I had to run a short errand. After jumping into my car, I headed south on Rt. 113 toward Berlin. Just prior to Showell, Maryland, there was a subtle curve in the road that had two lanes, one each way, at that time. As I negotiated the slight bend, I observed another vehicle headed at me in my lane. From that point on, everything became very surreal and almost out of body. The vehicle seemed to pass directly through my car like a wisp of air, and then it was gone. With my awareness quickly restored, I glanced into my rearview mirror only to see a vehicle in my lane traveling in the opposite direction. Startled (It was as if I was watching what I just described and not experiencing it—that is, until it was over and I realized that it had, in fact, happened.), I continued on my errand, not recounting my experience, for whatever reason, to anyone until doing so to my wife several years later. I want to stress two important facts that I believe are very relevant. First, I did not have a personal or any other sort of relationship with Jesus at that time, nor was I inclined to spiritual matters. And second, I did not use drugs of any kind, and there was zero alcohol in my system. The second story brings me to January 2019. I found myself in Cancun, Mexico, for my daughter, Sarah, and my son-in-law Shane's wedding. On the second day there, as we were returning from dinner, I found myself attempting to warm my hands over a fire ring that I believed to stand alone in a courtyard. As I would soon discover, it did not stand alone but was surrounded by an empty concrete fountain. It was dark outside, and there was nothing to warn of the impending danger. I lost my balance and began to fall into the three-to four-foot-deep concrete hole. I put my hands down as I was falling. To shorten the story, I should have hit the bottom headfirst. That did not happen. I did suffer a nasty wound on my left calf along with scrapes on my right forearm, both of which have since healed. Most importantly, I incurred a painful bruise on my back. Why is that so important, you ask? Because it means that I landed on my back and not on my head or neck. That could not and should not have been. The fall was not far enough for my body to turn. There had to be some explanation. There was! It wasn't long before the Holy Spirit allowed me to see how angels had turned my body, mid fall, protecting me from catastrophic harm. I was spiritually overwhelmed. By this time in my life, I was all in, fully engaged, and sold out to Jesus, which might lead one to wonder how this harm could come knocking at my door. God never promised that we would not have trouble. What He did assure us is that He would be there to see us through all of it. Rather than focus on why these incidents occurred, I choose to direct my attention upon four promises from God that, when viewed collectively, can be seen at work and used to explain both of my experiences. First, Ephesians 2:10 promises that "we are God's workmanship, created in Christ Jesus to do good works, which God prepared in advance for us to do." Second, "being confident of this, that He who began a good work in you will carry it onto completion until the day of Christ Jesus" (Phil. 1:6). Next, "the One who was born of God keeps him safe, and the evil one cannot harm him" (1 John 5:18). And finally, "the Lord watches over you… The Lord will keep you from all harm—He will watch over your life; the Lord will watch over your coming and your going both now and forevermore" (Ps. 121:5, 7–8). Four distinct assurances given to His children by which our Father declares the following. He has a plan for us, one that He will accomplish. He has a kingdom purpose for our lives. Things for us to do that we cannot complete if we are taken out by an erratic driver in Maryland or an empty fountain in Mexico. The enemy is aware of God's plans, and He does not care for them one bit. Enter harm, or at least an attempt to inflict the same, God has that fully covered also. Jesus keeps us safe, both now and forevermore. He watches over us and keeps us from harm. Whether it is by virtue of a vehicle turning to vapor or by angels twisting your body, the evil one cannot harm you. And why is that? It is because your God created you for a purpose(s), one of which is to complete the good work(s) that He has assigned for you, a plan that He is fully committed to and perfectly capable of equipping and protecting you for. Then there is that other reason: because He totally adores you.

April 29, 2020

I spent a portion of the day yesterday trying to convince myself that those of you who are reading this are not now completely convinced that I am totally crazy. That after hearing of cars passing through me and angels twisting my body, each of you have not put this down never to open it again. After a period of doubting and second guessing the decision to share my stories I was reminded of two very important things. First, it was not my decision to make, it was my Father's. He who makes *no* mistakes and whose timing is perfect guided my heart, my mind, and my hand; therefore, only blessing and good will follow. Secondly, I am not delusional. I know it, and those who are around me do as well. I believe that they would even vouch for it. I would hope that what could be viewed as questionable mentally is more than equally compensated for by my passion for my Father, His Son, and His Holy Spirit. ("If we are out of our mind, it is for the sake of God… For Christ's love compels us…" [2 Cor. 5:13–14].) Matthew relates an instance where a Pharisee asked Jesus which is the greatest commandment in the law, to which Jesus replied, "Love the Lord your God with all your heart and with all your soul and with all your mind" (Matt. 22:34–37). Whatever the Holy Spirit chooses to reveal to you through these writings, please know this. I have fallen completely, passionately, and unashamedly in love with my God, with His Son Jesus, and with His amazing Holy Spirit. They have captured my heart, my soul, and my mind. Funny thing is, I do not even have to work at obeying the greatest commandment directive. It just flows from my being in relationship with, trusting in, and surrendering to Them. And it is from that love, that trust, and that surrender that days like yesterday arise. Times where I share stories that to the human mind may appear farfetched and deranged but that are completely normal in the spirit realm. Paul wrote, "Do not conform any longer to the pattern of this world, but be transformed by the renewing of your mind" (Rom. 12:2). God's adoration of me, along with the great love for Him that it has birthed, has completely transformed my mind, my heart, and my spirit. I see things differently—hopefully, as He sees them. As for yesterday's stories, please open your minds, your hearts, and your spirits to the possibility that they are real and true; and be assured that I share them out of my obedience to and my love for my God, as well as from my love for each of you. Jesus asked Peter if he truly loved Him, and when Peter answered yes, Jesus replied, "Feed my sheep." My hope and my prayer is that you are being fed.

April 30, 2020

God has placed a passion in my heart to see His children discipled. So what exactly is a disciple, and what in turn, does that answer tell us about discipleship? The late Rev. Billy Graham defined a disciple as someone who believes in Jesus and seeks to follow Him in his or her daily life. A disciple of Jesus was and is someone who becomes like Him in everything, a dedicated follower of Jesus. In the Old Testament, a disciple actively imitated both the life and teachings of their master. It is in the New Testament, however, that a much clearer picture of a disciple is provided. Of much significance is the fact that the beginning and the ending of Jesus's earthly ministry accentuated discipleship. The very first task that He attended to upon returning from forty days in the desert was to gather together twelve men to be His disciples. What better means by which to define a disciple then through Jesus's interaction and relationship with these individuals—men who started by simply following Jesus and then who, after sitting at His feet for three years and absorbing every word that He spoke, became true believers dedicated to being like Him in every way; men who, unlike the many who merely followed Jesus, chose to stand and be associated with Him, leaving only at His moment of divine purpose and then being reinstated thereafter and called to imitate His life and teachings to the world around them; men who then committed to giving up their lives for their Lord; men through whom true discipleship is defined. Jesus Himself gave further insight into this concept of discipleship when He declared, "If you hold to my teaching you are really my disciples" (John 8:31). He also proclaimed, "By this all men will know that you are my disciples, if you love one another" (John 13:35). And finally, Jesus said, "And anyone who does not carry His cross and follow me cannot be my disciple" (Luke 14:27). Hold to His teachings, love one another, take up your cross and follow me—words of instruction spoken directly from the mouth of our Lord that define a disciple. Armed with a pretty clear picture of what a disciple is, we are left with the question of what we are supposed to do with it. Jesus again provides the answer. One of His final acts before ascending into heaven can be found in Matthew 28:16–20. There He commanded those who had become His disciples to "go and make disciples of all nations…" He directed those who He had taught to become like Him to do likewise to others, everywhere; to engage in discipleship throughout the world. He directs each of us to do the same. In order to fulfill that calling, we must first become like Him. We cannot make a disciple unless we are a disciple. He has provided us with a blueprint. It will not be easy, but the reward will be great. It resonates with me that the Son of God could have addressed any truth whatsoever before rising to take His rightful place in heaven. He chose discipleship. It has to be of the utmost importance to Him, and therefore to us. We must heed and obey His command. Oswald Chambers, in the April 24 entry of *My Utmost for His Highest*, states,

> Our work only begins where God's grace has laid
> the foundation. Our work is not to save souls,

but to disciple them…to disciple others' lives until they are totally yielded to God. We must reproduce our own kind spiritually.

In my experience, discipleship is best approached and most effective in one-on-one relationships or in smaller groups. Certainly, Jesus ministered to large gatherings of people; however, His disciples arose from more personal and intimate interactions. We would be well advised and much more effective in our calling by following His lead. Become His disciples, and then go and make others the same. It is *so important*!

May 1, 2020

Now may the God of peace, who through the blood of the eternal covenant brought back from the dead our Lord Jesus, that great shepherd of the sheep, equip you with everything good for doing His will, and may He work in us what is pleasing to Him, through Jesus Christ, to whom be the glory for ever and ever. Amen. (Heb. 13:20–21)

For almost two years now my Father, His Son, and His Holy Spirit have been joining me at this altar that I have established for Them in the front of my home. It usually goes like this. I rise early in the morning, turn on the desk lamp, gather my Bible and my devotionals, and begin to commune with Them. Instantly, without exception, They are with me. (I am certain that They were there first, excitedly anticipating my arrival!) They never miss a day. Not one. Just as They promised They are with me always, wherever I go. From that moment on, They stay with me for as long as is necessary. Necessary for what, you may ask? For as long as it takes each day to encourage me and to love me, to speak truth into and about me and to pour out Their compassion over me; to hear me and answer me; to equip me with everything good for doing Their will; and to work in me what is pleasing to Them. Some days we spend a couple of hours together; others, several more. Regardless of the length of time, it is the richest, most blessed part of each of my days.

About a year after we began, or almost one year ago, I was led to inject a journal that Megan had gifted me into our time together. I had never been one to chronicle my thoughts, but by this point, I had come to know my Father's voice, and I clearly felt Him directing me to begin writing down that which He was speaking over and into me as we met. Each day I would simply show up, spend time with my Father, listen for what His Spirit would say, and then write it in my journal. No other instructions from Him; no other intentions from me. That is until recently when I began to sense that God had another plan. Enter an amazing book written by Pastor Steven Furtick of Elevation Church entitled *Sun Stand Still*. I began to read, and as I did, the eyes of my spirit and my mind were opened. (Please get this book and read it!) God revealed that He has a specific purpose for that which He is giving me to write each morning and that at the perfect time, He will provide me with a clear vision of exactly what that purpose is. As I wait, I am to exercise an audacious level of faith just as Joshua did in chapter 10 of the book named for him in the Bible. Then, when He directs, I am to step out boldly, in strength that is not my own, and watch as He moves and His purpose is fulfilled. God desires that all His children receive the words of truth, identity, and purpose that He has ordained be written here over the last year. What God purposes shall come to pass. His will shall be done! Exactly how He will accomplish this plan has not yet been revealed to me. For now I am simply to pray and exercise a Joshua level of faith. That is what I am doing at this moment. This is very, very unchartered territory for me. I know that He is with me and that He will equip me with everything necessary to do His good and perfect will. I also know, from being attentive to His voice, that I am to complete two hundred entries and then wait upon Him. This is entry number 191. Nine more to go. I am a bit anxious, but mostly I am greatly excited. My Father adores me—of this, I am certain. Therefore, I can completely trust Him. What a great honor and privilege it is to be used by Him. For those reasons, I will show up tomorrow morning and be greeted by my Father. Then I will listen to Him and write down what He says. How extremely blessed am I! Thank you for going on this journey with me (Furtick 2010).

May 2, 2020

I began this journey in a place of great fear. Issues with my physical health and the uncertainty that accompanied them led me to the only place that I knew or would allow myself to go: to my own understanding, to my own thoughts. Our mind is fertile ground upon which the enemy sows the seeds of deception and untruth. It seems that his strategy of destruction always begins in the mind. While certainly no match for our Father, he is aware that if he can capture our minds, he is well on the way to achieving his goal. Jesus, on the other hand, desires our hearts. He knows that the path to gaining our belief and our trust is through our hearts. "For it is with your heart that you believe and are justified… As the Scripture says, 'Anyone who trusts in Him will never be put to shame'" (Rom. 10:10–11). And so the war is on. Satan wants to take hold of our hearts and our bodies by controlling our minds. His weapons are fear, heartache, anxiety, lust, greed, pride, and anger, along with anything else that is contrary to the very nature of God. His success depends entirely upon keeping our minds troubled and devoid of any concept of trust in our Father or in His great and unconditional love for us. Our God approaches us from a completely different perspective. He longs for our heart. To redeem our spirit and restore us to right relationship with Him by capturing the same. To gain our minds and the thoughts within them by opening our hearts to the gift of His Son Jesus and then filling them with the love, joy, peace, mercy, grace, presence, favor, and rest that only He has to offer. God created us. He knows our innermost being, our strengths and our weaknesses. He also knows that we will need His help to complete our journey back to Him. Help that is ours to have. Help that comes by way of trust. Trust that is birthed and then nurtured and sustained in our hearts, before overflowing into our minds and laying captive our thoughts. At a time, when His disciples were greatly troubled upon hearing the prediction of

His impending death, Jesus said to them, "Do not let your hearts be troubled. Trust in God, trust also in me" (John 14:1). An often-quoted passage found in Proverbs states, "Trust in the Lord with all of your heart and lean not on your own understanding" (Prov. 3:5). Satan continues to knock at the door of my mind with an arsenal of weapons. Only now something has changed. I am different. My heart has been captured by and filled with the unsurpassable love of my Father. Love that has generated a trust in Him, an awareness of my identity, and an unwavering faith in His promises. Love that overcomes all fear. Love that is past all understanding. Our Father longs for us to trust Him. It starts with our hearts. Will you surrender yours to Him?

May 3, 2020

This morning trouble lurks. The enemy is prowling around seeking to discourage me and cause me harm. God's plan and His purpose for me during this season are one step closer to completion. Lives will be changed for His kingdom. Satan cannot be happy. I am encouraged in the midst of his attack. My Father's hand is upon me. His promises of safety and protection cover and surround me. His Spirit dwells deep within me. "Greater is He who is within me than he that is in the world" (1 John 4:4). Please do not be deceived. The enemy's attack is real, and it is heavy, and I would be no match for it on my own. But praise be to my Father, I am not alone. I know who I am and to Whom I belong and am fully aware of the privileges and benefits afforded me by each. I can trust that He will fight my battle, and I stand upon the truth that He has already won it. All I need to do is wait, to be still, and to know that He is God (Ps. 46:10). And while I wait, I will worship and I will bow down before and exalt Him who is fully able to carry me as I stand upon His promise to do so. The Holy Spirit has led me to David's declaration found in Psalm 27. As I close, I make it mine this morning. It can be yours as well.

> The Lord is my light and my salvation—whom
> shall I fear? The Lord is the stronghold of my

life—of whom shall I be afraid? When evil men advance against me to devour my flesh (or slander me), when my enemies and my foes attack me, they will stumble and fall. Though an army besiege me, my heart will not fear; though war break out against me, even then will I be confident. One thing I ask of the Lord, this is what I seek: that I may dwell in the house of the Lord all the days of my life, to gaze upon the beauty of the Lord and to seek Him in His temple. For in the day of trouble He will keep me safe in His dwelling; He will hide me in the shelter of His tabernacle and set me high upon a rock. Then my head will be exalted above the enemies who surround me; at His tabernacle will I sacrifice with shouts of joy; I will sing and make music to the Lord. Hear my voice when I call, O Lord; be merciful to me and answer me. My heart says to you, "Seek His face!" Your face Lord, I will seek. Do not hide Your face from me, do not turn Your servant away in anger; You have been my helper. Do not reject me or forsake me, O God my Savior. Though my father and mother forsake me, (Not the case!) the Lord will receive me. Teach me Your way, O Lord; lead me in a straight path because of my oppressors. Do not turn me over to the desire of my foes, for false witnesses rise up against me, breathing out violence. I am still confident of this: I will see the goodness of the Lord in the land of the living. Wait for the Lord; be strong and take heart and wait for the Lord. (Ps. 27)

David cried out this prayer to His God and trusted Him for deliverance. This morning I am doing the same. You can do likewise. I pray that you do.

May 4, 2020

Chapter 8 of Paul's letter to the Romans provides God's church with a bounty of truth and promises, each purposed to establish and strengthen our faith; undergird us in times of doubt and trouble; and prepare us for the journey ahead. Time and again, the Holy Spirit has taken me to this fountain of reassurance and drenched me in the peace and confidence that flows from the mouth of my Father. Grace, love, and mercy that is unsurpassed and can be found only in His presence. Presence that is fully ours by way of His Word. This morning I am compelled to address a few specific passages found in chapter 8. I would encourage you to read it in its entirety, asking the Spirit to open your spirit, heart, and mind to the truth revealed there. God begins with one of the most powerful and life-altering passages in all of Scripture: "Therefore, there is no condemnation for those who are in Christ Jesus, because through Christ Jesus the law of the Spirit of life set me free from the law of sin and death" (Rom. 8:1–2). Take a minute to consider what God just declared. The world is filled with judgment and condemnation. It comes at us from every direction. Much of the time it simply arises from within. In the face of such an onslaught, our Father says, "I have a new way, a New Covenant. His name is Jesus. He is the Way, the Truth and the Life. Accept and receive Him. Come to me through Him and condemnation will be no more." Incredible! Verse 9 declares, "You, however, are controlled not by the sinful nature but by the Spirit, if the Spirit of God lives within you." We know that our sinful nature separates us from God. We also know that Jesus died for our sins, once for all (1 Pet. 3:18), and promised to give the Holy Spirit to those who are His followers. Therefore, God is assuring us that through Jesus, sin no longer has any power over His children. Awesome! Next this: "The Spirit helps us in our weakness" (Rom. 8:26). While we received power when we received the Holy Spirit, we continue to exist in these human, flesh-composed shells. Therefore, we experience weaknesses, a reality that our Father provides an answer for. And not just any solution but the best one of all. He gives us Himself. He gives us His Spirit. It just keeps getting better! Verse 28 proclaims, "And we know that in all things God works for the good of those who love Him, who have been called according to His purpose." Do you love Him? Then be assured that He is working for your good. Not just some of the time but all of the time. Not just when you are walking in obedience and/or in the fullness of His joy and peace, but all the time. That includes the hard and the weak moments. Your good is what He promises. You can count on it. He is so amazing! Two more. "No, in all these things we are more than conquerors through Him who loved us" (Rom. 8:37). There is that word "all" again. What exactly are "all these things"? The answer is found in verse 35: "Trouble, hardship, persecution, famine, nakedness, danger or sword." It is easy to be an overcomer when the sky is blue and the sun is shining. But our Father is promising that, with and through Jesus, we will not only conquer but more than conquer the hard times. That when the enemy shows up to destroy us, we will overcome him, and we will do so "by the blood of the Lamb…" (Rev. 12:11). Stand tall and strong, child of the Most High God, you are a conqueror. Your Father declares it. Lastly, God promises "that nothing will be able to separate us from the love of God that is in Christ Jesus our Lord" (Rom. 8:39). I am afraid that the magnitude of this passage escapes far too many of us. We read it and completely miss the depth of its significance. Recently, I was made painfully aware that no matter how deeply we are loved by those closest to us, there will always be something that will challenge and stretch the limits of that love. With God, that something ceases to exist. He will love us regardless, and nothing will ever separate us from that love. Love that, like every other promise spoken of in Romans chapter 8, begins, exists, and flows through His Son Jesus. Do you want to experience and walk in the fullness of God's love and of His promises? If so, then the answer is simple: get Jesus!

May 5, 2020

In Romans chapter 12, Paul, while addressing function and unity within the Body of Christ, speaks to the different gifts given to each according to God's grace. In so doing, he identifies prophecy, serving, teaching, encouraging, contributing to the needs of others (giving), leadership, and showing mercy as examples of those gifts. Today I will expound upon the gift of giving, or of generosity, as it is sometimes referred. Certainly there are those within the Body in whose heart God has placed a passion and a heightened desire to give and to do so abundantly. Megan and I have been graciously afforded that gift. The spirit within us longs to contribute to those who are in need as well as to those who have been called to advance the kingdom by other means. We thank our Father for the gift and for the provision to fulfill it. Having acknowledged the special gift of giving afforded to certain of God's children, I am compelled to remind of the trait of generosity that should be common to all His beloved. A spirit of charitableness that should flow from and reflect our love for Jesus. Are we not to emulate every witnessed characteristic of our precious Lord? And was He not the very essence of benevolence, giving everything, including His life, for those in need, each of us? Everyone may not have received the gift of an impassioned heart to give, but each of God's children has been given the Spirit of Christ—an endowment that is accompanied by a genuine love and concern for others as well as the needs that burden them. Needs, when presented and realized, our Father expects each of us to meet.

> Command them to do good, to be rich in good deeds, and to be generous and willing to share. (1 Tim. 6:18)

> But the righteous give without sparing. (Prov. 21:26)

> You will be made rich in every way so that you can be generous on every occasion, and through us your generosity will result in thanksgiving to God. (2 Cor. 9:11)

> See to it that you also excel in this grace of giving. (2 Cor. 8:7)

> He who gives to the poor will lack nothing. (Prov. 28:27)

Jesus declared that the greatest commandment is to love the Lord your God with everything within you and then to love your neighbor as yourself. He was fully aware that out of such love would flow every other quality that He desired for His bride to exhibit, including generosity. Giving is an element of our Christian DNA, one that we must exercise. Yes, some are gifted the privilege to give abundantly; but all are called to give as Jesus did—generously, sacrificially, and unconditionally—that the kingdom may be advanced and our God glorified. Is not all that we possess His to start with?

May 6, 2020

In case it has not become obvious by now, I have a very real control issue. I have this need to be in the front, in charge, steering the ship. Whenever I am in a car, I either have to be driving or driving the person batty who is. If I could, I would pilot the plane when I travel by air. (It drives me crazy that I cannot see out the front window of the airplane.) Leadership and command are beneficial qualities in many circumstances. In my relationship with God, not so much. He is God! The One who created everything, including me, and has control over it. He is perfectly capable of doing so. What He desires of me is surrender. It is one of the qualities that He is working out and perfecting in me on this journey. While I am certain that He will succeed, I nonetheless remain a lump of clay in His hands, which brings me to this place in my assignment. With only five more entries to go, I am experiencing feelings of concern and restlessness over how I am to finish. But I am reminded that it is not my responsibility to make that decision. I am only to surrender to Him, listen to His voice, and then wait for His provision. He has got this. By this time, I hope that it is very clear that my steps throughout this journey have been perfectly ordered. While it has oftentimes been necessary for the Holy Spirit to reroute my GPS, I have come to know that little or nothing transpires in my life outside of His direction. A recent case in point would be the book *Sun Stand Still*. At just the perfect time, my Father interjected this amazing writing into my journey as a means of revealing the next direction that I would be taking. A way by which He has rebirthed a dream and a desire that He placed within me years ago, and then connected it with a second and third passion raised up more recently. I believe that it is time for me to share that dream with you.

Several years ago, I got this crazy (to me) idea that was way bigger than me and therefore had to have come from God. I wanted, and still greatly desire, to give away as much as I possibly can during my lifetime. Many people that I have encountered desire to accumulate great wealth. I do not share that passion. My treasures are stored up in heaven. Blessed with the Romans chapter 12 gift of generosity, I long to give a large portion of the money that my Father has entrusted to me back to Him for the care of His people and the advancement of His kingdom. I shared my dream with Megan; and she is, not surprisingly, all in. We are together for a reason and a purpose. Pastor Furtick writes that your *Sun Stand Still* prayer has to be audacious, far beyond your normal thought process. This one is. That is where the level of faith that was released by Joshua to have God stop the sun from setting for twenty-four hours comes in. Over the last three years, God has been raising up that kind of faith within me and within my wife. We are convinced that God can and will complete the good work that He began in us. How He will do so is not for us to question or decide. We are only to receive, then believe, and then move. We have been given the vision and are in the process of exercising an audacious level of faith. When we are instructed what to do next, we will move. Spoiler alert: we believe that what you are and have been reading is part of the plan. We are very excited!

May 7, 2020

When I was in elementary school, the teachers had a practice of having students who had done something wrong write sentences by the hundreds declaring their commitment to refrain from such actions in the future. I also recall that later, particularly during high school and college, I would prepare for tests by either writing or stating a particular concept over and over. Both of these memories illustrate methods of learning by the use of repetition or redundancy. To this day, I continue to apply this concept when memorizing scripture. I am convinced that God uses this idea when He purposes to instill an especially significant truth into the lives of His children. He has done that with me as I have written here. There are times when He gives me something to write that I am certain He has given me on a prior occasion. Maybe you have noticed the same thing. I have mentioned my daily reading of the devotional *Morning and Evening*. Therein, Charles Spurgeon will often speak to the same biblical principle more than once in an effort, I believe, to imbed it deeply into the hearts and minds of his readers. I say all of this because this morning the Holy Spirit is directing me to expound upon a topic that I know He has had me address before. It must be important, so I am listening intently. I hope that you will do the same. The truth that is resonating in my spirit involves "victory." As I am often led to do, I looked up its definition and learned that it is "an act of defeating an enemy or opponent in a battle, game or competition; a conquest or triumph in a struggle; to overcome or gain control over someone or something." Man, that is really rich! When viewed from our perspective as followers and disciples of Jesus, it becomes even more so. Do we have an enemy? Are we in a battle, a struggle? Is it our longing to see him defeated? Do we strive to overcome him, to gain control over him? The answer is *yes* to each and every one of those questions. Yes, we have an enemy. His name is Satan. Yes, there is a battle raging with him, one for our very souls. A struggle that is being waged this very second. Yes, it is our heart's desire to see him defeated. Yes, we need to overcome him, for control to be gained over him. Sounds like we need a victory. Praise be to God, we have one! Lift up your heads, raise your hands high, and shout to God with a voice of triumph. The victory has already been secured. It is ours. The battle has been won and glory to our God we did not even have to lift a finger. "But thanks be to our God! He gives us victory through our Lord Jesus Christ" (1 Cor. 15:57). By virtue of Calvary, victory has been achieved, and it has been given to us as a gift by our Father. Do you find yourself constantly struggling with someone (Satan) or something (sin, fear, anxiety, greed, lust, pride)? Are you a blood-bought, blood-washed child of the Most High God? If your answers are yes to both questions, then stand on this promise from your Father: "For everyone born of God overcomes the world, even our faith. Who is it that overcomes the world? Only he who believes that Jesus is the Son of God" (1 John 5:4–5). Are you born again of God? Do you believe that Jesus is His Son? If so, then victory is your birthright. By faith, receive what is yours and struggle no longer. The someone or something with which you do battle has been overcome. Hallelujah! During the night, I received another song: "See a Victory" by Elevation Worship.

> I'm gonna see a victory, I'm gonna see a victory, For the battle belongs to You, Lord. There's power in the mighty name of Jesus, Every war He wages He will win. Gonna worship my way through this battle 'cause I know how this story ends.

There are more awesome lyrics, please check them out! Seems pretty obvious that our Father places a high priority and a great significance on "Victory." Maybe that is because it was paid for with such a high price. We cannot allow that sacrifice to be neglected or ignored. Walk in what is yours: *victory!*

May 8, 2020

I am confident in saying that virtually everyone, even those with a paltry knowledge of scripture, would concur that there was nothing ordinary about Jesus and His life on earth. "Ordinary" is defined as having no special or distinctive features. An ordinary person is one who does things that are accepted by society (the world), someone who proceeds as those around them expect. Synonyms for *ordinary* include *normal, standard, expected, routine, traditional,* and *established.* The opposite of ordinary is extraordinary. It means beyond what is regular or established; exceptional in character and degree; noteworthy and/or remarkable. Jesus was nothing if not extraordinary. Everything about His life from the words He spoke to the people He associated with; from the love and compassion that He poured out to the acts of wonder that He displayed, even the manner in which He gave His life, were beyond regular, exceptional in character and degree and remarkable. Jesus did not conform to the norms of this world. He answered to and was led by a much higher Authority. Even though He was in this world, He was clearly not of it. Jesus spent most of the evening that He was betrayed with His disciples partaking of the Last Supper, administering the elements, teaching service by washing their feet, and imparting great truth. One example of the latter is found in the Gospel of John chapter 14 verse 12. There Jesus declared to His disciples, "I tell you the truth, anyone who has faith in me will do what I have been doing. He will do even greater things than these, because I am going to the Father." As the time was approaching for Him to leave them, Jesus was instructing these seemingly ordinary men, who had begun by following Him and now had grown to be His disciples, that it was their time to become extraordinary. To become like Him. This morning He is declaring the very same directive to you and to me, to His entire church. Peter, James, John, Matthew, Philip, Thaddeus, Andrew, Thomas, Matthias, James, Bartholomew, and Simon the Zealot would no longer settle for normal, standard, routine, expected, or traditional lives. Their prior ordinary existence had been set ablaze by the glory of God. They had witnessed exceptional and remarkable firsthand; and they would proceed, by faith, to impart what they had experienced, and even greater things, to a lost and dying world. Our Father is declaring to each of us that we must do the same. He is calling us to move on from the ordinary, to take the glory that He has bestowed upon us in answer to Jesus's prayer found in John 17:20–26 and pass it on to those around us. The ordinary disciples were not up to the task; the extraordinary ones changed the world, one person at a time. We can do the same. Jesus said that we would do what He had done and more. He did exceptional and remarkable things, so will we. It is time to get started. Time to move on from the ordinary and become extraordinary for the kingdom.

May 9, 2020

I am led to the sixty-first chapter of Isaiah to serve as a means by which to reflect upon the depth of despair and brokenness from which this journey began as well as to rejoice in the riches of blessing and favor in which I bask as I write. As I ponder Isaiah's words, spoken prophetically for Jesus long before his arrival upon earth, I am compelled to rejoice, to worship, and to give thanks to my Father in heaven for the great things that He has done in my life. Join with me as I celebrate the riches of His glorious grace poured out over, not only this servant but over all of His children, yourself included. First, let me reiterate that the words spoken by Isaiah are prophetically those of our Lord. Jesus begins by affirming that He is blessed and empowered by the Spirit of the Lord God and that what He is about to declare is anointed and straight from the throne of heaven. He next asserts the purpose of His ministry: to bind up the brokenhearted, to free the captives, to release from darkness those who are prisoners, to comfort those who mourn, and to provide for those who grieve. Three years ago, my heart was broken; for that matter, I was broken. I was captive to and a prisoner of the darkness of sin. My spirit, heart, and soul grieved and mourned over my separation from my Father. Enter Jesus who, just as He promised in verse 3, began the process of restoring everything that sin had stolen. He bestowed upon me a crown of beauty that was rightfully mine through Him. He anointed me with the oil of gladness and thus reactivated the joy of my salvation. He took away the spirit of despair that enveloped me and replaced it with a garment of praise. Then, exceeding my highest hope or expectation, He declared me to be an oak of righteousness, planted by God, that I would be a display of His splendor. No longer would I be blown to and fro by the winds of worldly desires, but instead, I would serve as a most firmly rooted witness to His glory and majesty. *Wow!* Want to know why we are called to set our hearts upon a pilgrimage of the highest honor? (Ps.

84:5). The answer is found in the words of Jesus spoken through the prophet Isaiah. Amazingly, Jesus did not stop there. He declares that I (me) will restore the places long devastated. That begins with my life and proceeds to places yet unnamed and beyond limitation. Whether that restoration be of people or places or relationships, Jesus has declared it; therefore, it will be so. In verse 6, our Lord proclaims that we will be called priests and ministers of our God. That we will be afforded the honor and the privilege of serving by declaring the truth to all who will receive it. Such is already coming to pass. At the beginning of this journey, my life was marked by shame and guilt. Jesus promises to not only replace each, but to do so with a double portion: to restore to me my rightful inheritance in His Father's kingdom, to fill my heart and my spirit with rejoicing and everlasting joy. That which He has promised now exists within me. At verse 8, Jesus proclaims His faithfulness and promises to reward His church with an everlasting covenant—a promise to give His life for our sins and to reward us with eternal life with Him, an assurance that I did not walk in three years ago. One that I absolutely do today. Prior to this journey, few would have acknowledged or even noticed that I was a child of God. Now I pray and I strive each day to reflect His presence and His favor in my life. Why? Because I love Him greatly and long to honor Him and because Jesus declared that I would (vs. 9). For most of my life, I did not understand the true meaning of delighting or rejoicing in my God. After this season of sitting at His feet and allowing Him to restore the joy of my salvation; to clothe me in righteousness; to reveal to me my true identity; and to open my heart, mind and spirit to His plan and purpose for my life, I am changed. I am no longer the same. Just as Jesus declared through the words of the prophet Isaiah, God has made righteousness and praise spring up within me, before all nations—for all to see. Has this journey always been easy? It has not. Would I change one second of it? Never! I am so grateful that you have chosen to travel it with me. I pray that there are more to come.

May 10, 2020

I have to admit that I have wondered what God would have me write on this day. As I often find myself doing, I spent a good portion of yesterday conjuring up a message in my mind that I believed to be the perfect one to finish with. It was really a good one too. And then as I began to pray the Holy Spirit flooded my mind with what is the actual perfect truth that my Father desires to be imparted on this day. I was reminded that all of this is His, including me, to use and do with as He in His sovereign, infinite wisdom deems best. That both I and this assignment that He has so graciously honored me to complete are His tools and that He has a purpose for each. A plan that is infinitely superior to anything that my human mind is capable of creating. This journey began at His direction. It has proceeded only with His hand guiding it, and it will be completed in no other manner. He is God, and I am not. What I am is His child and His servant. Therefore, I will worship and serve Him. I will strive to bring honor and glory and praise to He that is truly and infinitely worthy. Forgive me, Lord, should I ever do otherwise. What my Father wants for me to do is to speak from my heart, to impart that which He has placed there to each of you who have been led to complete this pilgrimage with us. The words that I have been given to write on these pages for the last year have spoken life and truth deep into my heart and my spirit. They have ignited a fire of passion for my Father and His Son Jesus that rages within me. That would in no way be the case without the absolutely necessary and vital presence of His Holy Spirit. God's Word assures that when we receive His Son into our hearts, He sends His Spirit to dwell within us. To lead us and to guide us into all truth. To comfort us in times of trouble and to convict and correct us should we wander astray. To stir up a passion within us for our God and His Son that we are incapable of discovering without His (the Spirit's) help. Help that requires the opening of our hearts and the surrendering of our wills. Help that is ever-present and freely given. Help that is essential and requires an awareness of its necessity. For thirty-five years, the Holy Spirit has dwelled within me. God declared it; therefore, it is so. For far too many of those years, I refused to open my heart and surrender my will to His presence, thus depriving myself of the truth and the power thereby available to me. Only when I laid aside myself and handed control of the reins of my life to Him who is worthy of sitting on the throne of my existence did the Holy Spirit's presence come alive within me. Sadly, it took hard trials and painful troubles to grab my attention. Wonderfully, it took hard trials and painful troubles to open the eyes of my heart. I am eternally grateful! I realize that what I have been led to write over the last year are only words upon the pages of a journal without the special ingredient that is sent from heaven. I am now keenly aware that, fused with the welcomed presence of God's Spirit, those words become empowered and emboldened with the presence and the favor of Him that birthed them. They reveal the truth that is embodied in His Son; and maybe most importantly, they stir up a passion, a burning desire, within those that receive them for all three members of the Godhead. My very earnest prayer at this moment is that They will each impact your life as They have mine. That They will capture your heart, your mind, your spirit, and your soul and fill each with the richness and wonder of Their indescribable love for you. That you, like me, will be changed eternally. In Jesus's name, let it be so!

The Holy Spirit Recalibrates One Last Time

Right about now, you may be wondering where God is taking us next. Shouldn't this be the end of the book? Where is the chapter titled "Conclusion"? Didn't the Holy Spirit say two hundred entries? Your questions are legitimate, and your confusion is justified. I have been making similar inquiries myself for several months. As always, the answer lies with the One that created heaven and earth and knows exactly what we need and when we need it.

As I write on this Friday afternoon in late August 2020, I am convinced, and therefore trusting God, that His Spirit has revealed to my spirit the direction in which I am to proceed next. My spiritual GPS has been recalibrated for what I believe is the final time on this particular journey/assignment for the kingdom of God. Let me bring you up to date.

After completing entry number 200 on May 10, 2020, I proceeded to do the only thing that I was certain that my Father desired of me. I rose early on the morning of May 11, and I met Him, His Son, and His Holy Spirit at the place where I had done so for two years prior. Then I did likewise on May 12, May 13, and so on. Each and every day being still, waiting, and listening for Them to speak, trusting that They would lead and guide me to and through the next steps that I was to take on my journey for Them.

My first indication came on the morning of May 13 when I was once again unmistakably led to write in my journal. Then as the days and weeks passed, He continued to do likewise, just as He had for the year prior. Still uncertain of what I was to do with these additional revelations, I simply listened, received, and wrote—all the while striving to exercise the Joshua level of faith that my Father has revealed to and birthed in me.

At some point after May 10, I am uncertain of the exact date, I clearly sensed God instructing me to begin to formally transcribe what He had led me to write up to that time. I have to admit that I was a bit reluctant inasmuch as this directive presented a daunting task. As you have witnessed, it is a lot of pages, and as you might guess, my typing skills are extremely limited. With that said, I put on my best Joshua shoes and began to obey my Father's instructions.

Viewing my assignment as a marathon and not a sprint, I began typing, a few pages each day, the truths, messages, and experiences that had been placed in my heart and my spirit each morning. Not surprisingly, my Father did not cease to commune with me, nor did He stop having me chronicle the same in my journal.

Over time the typed pages grew in number as did the post-May 10 written entries. All of which fueled my confusion regarding what I was to do with the additional revelations. While my human mind struggled to obtain the answer, my spirit heard God's Spirit clearly reassuring that He had everything under control and would clue me in when I needed to know. Just obey, trust, and exercise that which I have given you, He reminded me.

During the month of August, as I was about to complete the transcribing of the initial set of writings, I came across entry number 191 dated May 1, 2020. There I read these words: "I also know, from being attentive to His voice, that I am to complete two hundred entries and then wait upon Him." My eyes were opened. It didn't say that I was to include only two hundred entries, but instead that I was to complete that many and then wait.

Additionally, on August 5, 2020, while participating in twenty-one days of prayer at my church, I heard a message spoken by Lysa Terkeurst of Proverbs 31 Ministries. She related how God had led her to participate in a previous twenty-one day prayer and fasting experience, at the end of which He directed her to complete an additional seven unexpected days. She admitted that she was confused and reluctant, but obedient. Most importantly, she conveyed how those additional seven days had forever changed her life and the lives of those around her. I heard God loud and clear. He was not finished.

He was recalibrating my GPS once again. My assignment was not complete. He had more to say.

Recently, the thought crossed my mind that maybe this work should be retitled, *He Must Increase; I Must Decrease: A Journey of Recalibration.* At first, I did not give the idea much consideration; and then, as I contemplated it some more, I realized that recalibration is one of the primary means by which our Father increases our faith and trust in Him. By continuously redirecting our steps onto the path that He has ordained, He teaches us to surrender control of our journey to Him and thereby to remove our own hands from the wheel that is steering the direction of our pilgrimage. In so doing, He also restores our relationship with Him, establishes our identity in Him, and reveals His kingdom purpose for our lives. With His guidance and direction, we arrive at a place where it is no longer we who are on the increase, but instead, it is He who was and is the only One truly worthy of being on the throne of our existence.

While my Father has not chosen to change the title of this assignment, He has sovereignly decided to recalibrate its direction. Therefore, here are thirty-six additional messages from Him. As before, my earnest prayer is that they will minister to you as they have to me, and that through them, you will experience the fullness of His presence and the richness of His favor, just as have I.

May 13, 2020

Two days have passed since I have been led to write. Having completed the two hundred entries directed by the Holy Spirit, I was not certain of when, or if, I would be moved to do so again. I received guidance this morning. As I arrived at the place where I meet with my Father, I began to examine several books that I have gathered there. I sense a new season in my journey and was searching for direction from the Holy Spirit. What I found was something completely unexpected. If I have not said so definitively before, then let me do so now. I believe that God has given me a clear vision that these writings are to be published and dispersed. It is a proposition that I struggle to wrap my human mind around and one that overwhelms me in my flesh. At the same time, it is a promise from God that my spirit receives and embraces, one that is only conceivable by faith. Faith that comes from Someone greater than me. Faith that flows down from heaven. Faith that conquers the doubt that arises from my sight. As I opened each of those books on my desk, I saw with my human eyes publishing, disclaimer, and legal language that immediately gave rise to daunting negative thoughts within my legally trained mind. This dream, this vision that is before me is way too big, if not impossible, for me to undertake, let alone to accomplish. I am just one man sitting in a house in North Carolina. Discouraged in my flesh, the Holy Spirit immediately led me to where I should have been all along. I cried out to my Father, "Lord, you are going to have to take this. It is too large for me. If this is of Your doing please show me." And then He did just that. By way of a writing that He has divinely placed before me, He spoke these words over the vision that He has given me.

"Yes, it is too large for you alone. That is why it is My vision given to you. What overwhelms you is of no challenge to me. Have I not made the direction in which you are to proceed clear? Are you not certain that I am with you in this? Have I failed you before, even once? Exercise the faith that I have placed within you. Seek my direction every day, and do not move until you have received it. My presence and my favor are with and upon you. Do not hesitate to go where I lead. I have declared Isaiah 42:16 over you. That I would lead you by ways that you did not know and guide you along unfamiliar paths and not forsake you along your way. Do not be afraid to move, but only when I say so. Go forward as I have directed. Be strong and courageous as you do, for I go before you. Walk by faith and trust in what I have said, in that which I have promised. I adore you! I have got this!"

I am speechless. My cup runneth over.

May 15, 2020

If you have ever wondered why it seems that some of God's children would appear to experience a lesser degree of trials and tribulations than others, you are not alone. I have made the same observation. I have also noticed that some who seemingly encounter more difficult hurdles along their heavenly journey struggle to accept the same, becoming discouraged and possibly angry or bitter, even believing the enemy's lie that they are less favored by their Father than those receiving a lesser burden. If that is you this morning, please be encouraged that nothing is further from the truth. Our Father loves each of His children equally and to a depth and degree that is unfathomable to our human minds. He created each of us and knows our makeup, our strengths and our weaknesses intricately. Jesus declared, "I am the good shepherd; I know my sheep..." (John 10:14). A shepherd is responsible for every one of his sheep. "He gathers them in His arms and carries them close to His heart" (Isa. 40:11). Know that your Father has a specific plan and purpose for your life, a good work that He will carry onto completion (Phil. 1:6). The road that we will travel to fulfill that assignment is not ours to choose, but His. "He will carry" the good work to completion, and as He does, Jesus will carry us close to His heart. Will it be difficult at times? Most likely, yes. "In this world you will have trouble" (John 16:33). How much trouble? That is up to Him who is sovereign and who knows what is necessary and what is best for each of His sheep. Regardless of the degree of difficulty that you are called to encounter along the path set out for you, count it pure joy that you are divinely placed there by a God who knows you perfectly and is fully aware of that which is necessary to complete you. A Father who adores you and will never leave or forsake you. One who has provided you with a Good Shepherd to carry you close to His heart along the way. "In this world you will have trouble. But take heart! I have overcome the world" (John 16:33).

May 17, 2020

"All scripture is God-breathed and is useful for teaching, rebuking, correcting and training in righteousness, so that the man of God may be thoroughly equipped for every good work" (2 Tim. 3:16–17). Take a moment and consider what Paul is writing to Timothy, or should I say what God is speaking to us. He is declaring that every last word recorded in scripture (the Bible) originates with Him. Not just some of them; not only the ones that suit our whims, our desires, or our lifestyles; but all of them! So important is scripture, the very words of God, that in the last full paragraph of the last book of the Bible, He declares,

> I warn everyone who hears the words of the prophecy of this book: If anyone adds anything to them, God will add to him the plagues described in this book. And if anyone takes words away from this book of prophecy, God will take away from him his share in the tree of life and in the holy city…" (Rev. 22:18–19)

Grave consequences await "anyone" who "adds anything to" or "takes words away" from "this book of prophecy." Many biblical scholars concur that these words of warning apply not only to the book of Revelation but to the entirety of Holy Scripture. I fear that far too often this stern caution and its dire ramifications spoken to and through John on the Island of Patmos are either ignorantly or even openly ignored. That either an act is engaged in or a philosophy espoused that adds to or takes away from the God-breathed truth contained in His Word. I myself have in the past been guilty of such a haphazard and dangerous course of action. With the constant presence and guidance of the Holy Spirit, such is no longer the case. How, you ask, did God's Spirit redirect me from my calamity bound path? Interestingly enough, the answer is found predominantly in scripture itself, or more specifically in the manner in which we receive it. Too many times I have heard it stated, when referring to scripture, that what is written is not what God intended and should therefore not be taken literally. That school of thought belies all logic and common sense and removes faith and trust completely from consideration. Why would God have over one thousand pages worth of His truth written and mean something entirely different or intend that we accept some but not all of it? He would not! A conclusion that I arrived at with the guidance of the Holy Spirit. One that is based upon a belief in the Word of God itself and its divine nature and origin, one that is grounded in and dependent upon faith—faith that leaves no room for my own understanding and absolutely no allowance for adding to or taking away. The righteous are called to walk by faith in and obedience to every last word that comes from the mouth of our Father. All of them!

May 18, 2020

> Be completely humble and gentle; be patient, bearing with one another in love. (Eph. 4:2)

> Bear with each other and forgive whatever griev-ances you may have against one another. (Col. 3:13)

> We who are strong ought to bear with the failings of the weak and not to please ourselves. (Rom. 15:1)

Each of these directives was made in letters addressed to the church, to you and me. Commands to "bear with" our fellow believ-ers, our brothers and sisters in Christ. To "bear with" means to be patient or tolerant with, to hold up, to support, to cope with, or to endure. I cannot speak for anyone else; but I find myself struggling, from time to time, with fulfilling this instruction. More often than I would like to admit I become disappointed, frustrated, impatient, and even distrusting of and angry with those around me. Sadly, even embarrassingly, that would apply to those within the church as well as those who are not. Sometimes it would seem that my tolerance level is even lower with believers. Why is that? I am not certain. Regardless of the reason, it is behavior that does not line up with my Father's will for me, or for any of His children, and for which I shall repent and, with the help of the Spirit, turn from. As I hope you have come to know, I love my Father, His Son, and the Holy Spirit with all that is within me; and out of that adoration flows a great love for my fellow believers. That part comes easily. My occasional struggle would appear to be with accepting and tolerating the little eccentricities and idiosyncrasies that we all exhibit. Peculiarities that God is completely familiar with and accepting of. Characteristics that are not only a part of who we are but to which He commands us to "bear with." Sounds like God has both a plan and a purpose behind this whole tolerance and patience thing. He is constantly working to perfect and finish our faith. He desires that we be like Jesus, who, considering not Himself, bore our sins and the insults intended for us. We are to emulate our Lord who is never impatient, intolerant, frustrated, discouraged, or angry with us but instead is always compassionate, kind, humble, gentle and patient, bearing with, and forgiving us—in a word, "loving" us. I say all the time that I want to be like Jesus. I ask my Father to help me accomplish that goal. I know that He is pleasingly answering my prayer. How do I know? Because it is His will that we reflect and bear witness to His Son, and it is His plan that one of the ways that we do so is by "bearing with" one another.

May 20, 2020

With each passing day, the dream that my Father has placed in my heart, the vision of His plan and His purpose during this season of my journey, becomes more real, more clear, and closer to its fulfillment. A great excitement wells up within me. At the same time, I am called to take up the armor that has been provided to me in order that I can stand my ground against the devil's schemes. The enemy of my soul will stop at nothing within his power to attempt to derail the plans for good that my Father is bringing to completion in me. Flaming arrows of doubt and discouragement are being shot in my direction daily, specifically targeting the vision that has been divinely imparted to me. Praise be to my God that He is greater and more powerful than Satan. Glory be to His name that He has defeated my adversary and that He has equipped me to stand firm against him. He has given me armor with which to fight the battle: the belt of truth, the breastplate of righteousness, the gospel of peace for my feet, the helmet of my salvation, and, in particular in this instance, the shield of faith to extinguish those flaming arrows that are hurling my way. I have spoken before of the Joshua level of faith that my Father has called me to exercise regarding His vision for me. It is time that I allow the Holy Spirit to raise such a level of trust and belief in me. This assignment is so much bigger than I alone am able to fathom or to undertake, a reality of which my enemy is well aware. Satan is scheming by attempting to discourage me and cause me to doubt. He is doing so by firing arrows that I can see before me. At the same time, God is moving, bringing to completion the good work that He has begun in me. A truth that I cannot always see with my eyes but that which, by faith and trust, I know to be real. Today I choose to exercise that radical, Joshua degree of faith and to walk in it as opposed to the lie that Satan is trying to place before my eyes. Get behind me, Satan. I resist you in the name of He who has defeated and been given full and complete authority over you—Jesus Christ, the Son of God! Glory be to His name!

May 22, 2020

Two days ago I was drawn to Matthew chapters 5 through 7. It is in this portion of his gospel that Matthew records what is known as the "Sermon on the Mount." First, through my brother Arzie and then later by way of Dr. David Jeremiah, the Holy Spirit led me to these passages of scripture that are chocked full of the richness of Jesus's teaching regarding our day to day walk with Him. Over the days and weeks to come, as He leads, I will address the truths revealed there. To begin to understand that which Matthew describes in chapter 5, we must first look at chapter 4. There we learn that Jesus has returned from being in the desert for forty days, where He endured Satan's temptations. Upon doing so, He traveled to Galilee where He began His preaching ministry and called His first disciples (Peter, Andrew, James and John). As Jesus went throughout Galilee, declaring the Good News and healing every disease and sickness, large crowds from throughout the region gathered and followed Him. It is upon this backdrop that we arrive at Matthew chapter 5.

Jesus sees the throngs of followers and, upon doing so, goes up on a mountainside and sits down. As He does so, His disciples come to Him. It is unclear if the disciples spoken of included all twelve or only the four mentioned in chapter 4. In either case, we know that Matthew was present and recorded the words of our Lord for all to receive. Matthew 5:2 tells us that "And He began to teach them, saying…" (It is also uncertain whether the crowds described earlier could hear Him). Jesus begins with what have come to be known as the Beatitudes. Beatitude is derived from the Latin word *beatus*, meaning both happy and blessed. Because Jesus proceeds to enumerate eight groups of people who are "Blessed," I searched for its meaning. I learned that "blessed" means to be made holy (dedicated to God); to be consecrated (set apart for God); those who live with God in heaven. So therefore, Jesus was instructing these men, who had been with Him for only a short period of time, regarding who it is that are "Blessed" by His Father. Eight traits which He proclaimed would dedicate and set people apart for God. Let's examine what exactly they are: the poor in spirit (those who acknowledge their own spiritual inadequacy), those who mourn (grieve their fallen state), those who hunger and thirst for righteousness (long for right relationship with God), the merciful (who forgive), the pure of heart (sincere inner nature), the meek (willing to submit to authority), the peacemakers (merciful, kind, and patient), and those who are persecuted (punished for their faith). What must have surprised the disciples most is that at no time did Jesus mention the Pharisees, the Sadducees, the teachers of the law, or any other of the religious leaders of the time. Right from the beginning, Jesus was declaring a New Covenant. One that focused on a man's heart as opposed to his status, one that would turn the religious world upside down. Jesus not only declared these groups of people "Blessed" but went on to specify exactly in what manner. They would be comforted (receive love, peace, joy, and compassion), inherit the earth (find happiness here), be filled (with righteousness), be shown mercy (forgive and it shall be forgiven unto you), see God (His power and majesty both in heaven and on earth), be called sons of God (be a part of His family), and, most importantly, inherit heaven (eternal life with Him). Jesus started His ministry with a bang. He came with a purpose, and He wasted no time in declaring the truth that His Father had given Him to anyone who would receive it. It is not insignificant that His first message was one of hope; a promise of reward for those who are His, who are chosen by Him—a message and promise that continues to be available to us today.

May 23, 2020

Today I will continue with Matthew chapter 5, speaking of verses 13 through 16. These passages are gathered under the subtitle "Salt and Light." Jesus begins by declaring to His disciples, "You are the salt of the earth." Salt was the most valuable of minerals during early times. Just as today, it was used as a preservative and for flavoring food in addition to for medical purposes. Salt was essential to and enhanced the lives of those to whom Jesus was speaking. He was providing them with a point of reference to which they could easily relate. He was instructing them that just as salt enhanced and preserved life physically, they could do so spiritually. What an awesome analogy. He then proceeds to remind them that once salt loses its saltiness, it cannot regain it again and therefore can no longer be useful for its assigned purpose. He even goes so far as to say that "it is no longer good for anything, except to be thrown out and trampled by men" (vs. 13). While Jesus's words would at first impression seem harsh, He was stressing what immense impact He would have upon the world and that they (and we) would be given an assignment of great importance thereto. That in order to complete that role, it would be necessary that they maintain their spiritual fervor, their connection to Him. That like salt needs its saltiness, they needed His presence and His favor, for if they did not have it, they would not be up to fulfilling their calling. This is such a good Word.

Next, in verse 14, Jesus tells the disciples they are the light of the world and uses two illustrations to drive home His point. First, that a city on a hill cannot be hidden and, second, that a lamp is not placed under a bowl but on a stand where it can be seen by everyone. Again the city and the lamp are examples of physical light that Jesus uses to impress upon the disciples (and us) that they are called to bring spiritual light (Jesus) to a dark world. In verse 16, He commands that they (we) let their light (the spiritual truth imparted to them) shine before all men to see. And why are they (we) to do so? "That they may see your good deeds and praise your Father in heaven" (vs. 16). That they (we) may be a living, breathing testimony to the goodness of God. That people may be drawn unto Him by what they see in us (the light of the Holy Spirit). We are to let that light shine for the world around us to see, to put it on a stand and not under a bowl.

There it is. Three simple verses that reveal the depth and power of Jesus's teaching. Instruction purposed to equip us to fulfill the calling that is divinely placed upon our lives: to point people to Him.

May 24, 2020

I sense a leading to write with regard to fighting our battles. During the night and as I rise, my spirit is flooded with a song "Surrounded (Fight My Battles)" by Bethel Worship and Kari Jobe.

> This is how I fight my battles, This is how I fight my battles, (repeat); It may look like I'm surrounded but I'm surrounded by You, It may look like I'm surrounded but I'm surrounded by You, (repeat).

I searched the scriptures and as He often does, I was quickly taken to the exact place that God desired: 2 Chronicles chapter 20. There we find the story of Jehosaphat and his battle with the Moabites and the Ammonites. Jehosaphat was the king of Judah. The Lord was with him because he walked in the ways that his father David had followed. He did not worship idols, as did many other kings, but sought God and followed His commands (2 Chron. 17:3–6). During Jehosaphat's reign, vast armies from Moab, Ammon, and Mt. Seir rose up against Judah. Rather than panicking in fear, Jehosaphat resolved to inquire of the Lord and proclaimed a fast for all of Judah. Then he rose up in the assembly and, before all of the people, declared God's greatness and prayed for His help and guidance. After Jehosaphat was finished, the Spirit of the Lord came upon Jahaziel, son of Zechariah and a Levite, as he stood in the assembly. And he said, "Listen King Jehosaphat and all who live in Judah and Jerusalem!... Do not be afraid or discouraged because of this vast army. For the battle is not yours but God's. Tomorrow march down against them... You will not have to fight this battle. Take up your positions; stand firm and see the deliverance the Lord will give you" (2 Chron. 20:15–17). Jehosaphat and all the people of Judah and Jerusalem fell down with their faces to the ground and worshiped God. The next morning they did as the Lord had commanded, and Jehosaphat appointed men to sing and to praise God as they took up their positions. Immediately, the Lord set ambushes against the vast army, and the men of Ammon and Moab rose up and destroyed the men of Mt. Seir. When they finished, they destroyed one another. The men of Judah looked toward the vast army and saw only dead bodies. No one escaped. They gathered such a great plunder that it required three days to collect it. Then on the fourth day, they assembled and praised the Lord. Upon their return to Jerusalem, they went to the temple with harps and lutes and trumpets. The kingdom of Jehosaphat was at peace, for God had given him rest on every side (2 Chron. 20). The God who fought and won the battle for Jehosaphat is the very same God who we love and serve today. Our battles may not be against vast armies of Moabites or Ammonites, but they are daunting struggles all the same. Ones that our Father is fully capable of and longs to fight and win on our behalf. This morning He desires that we hear and follow what His Spirit is teaching through the lyrics of a song and passages from His Holy Word:

> It may look like you are surrounded but fear
> not for the battle belongs to Me. Trust me, walk
> by faith in Me and not according to that which
> your eyes see. Follow the example of my servant
> Jehosaphat and resolve to seek Me. Call a fast.
> Declare my greatness. Bow down and worship
> and praise me. Then stand before me and wait to

receive your deliverance. You will not be required to lift a finger. Simply sing to and praise Me through the battle and receive your victory. And when you do, praise and worship your God and live in the peace and the rest that I have given you.

Thus saith the Lord. Glory be to His name!

May 27, 2020

I am reminded again of how physical comfort is a tool of Satan and an enemy of us all. Far too often we search for peace and joy and stability in temporal as opposed to eternal things. We place our hope in the fullness of our paycheck, our bank account, and our cupboard as opposed to in the richness of the presence and the favor of our Father. When our provisions and our health are abundant and well, our need for and our reliance upon our God dissipates. More comfortable, less need for Him. We refrain from calling upon and worshiping the One from whom our provision comes: our Father who "gives us this day our daily bread." That is, until the next storm arises and causes us to scurry back to Him who calms the seas. And so a cycle is formed. A journey through life on which the level of our faith and trust in the God of all things rises and falls based upon the degree of comfort we are experiencing in our flesh. We find ourselves being tossed to and fro spiritually, never truly experiencing the promises, privileges, and benefits that are ours to walk in, every day. Not just on those days during which trials and troubles appear. Our Father never intended for His children to live their lives in this manner. Nor is He deserving of such inconsistent, wavering attention and affection. He is worthy of so much more. Amazingly, His love for us never wanes, regardless of our neglect and inattentiveness to Him. During our seasons of wandering in self-reliance and comfort, He continues to pursue us, being fully present with open arms to rescue us when the seas of trouble again rise. How could that be? Actually, the answer is quite simple: so great is His love for us, so enormous is His desire for relationship with His children, so amazing is His grace, so deep and endless are His mercies. Oh, dear child of God, I implore you not to be deceived by the pleasures and comforts of this world. I beseech you to resist the lie that what you have is enough and somehow better than that which He freely offers you, that you rebuke any thought of only needing Him when all else fails or when trouble knocks. As I observe many longing to return to the normal comforts of life during this season of COVID-19, the Holy Spirit is impressing upon my heart our need to stand firm in our faith in, our trust upon, and our surrender to our Father; to not return to our reliance upon the fleeting comfort provided by the things of this world. It is only temporary. Another storm will come, and then another and another. Let's put an end to this cycle of reliance upon ourselves and our stuff and place our total and complete faith, hope, and trust in the only One who is worthy and deserving of the same—the God of all comfort.

May 28, 2020

Today I will examine, with the help of God's Spirit, verses 17 through 20 of Matthew chapter 5, which are written under the heading "The Fulfillment of the Law." Many have espoused the belief that because Jesus came to establish a new covenant, the old covenant and its many laws and commandments would be thereby abolished. In this portion of His Sermon on the Mount, Jesus declares otherwise. He begins by cutting directly to the chase. "Do not think that I have come to abolish the Law or the Prophets; I have not come to abolish them but to fulfill them" (vs. 17). Notice that Jesus does not speak to the Law of the prophets but instead uses the conjunction "or" to refer to both the Law and the prophets. Therefore, His words can be interpreted to announce His purpose in coming to earth to include the fulfillment of both the written Law and the words of the many prophets. In verse 18, Jesus more clearly states His point: "I tell you the truth, until heaven and earth disappear, not the smallest letter, not the least stroke of a pen, will by any means disappear from the Law until everything is accomplished." Jesus did not come to abolish but to fulfill the Word of God by correctly interpreting it. At no time did He add to or disobey the Law that His Father had established. He simply fulfilled it by revealing the truth declared. He completed it through His perfect obedience to each and every written word. *Wow!* Jesus came to establish a new means of restoring right relationship with our Father. By doing so, He both fulfilled the Law and declared it to be the absolute expression of God's character. Truth to be practiced and taught and not to be broken.

> Anyone who breaks one of the least of these commandments and teaches others to do the same will be called least in the Kingdom of Heaven, but whoever practices and teaches these commandments will be called great in the Kingdom of Heaven. (vs. 19)

Of much importance here is that Jesus is speaking to His disciples (His followers, the church) and does not say that those that break the Law shall not enter the kingdom of heaven. His followers' eternal destination would be secured in three years at Calvary. What He was saying was that those who break the Law would be "called least" while those who practiced and taught it would be "called great" in the kingdom. In other words, obey the Law and teach others to do likewise, and your reward will be "great." Finally, in verse 20, Jesus speaks to entrance into God's kingdom by addressing righteousness: "For I tell you that unless your righteousness surpasses that of the Pharisees and the teachers of the law, you will certainly not enter the Kingdom of Heaven." In this single verse, our Lord was proclaiming the magnitude and purpose of His mission. None of us is righteous, not even one (Rom. 3:10). Without being in right standing with our Father, we cannot enter His kingdom. Jesus is truly righteous, and He came to impute that right relationship with His Father to any of us who would accept it, to establish a path by which we can enter the kingdom of heaven. The Pharisees and the teachers of the Law refused to accept Jesus, or the gift of His righteousness, instead choosing to rely on their own merits. That is a bad plan, one which certainly will fail. Right relationship with our Father is necessary to spend eternity with Him, and Jesus is the only way by which we can receive it. He is an amazing gift. Will you receive Him?

May 30, 2020

Recently, I was asked by a brother in the Lord in what manner the Holy Spirit spoke to me and how I knew it was Him. My response to the first portion of his question was that I have come to hear from God by several means, all of which require that I be intentional about being alone with Him, about being still before Him, about waiting upon, being attentive to and listening for Him. At first, obeying His instruction that I apply this approach was not easy. Looking back, it was then that trials and troubles seemed to rise against me in waves. I struggled to understand why it was that at the exact time when a desire for my Lord was welling up within me, I faced a plethora of difficulties in my life. What I could not see then, but what is completely clear to me now, is that during that season of desperation, an increased desire to hear from my Father was rising inside of me. A willingness to be still, to wait, and to listen for Him to speak, by whatever means He divinely chooses, was birthed within me. As time passed, my patience in doing so increased, and I grew to recognize when the Holy Spirit purposed to communicate with me. And make no mistake, He did and does, in fact, speak to me. How, you ask, does He do so? However He chooses. Sometimes He gives me songs in the night or, at other times during the day, the lyrics of which speak a particular word of truth, instruction, or revelation that He desires for me to hear. Other times, He does the same by way of scripture passages that arrive through fellow believers or directly from Him imparted into my spirit. On yet other occasions, He communicates with me through words spoken or written by anointed men and women chosen by Him to be messengers to me and to others. Almost always it is during times when I am still, when I am waiting, and when I am listening. Not surprisingly, what I have come to realize is that the more I intentionally purpose to be open and to receive from Him, the broader the means by which I do.

As for the second portion of my friend's question (How do I know that it is Him?) that too required time. Time that establishes relationship. Time that creates familiarity, builds trust, and increases faith. I once heard a preacher say that believers have a "knower" inside of them and that as they grow and mature in their faith, it allows them to simply "know" that which is truth, and therefore from God, and to distinguish that which is not. Does it line up with Scripture? Does it speak life? Is it filled with love and mercy and grace? Does it arrive at just the right time and speak perfectly to where we are in our journey? Does it glorify Jesus and advance the kingdom of God? If the answer to most, if not all, of these questions is yes, then you are hearing from God. Does God speak to me? Call me crazy if you like, but absolutely, He does. Why does He do so? Because He loves me passionately and because it is what a good father does. Give Him the chance, and He will do the same for you.

May 31, 2020

Acts chapters 10 and 11 tell the story of Cornelius, a centurion in the Italian regiment, and his divinely purposed encounter with Peter the disciple. We learn that Cornelius, although a Gentile, was a devout and God-fearing man who gave generously to those in need and prayed regularly. God sent an angel to Cornelius who directed him to send for and have Peter brought to him. Almost simultaneously, the Spirit of God spoke to Peter and instructed him to go with the men who were coming to retrieve him. There was just one problem, Peter was hesitant and reluctant. You see, Cornelius was a Gentile; and Peter, who was Jewish, was therefore forbidden by the Law from associating with him. What Peter had not yet grasped was that God sent Jesus to establish a New Covenant, one that offered His love, grace, mercy, and righteousness to everyone, not just the descendants of Abraham. He was about to witness this truth firsthand as he was led by God to Caesarea and the house of a Gentile centurion. Peter was being called to go on a journey of faith, one that would divinely impact the Gentile community and the world for generations to come. Did he fathom the magnitude of his assignment? I believe that he did not. Did he have doubts and reservations? I am certain that he did. Did he fully understand what lied before him? Not in the slightest. Did he choose to wait until he fully understood everything before obeying God? He did not. Peter chose to step out in faith and travel to an unfamiliar place for an unknown purpose, trusting that His Father's plans were good and perfect and that He would be with him throughout his journey. We too are called by our God to embark upon journeys for His kingdom. Oftentimes, like Peter, we do not have all the details of our assignment up front. We begin with doubts, questions, and uncertainties. Therein lies the element of trust. It is from that place that faith begins to increase and joy starts to well up. Along his sojourn, Peter began to change. His eyes began to open, and God's perspective came into focus. By the time he had completed his assignment with Cornelius, his mindset was completely new. The revelation that God's love and the gift of His Son were for all people was firmly embedded in his spirit. Because Peter had chosen to trust his Father and in the face of doubt to not wait for all the answers, the heart of God was revealed to the world. My prayer is that we too, when called by God to go on a journey of faith, will look beyond the unanswered questions and the uncertainties and, seeing the face and the hand of our Father, will choose to not hesitate or wait but to step out and follow Him, trusting that along the way we will be changed and that in the end His kingdom will be advanced (Cooke 2017, 17–34).

June 1, 2020

I am reminded that God's ways and His instructions to His children are different from and above those of the world. That as His children we are to no longer conform to the patterns of this world, but to be transformed by the renewing of our minds (Rom. 12:2). That although we are in this world, we are to be set apart from it. That we are called to live according to every word that comes from the mouth of God (Matt. 4:4). In verses 21–48 of Matthew chapter 5, Jesus provides us with just that, words of direction straight from the mouth of God. Truths that renew our minds with our Father's wisdom and by which we are to be transformed and set apart from the patterns of this world. Let's examine God's instruction imparted to us through His Son. Jesus begins with the subject of murder and teaches that not only are we to refrain from taking another's life, but if we are angry with or call our brother a fool, we risk judgment. Much of the world deems anger and harsh words toward another acceptable and commonplace. God does not. He calls upon us to renew our minds and to not conform to the world's ways. We are to love our brother and live peacefully with him. Next, Jesus speaks to adultery. The seventh of the Ten Commandments directs that "You shall not commit adultery." Jesus expounds upon that command in verse 28: "But I tell you that anyone who looks at a woman lustfully has already committed adultery with her in his heart." The world in which we live adheres to the philosophy that one can look at, but not touch, a member of the opposite sex. Actually, in some factions of society, touching is not even discouraged. In God's eyes, all adultery is sin and that includes gazing lustfully. First Corinthians 6:9–10 declares, "Neither...nor adulterers...will inherit the Kingdom of God." We must transform our minds. Verses 31 and 32 recite our Lord's words regarding divorce. The Law of Moses provided that a man could divorce his wife for just about any reason. In our society, divorce can be granted based upon several grounds, including mutual consent. God's view is very different. He created marriage, and He opposes divorce. Therefore, His Way is that one who divorces their spouse, other than for marital unfaithfulness, commits adultery, and, as we were instructed earlier, subjects himself to judgment. Again, renew your minds and be set apart. Jesus next addresses oaths and swearing. Rarely does a day go by that I do not witness someone around me swearing by something or someone. The one that cuts me deepest is the wrongful use of both the name of Jesus as well as that of my Father. The world openly and blatantly accepts such practice. God's children are directed otherwise. Jesus clearly instructs, "Do not swear at all... Simply let your 'Yes' be 'Yes' and your 'No' be 'No.'" Moving forward, the world often says that submission and gener- osity are signs of weakness. Jesus presents an alternative view and approach in verses 38–42. We are to set ourselves apart by turning the other cheek, giving more than what is asked for, lending freely, traveling the extra mile, and not resisting an evil person. Are these easily accomplished objectives? No, they are not. Are they words from God's mouth? Yes, they are. And what, therefore, are we to do with them? We are to live by each and every one. Finally, Jesus provides God's instruction regarding our enemies. The world in which we live is split into many factions. Enemies are common throughout. Hating them is commonplace and acceptable. Jesus proclaims a new approach: "Love your enemies…" And not only are we to love them but He further directs that we "pray for those who persecute you…" Why would He say that? The answer is found in verse 45: "That you may be sons of your Father in heaven." Our Father loves the righteous and the unrighteous. He is perfect, and He calls us to rise above and "be perfect as He is perfect" (Matt. 5:48). Difficult teachings from the very mouth of God, purposed to transform the manner in which His children are to think and act from that of the world to the viewpoint of heaven. Did everyone who heard our Lord's words receive and obey them? Some did, and many did not. My prayer is that you will join those that received and obeyed, those whose lives were transformed. If you do, your reward will be great.

June 3, 2020

Most, if not all, of us are familiar with the apostle Paul and would not hesitate to acknowledge that God used him mightily in fulfilling His purpose of evangelizing and discipling the Gentiles during biblical times. Fewer may be aware that Paul the Apostle was once Saul, the Pharisee and persecutor of God's children. Today I will speak to Saul's conversion, a man named Ananias and the truth that our Father desires for each of us to consider as a result of their divinely ordained encounter. Luke's account can be found in the ninth chapter of the book of Acts and begins with Saul continuing his murderous crusade of persecution against the Lord's followers. Armed with arrest letters from the high priest, we find him traveling to Damascus to capture as many Christian prisoners as possible for transport to Jerusalem. What Saul did not know, but what he would soon discover, was that his life and his future were about to be turned upside down in the most glorious of ways.

As he neared Damascus, a light from heaven flashed, and Saul heard a voice inquire, "Saul, Saul why do you persecute me?"

"Who are you, Lord?" he replied.

The answer to his question was simple yet life altering.

"I am Jesus… Now get up and go into the city and you will be told what you must do."

No lengthy diatribe. No words of condemnation. Just who He is and what Saul was to do. That was all that Saul needed to know. He had experienced the presence of Jesus. He had heard His voice and received His direction. There is a valuable lesson here for each of us. We hear His voice, we know it is Him (He declares it), and we receive His instruction. Why then do we hesitate or tarry? In Saul's case, Jesus added an additional element to ensure His compliance. Saul could not see. He was blind. Sometimes our Lord does likewise with us. It may not be blindness but rest assured that His plan and purpose for you will be fulfilled. He will not lose one that His Father has given Him. Count it all joy that such is the case. Call yourself blessed. Saul's men led him into Damascus where he remained blind for three days. Luke tells us that "neither did he eat or drink" (Acts 9:9). Enter into the story a disciple by the name of Ananias. We are not told so, but Ananias was a child favored by God. So too are you and I. Jesus spoke to Ananias in a vision and instructed him to go to Saul, who was at the house of Judas on Straight Street (interesting address!). Once there, he was to place his hands on Saul to restore his sight. Being a devout disciple of Jesus, Ananias was fully aware of who he was being told to go to, and he had questions. You see Saul did not just persecute God's church, he attempted to destroy it, and killing its members was always an option (Gal. 1:13). He had come to Damascus for that purpose, and Ananias knew it, so he had reservations—but only briefly. As soon as Jesus assured him, compassionately, that he had a plan for Saul, one that would advance His kingdom, Ananias did just as his Lord had directed; and Saul's sight was restored. To the best of my knowledge that is the first and the last that we hear of Ananias. But not of Saul, later to be known as

Paul. Not by a long shot. The world then, and for every generation since, was and has been gloriously changed by Paul's writings. And it all began with a child of God obeying Jesus and going to a person to whom, in his own understanding, he would never have given thought to ministering to. Consider for a moment your response should Jesus give you a similar command. Then substitute your most dreaded enemy for Saul. Ask yourself if you would respond with obedience, however reluctant, as Ananias did. Then finally contemplate the impact upon the kingdom, both now and forevermore, that your decision will have.

June 4, 2020

"Therefore, if anyone is in Christ, he is a new creation, the old has gone, the new has come" (2 Cor. 5:17). The truth and the significance of these words that Paul wrote to God's church at Corinth is flooding my mind and my spirit as I sit and wait to hear from my Father. When something is new, it usually replaces another thing that has been in existence for a period of time. Normally, that which is new is a better, more improved version of that which is old. And most of the time there is no longer a need for the old model, so it is discarded. The example of purchasing a new car comes to mind. We shop for and eventually buy a new vehicle because we desire something better. Our old one may be functional but does not provide us with all of the best choices available. Once we make the purchase, we drive away and from that moment forward avail ourselves of all the options and benefits afforded by our new possession. We do not operate or treat our new asset in the same manner as we did our old one. As a matter of fact, the odds are great that we no longer even possess the prior one. It is of no use or value to us moving forward. Our Father wants us to receive the teaching found in this example and, by it, to embrace the truth declared in 2 Corinthians 5:17. Are you His son or daughter? If so, then you are completely changed. You are new, and you are better. You are an improved version of what was. Benefits and privileges that were not afforded to your old self are now yours. The old you is gone and of no use or value where the new you is going. Just like your old vehicle, it is time to part ways with him or her, to let him or her go. You do not keep your old car in the driveway, so why do you allow your old self to hang around? God declares that the old is gone and the new has come. That you were of the world, and now you are not. That you are His. That He has a purpose for the new you—a plan that does not include your old self. The new has come; it is time to let go of that which is no more.

June 5, 2020

Six of the most impactful words that Jesus spoke during His three years of ministry can be found in Mark chapter 5 verse 36: "Do not be afraid, only believe." Beginning at verse 21 and then throughout the remainder of chapter 5, Mark tells the story of Jairus, his daughter, a woman with an issue of blood and their divine encounter with the Son of God. We learn that Jairus was a synagogue ruler, which meant that he was a man of earthly influence and authority. People answered to him and not the other way around. Yet at this moment in time, Jairus found himself in a situation that many of us likewise do. A place where no human authority or strength can help us. You see, his daughter was gravely ill. Mark tells us that Jairus told Jesus, "My daughter is dying." It is important to note here that Jairus was a Jewish religious leader. Why is that significant? Because he was a member of a group of people that spurned our Lord and denied His power and authority. What is also important to point out is that Jairus did not appear to share his colleagues' opinion of Jesus, at least not at this particular moment in time. Regardless of whether it was desperation or faith that brought Jairus to the Messiah, both were evident when he found Him. "Seeing Jesus, he fell at His feet and pleaded earnestly with Him, 'My daughter is dying. Please come and put your hands on her that she will be healed and live" (Mark 5:22–23). While we are not specifically told so, I am absolutely certain that Jesus was moved. Why? Because His compassions never fail; they are new each morning (Lam. 3:22). Jairus's status did not matter to Jesus. His faith and his need did. "Come to me all of you who are weak and heavy laden and I will give you rest" (Matt. 11:28). In verse 24, Mark provides us with our Lord's response: "So Jesus went with him." It is what happened along the way that led to Jesus's declaration found in verse 36. As they traveled to Jairus's house, a crowd followed. A group that included a woman who had been subject to bleeding for twelve years. Take a moment and consider the reality of that statement and then try to imagine the depth of her despair and torment. A level of desperation that led her to Jesus. A degree of distress coupled with a magnitude of faith that drove her to believe that merely touching Him would make her whole. She did just that, and her faith was rewarded. After seeking her out, Jesus declared, "Daughter, your faith has healed you" (Mark 5:34). What an amazing testimony of the love, compassion, and power of our Lord. But it is back to Jairus that I am led this morning. Imagine what confusion must have been overwhelming his mind as Jesus stopped to search out a seemingly random person who had touched His cloak. No doubt his heart was filled with worry and concern as Jesus tarried. Fears that appeared to be realized when he received the report that "Your daughter is dead." News that no doubt obliterated any hope and/or faith that Jairus was clinging to and crushed his heart (a depth of despair that many of us have also experienced). Devastation that Jesus was, and is, fully aware of. Pain and heartache that only further moved, and moves, our Lord. Compassion that led to those six words that I began with, "Jesus told the synagogue ruler, 'Do not be afraid; only believe" (Mark 5:36). The rest of the story is of no surprise to those of us who believe and trust in the love, compassion, and power of our Lord. Taking only Peter, James, John, Jairus, and his wife into the little girl's room, He commanded her to get up. And she did! While there are so many messages of truth to be found in verses 21–43 of chapter 5 of Mark's Gospel, it is the six words in verse 36 that our Father wants us to receive and walk in this day. There will be times when our faith and our desperation will lead us to the only place where healing and deliverance can be found: to the Master, to Jesus. Rest assured that during those instances He will, out of His great love and compassion, set out to answer our request and meet our needs. We can count on it. Also know that should the answer be delayed and seemingly bad news give rise to fear, you can be certain that Jesus will be declaring the same six words to you that He did to Jairus and that He has to me for over three years now: "Do not be afraid, only believe."

June 6, 2020

We are so easily distracted. In the blink of an eye, our focus and attention are lured away from that which matters to something which is usually, if we will be honest with ourselves, of much lesser importance. For somewhere around fifteen years, my family included Toby, a Jack Russell terrier who was as loving and energetic as he was adorable. Toby was completely devoted to each of us and was never happier than when he was hanging with either my wife, my children, and/or me. We had his complete attention. That is until a squirrel would show up. Regardless of what that dog was doing, if he spotted a squirrel, his attention redirected, and he was gone. To this day, we joke with one another when our attention drifts by emphatically declaring, "*Squirrel.*" I am absolutely certain that Toby believed that each squirrel that he caught a glimpse of was the most important discovery of his life. I am also convinced that he was mistaken! In every instance, after hopelessly chasing those furry little creatures for far too long, our beloved little dog would make his way back to that which was most important to him, to the ones who provided for and loved him greatly and unconditionally, to us. Recently, I have been reminded of just how much my relationship with my Father is like Toby's was with my family. God is my Creator, my Provider, my Helper, and my Protector. He is everything to me. His love for me is immeasurable and unmatched and has captured my heart, my mind, my spirit, and my soul. There is no place that I would rather be than sitting at His feet, engaging in that for which I was created, communing, and being in relationship with Him. It is what matters most. It is of the greatest import to me. That is, until I spot one of those squirrels of life and, inexplicably, without excuse, dash away from Him, allowing my focus and my attention to be lured from that which matters exclusively to that which does not. Why do I allow that to happen? I do not have a good answer. But this is what

I do know. Just like we were always there for Toby upon his return from the squirrel distraction, my Father is there waiting with open arms for me. He is likewise there for you! That is how great His love is for us. Such love deserves all our attention. I am going to strive to do better.

June 9, 2020

It has been about three and one half years since my Father called me out of the darkness that I had allowed myself to be overtaken by and began the process of restoring me to right relationship with Himself. During that time, He has been constantly with me. He has not once forsaken me. He has been my refuge and my strength, my ever-present help. He has done great things in my life. He has, through His Holy Spirit, completely changed my perspective from that of the world to that of His kingdom; firmly established my true identity in Him; and revealed, to the extent that He pleases, His plan and purpose for my life. He has led me on a pilgrimage of the highest honor. And He continues to do so. I am so greatly blessed, so highly honored, so immensely privileged, and overwhelmingly humbled by His presence and His favor in and over my life. He has brought me so very far. I am no longer the person that I was just a short time ago. I am different, and I am changed. And yet this morning, I am being reminded that there is much more road left for me to travel. That I am greatly mistaken at those times when I harbor any thoughts of having arrived at my destination, of having completed my journey, or of having garnered all the truth. That He is God, and I am not. That were I to exist for all the days ever created and receive wisdom and revelation from Him on each one, the sum total of that which I would have gained would be equivalent to a few drops of water from the sea of His knowledge and His understanding. The depth and the extent of His truth is immeasurable and unfathomable to my human mind, and woe to me for at any moment considering that I have mastered it. Only when I gaze upon Him face-to-face will I even begin to see as He sees or understand as He does. Until that time, I remain a lump of clay on His potter's wheel, a work in His hands.

Father, forgive me for thinking, even for a brief second, that I am anything else or that I have yet arrived where you are leading me.

June 11, 2020

When asked, Jesus declared that the greatest and most important trait that should emanate from those of us who are His followers and His disciples is love. Love first for the Lord our God and then for one another. And not just a lip service level of affection but a deep, abiding love. One that captures and moves your heart, overwhelms your mind, and stirs your soul. In the world, the concept of love is tossed about loosely and far too often focused upon one's self. In the kingdom of God, love is the source of life and the essence of being. Its focus is outward and is a pure reflection of Him that birthed it. Here, where we exist temporarily, we are commanded to reflect our Father's amazing love. First back to Him and then outwardly to those around us. Not in the manner in which the world loves, but instead in the way that He has shown us. What does that look like? The answer is clear and can be found in chapter 13 of Paul's first letter to the church at Corinth. I have heard this passage most often recited at wedding ceremonies, and while it is certainly important that a husband and wife love one another as Paul describes, it is equally essential that each of us love our God and those around us in like manner. Paul begins by proclaiming that what God is about to speak, and he is about to write, is the most excellent way. Not one of or simply a good way, but the best one. Then God continues by enumerating several of His gifts to His children. All of which are considered to be, and are in fact, excellent. Each of which are of no good or of no value without this ingredient known as love. The gifts of speaking in tongues, prophecy, and giving generously mean nothing if not exercised out of love, first for our Father and then for those to whom they are manifested. Next, real love is clearly defined by proclaiming the very qualities that must flow from it. It is patient. It is kind. It always protects, always trusts, always hopes, and always perseveres. Are you patient with and kind to your Father and to those that He has placed in your life? Do you always protect what He has given you, trust Him always, place your hope in Him continuously, persevere unceasingly? If you are like me, you cannot answer yes to all those questions; but you are striving, with the help of God's Spirit, to do so. Now what love is not. It does not envy or boast. It is not proud, rude, self-seeking, or easily angered. It keeps no record of wrongs and does not delight in evil but rejoices with the truth. Can any of these qualities be found in you? Again, we are each a work in our Father's hands. Verse 10 reminds us that we remain imperfect until He that is perfect comes. That when Jesus returns prophecies will cease, tongues will be stilled, and knowledge will pass away; but faith, hope, and love will remain, with love being declared the greatest of the three. It never fails. It is the most excellent way. It was created in heaven and flows to us. We are incapable of giving it without first receiving it ourselves. Not from any source but from the only Source. What do each of the characteristics of love written by Paul have in common? They all describe the very essence of Jesus. That is because He is love. Want to obey your Father and follow the most excellent way? Then turn your eyes toward Jesus and strive to reflect His love for His Father and for each of us. Only then will you find yourself able to fulfill the most important purpose to which you have been called.

June 12, 2020

One of what I like to refer to as my life scriptures is Lamentations 3:21–25. I was praying that passage back to my Father; and as I came to verse 23, which states, in part, "Great is your faithfulness," the Holy Spirit stopped me immediately and had me recite it over and over again, not allowing me to proceed forward through the remaining portions of the passage. I knew right away that it was my Father's desire that I write in this regard. I looked up the biblical definition of "faithfulness" and learned that it means to be steadfast in affection or allegiance; firm in adherence to promises. The list of its synonyms seems endless: *fidelity, loyalty, constancy, devotion, dedication, commitment, reliability, closeness, trustworthiness,* and *steadfastness* to name a few. As I write these words, my attention is drawn to how each describes a specific trait of the very nature of God. Not one of these descriptions of faithfulness fails to depict the Father that I have come to know intimately and personally. While mere words cannot capture the essence of who He is, I am impressed by the Spirit of God that "love" and "faithfulness" together provide us with an accurate glimpse into the nature and character of our Father. One that we are able to comprehend. God is love. He is the only source of real, pure affection, and He pours it down upon all of creation, especially His children. He is also steadfast in His love, firm in His adherence to His promises, loyal, constant, devoted, dedicated, and reliable in His commitment to us. He is faithful! We can count on and trust in not only His great love, but also in every word that He speaks over us as well. Not only is He faithful to us, He is "greatly faithful." His Word declares so. Psalm 57:10 proclaims, "Your faithfulness reaches to the skies." Psalm 33:4 states, "He is faithful in all He does." Psalm 146:6 says, "The Lord, who remains faithful forever." Second Timothy 2:13 states, "He will remain faithful…" And Lamentations 3:23 says, "Great is your faithfulness." The hymn writer declared, "Great is Thy Faithfulness." God's love is everything to us, but without His faithfulness, it is of little comfort. We must be able to count upon and trust in His steadfast affection. And we absolutely can. How do we know so? Because He promises. Still have doubts? Put it to the test. His love and His faithfulness will never cease. He will not fail you. He is incapable of it. He is loyal, constant, devoted, dedicated, committed, trustworthy, and steadfast. In a word, He is *faithful!*

June 14, 2020

I return to the Gospel of Matthew and write that which God's Spirit imparts regarding chapter 6 verses 1–4, "Giving to the Needy." My Father has had me often address giving and generosity among His beloved, and so I questioned what more He would desire to say on the matter. Upon reading the text in Matthew, I received my answer. There Jesus focuses upon our "acts of righteousness" and the manner in which we complete them by using the principle of giving to the needy as an example of one of such "acts." The truth that our Lord is imparting addresses not so much our actual service for the kingdom as it does upon the attitude and method with which we go about them. He begins with a warning: "Be careful not to do your 'acts of righteousness' before men, to be seen by them. If you do, you will have no reward from your Father in heaven" (Matt. 6:1). He then proceeds to teach how to correctly, and how to incorrectly, obey this command by way of the example of giving to those in need. At the very heart of what Jesus is teaching are the words of John the Baptist that form the foundation of our journey: "He must increase; I must decrease" (John 3:30). Our righteousness flows solely and directly from Calvary, from Jesus. Any act that we perform that bears witness to said right standing must be to honor Him and to advance His Father's kingdom. What it cannot draw attention to in any way, shape, or form is ourselves. So much contrary to our Father's will and so very dangerous is any such motivation that Jesus clearly warns that it will result in your heavenly reward being stripped from you. In no way is our Lord attempting to discourage us from honoring our Father through serving Him and ministering to His children. Clearly, we are called to do just that. What Jesus knew and witnessed firsthand was that many would do so in order to draw attention to themselves, to be honored by others and for their own personal gain. Such motives are abhorred by God and will not go without consequences. The answer? (Jesus always provides one.) Serve your Father quietly, uneventfully, even secretly, in a manner that will be visible to Him and will please Him but not draw attention to yourself. At its core, this teaching speaks to the condition of our hearts. Jesus wants us to search ours to ensure that what fills and moves it is centered upon Him and the kingdom of His Father and not upon ourselves, our gain, or our honor. Do you love your God with every fiber of your being? Has he captured your heart completely? Do you long to serve and honor Him above all else? If so, then rest assured that your Father will clearly see that the motivation behind your "acts of righteousness" is pure.

June 15, 2020

This morning I will continue to write that which the Spirit of God is speaking regarding Matthew chapter 6, specifically addressing Jesus's words of instruction pertaining to prayer and fasting. I have found there to be a common theme present in our Lord's teaching on these two matters as well as in His instruction regarding "Giving to the Needy." A reading of each reveals clearly that our Father desires and commands that when we perform "acts of righteousness," when we pray and when we fast, we must never do so to draw attention to or honor ourselves. That each presents us with an opportunity to commune with and to worship Him and must be exercised as He directs in order to receive the blessings for which they were imparted. Prayer is a gift from our Father, indisputably one of the most important of His benevolences. The privilege of entering into the presence of and engaging in dialogue with the Creator of all things presents us with an honor beyond description. One that must be practiced as our Father directs. How is that? Jesus tells us in Matthew 6:5–14: "Go into your room, close the door and pray to your Father…" (vs. 6). "Do not do so on the street corner so as to be seen by men and do not babble on with many words" (vs. 5 and 7). Our Father longs to be in relationship with each of us individually. He has this amazing capacity to interact with us, one on one, as if we were the only person in existence. He created prayer as a means by which to do so. He desires that it be between you and Him. It matters not that others hear or see it. Actually, He directs that they do not. What then should we say when we are with Him? Jesus provides a template for just that in verses 9 through 13. There He gives us what has come to be known as the Lord's Prayer. Jesus's words regarding how to pray. Use them! And do so as He instructs. Our Lord concludes His instruction on the subject of prayer by stressing our need to forgive others as God has forgiven us. I wondered why He would emphasize this teaching here, at this time, along with prayer. It is because forgiveness lies at the very core of our faith. Without it, we remain lost and void of righteousness. It is important to our Father so much so that He commands that we exercise it prior to presenting our gifts to Him (Matt.

5:23–24). Next, Jesus speaks to fasting. I have found the concept of fasting to be unchartered territory in the contemporary church. Although spoken of throughout Scripture, it is a practice that I have seldom heard taught or put into practice. Fasting, like prayer and service, originated with God. It too is His gift to us. One that should be availed of. Jesus says "when" you fast, not "if" you do so. And not surprisingly, He instructs that we do so quietly and privately, purposing to gain the attention of God and not men, not in any way seeking praise or honor for ourselves. As with prayer and other acts of righteousness, fasting has to arise from and be motivated by our love for our Father and His adoration of us and can never be about ourselves. If it is otherwise, our reward in heaven will be taken from us. Jesus declares the need for prayer and fasting and then teaches the manner in which we are to do so. As always, let's obey His words.

June 17, 2020

There is a song by Elevation Worship (feat. Tauren Wells) that has been resonating in my mind and my spirit for about a week now. It is entitled "Never Lost." The chorus declares:

> You can do all things, You can do all things, but fail; 'Cause You never lost a battle, never lost a battle, never lost a battle; And I know, I know You never will...

It is the assurance asserted through those lyrics that is filling my mind and my spirit this morning. Promises from our Father that He desires to instill deep inside of our hearts, our minds, and our spirits in order to strengthen and undergird us for the journey that lies ahead. I will begin where the chorus ends with "a battle." Make no mistake and do not be deceived, we are in the middle of a war. One that is being fought in the spiritual realm. A struggle between the forces of good and evil over the souls of men. One that, even with its victory secured at Calvary, will continue until the end (Dan. 9:26). A war that will include individual battles in the lives of each and every one of God's children. Struggles, trials and tribulations that must be encountered and cannot be avoided. Jesus declared so: "In this world you will have trouble. But take heart! I have overcome the world" (John 16:33). Now onto the really good news. These battles are not ours to fight. "For the battle is not yours, but God's" (2 Chron. 20:15). The Word of God is chocked full of battles being fought and won by our Father for His children without even so much as their lifting a finger. Our Father promises to go before and to fight for us (Exod. 14:14; Deut. 1:30; Neh. 4:20). Battles are a reality but be not discouraged, for you have the mightiest of warriors on your side. As the words of this morning's song promise and assure us, He has never lost a battle, never lost a battle, and, news flash, He never will. As I am often reminded: He has got this! All that is required from us is that we stand firm in our faith and trust His promise to fight and to win the battle. Stand and wait to see the glory of the Lord. And should the lies of fear and doubt attempt to worm their way through your armor as you wait upon Him, be sure to rest upon the second prong of His promise spoken over us this morning. Not only has He never lost a battle but He can do all things, which includes fighting and winning your battles. All things—that is, but fail.

June 19, 2020

One of God's greatest gifts to us, one of the most powerful resources that He has placed at our disposal, is one another. Second only to relationship with Him, His Son, and His Holy Spirit, fellowship with our brothers and sisters in Christ empowers us to fulfill the plan and the purpose to which He has divinely called us. Certainly, our Father possesses full knowledge of our human limitations. He is keenly aware of our inability, on our own, to complete that which He has purposed for our lives. Our Father made us, and He knows that we need help. Enter the Holy Spirit. God gave us Jesus to be a means by which our relationship with Him could be restored. Once we have accepted that life-changing offering, He then bestows the gift of His Spirit to empower us for the journey ahead. In addition, and for several reasons, He gave us the gift of one another, the fellowship of the believers. Clearly, He did not do so because He, His Spirit, is not up to the task of carrying and guiding us. That fact is beyond debate. However, like any good father, our God derives great joy from and longs for His children to love and to interact with one another. He also knew that together we would grow stronger and closer to Him.

> Two are better than one, because they have a good return for their work: If one falls down, his friend can help him up. But pity the man who falls down and has no one to help him up!... Though one may be overpowered, two can defend themselves. A cord of three strands is not quickly broken. (Eccles. 4:9–12)

Relationship and strength that our Father provides and encourages us to avail ourselves of. Fellowship and bonding that the early church not only recognized but embraced. "All the believers were one in heart and mind...but they shared everything they had" (Acts 4:32). "And all the believers used to meet together..." (Acts 5:12). It has been my observation that many in modern times are not as fervent in their willingness to receive and to walk in this benevolence from heaven. Maybe that is a product of the ease and availability of resources and technology. Possibly, it derives from some fear of or anxiety from contact with others. Whatever the cause, its consequence is the same: failure to avail oneself of the entire cache of resources provided by our God to enhance and fulfill our relationship with and purpose for Him. The apostles got it. Peter wrote, "Love the brotherhood of the believers..." (1 Pet. 5:17). Brotherhood entails interaction and fellowship. John penned, "But if we walk in the light, as He is in the light, we have fellowship with one another" (1 John 1:7). And finally, the writer of Hebrews stated, "Let us not give up meeting together, as some are in the habit of doing, but let us encourage one another—and all the more as you see the Day approaching" (Heb. 10:25). I know that it is oftentimes easier and less stressful to simply retreat into a solitary existence that requires no effort or risk. The problem is that when we do, we disobey our Father and deprive ourselves of a valuable gift and a vital resource sent from Heaven. One that will assist us in fulfilling our purpose and completing our sojourn for the kingdom. Therefore, God declares, "Gather together!" Are we listening?

June 21, 2020

"Hero" is defined as a person of distinguished courage or ability, admired for their brave deeds and noble qualities. Heroes can present in many forms, ranging from one's family and friends to athletes, actors, or leaders. Predominantly, heroes arise during one's youth, although they can be realized at any stage of life. Growing up, I do not recall identifying any such individuals in particular. Sure, there were athletes that I followed and admired, but none that I elevated to hero status. Television and movies did not play a significant role in my early years, so no actors or movie stars. The closest thing to a hero that I experienced during my youth would have been my dad. Certainly, I admired my father and believed him to be brave, courageous, noble, and selfless. His mother died when he was born. (He almost died as well.) He was raised by his aunt in somewhat trying circumstances. My dad served in the army during the Korean War, which in my mind rendered him brave and courageous. The quality that most left an impression was his selflessness, his willingness to sacrifice his own wants and needs for those of others, especially his family.

On this Father's Day, let me honor my dad by declaring him to be the second greatest hero of my life. It was not until after I became an adult and a father myself that I acquired a clear vision of what and who a true hero is. It was then that I was introduced to the real standard bearer of this concept of a hero, the hero by and against whom all other heroes are measured. In my mind, the only true hero to have ever existed. If a hero is someone who possesses distinguished courage and ability, then He checks that box. If they are to be admired for their brave deeds and noble qualities, then no one has ever matched His bravery or His noble presence. Add in my personal requirement of selflessness, and this person laps the field, many times. Hero status should not be bestowed lightly. In fact, in my mind there is only One who is truly deserving. Only One whose courage, ability, bravery, nobility, and selflessness rise to such a level. By now you know of whom I speak. It is Jesus, the only true hero to have ever existed. When compared to Him, are there really any others? There are not. Some, but very few, may lay down their life for another whom they care for. None would or have ever given their life for all mankind, even those who despise and spit on them. That's a hero! That's my Jesus! I want to ask you to consider the simple yet power packed lyrics of a song that I heard yesterday for the first time. "What Would You Do?" by Isaiah Templeton and Elevation Worship: "What would you do if He walked into the room? What would you do if Jesus walked into the room?" How would you react? Ponder those words because He does walk into your room and into your life each and every day. He wants to be your hero! Your everything! My friend Stephanie sent me the video and told me that I would cry. I did. So did over a thousand people at Elevation Church. So will you. That is the impact that a true hero has on one's life.

June 23, 2020

I have written before of the parallel that is sometimes present as I awake in the morning: heaviness from the burden of a struggle that I am striving to surrender to my Father battles to steal my precious, sweet time of basking in the peace, richness, and splendor of His presence. The Holy Spirit has taught me and helps me to recognize each of the spiritual forces warring for my focus and my attention. My heart and my spirit are not open for bidding. They have been captured by and belong completely to Jesus and to my Father. My mind is the battleground. There lies the territory that the enemy, his quiver filled with deceit-laced arrows, schemes to seize. Such is the part of me that the Holy Spirit ministers to day by day, hour by hour, minute by minute. Make no mistake I belong to Jesus. Not just part or some but all of me, including my mind. Satan doesn't even attempt to occupy my heart, my spirit, or my soul. He is fully aware of to whom they completely belong. Instead, he attempts to inflict fear and discouragement by buffeting my mind with lies. Falsehoods intended to distract me from the truth of my Father's great love for me and the promises that accompany it. Such ploys shall fail. How do I know that? Because my Lord, the King of kings and the Lion of Judah, has already crushed and defeated Satan, and his weapons formed against me, at Calvary. Does that mean that the enemy will give up? It does not. Not just yet anyway. So what am I to do in the meantime? I am to resist him by putting on the full armor of God and standing. I am to fight with the spiritual weapons that my Father has provided for me and to not forget that I never stand alone. This morning one of those weapons, the belt of truth, is to be applied, as it often is, through the lyrics of a song: "With You (Paradoxology)" by Elevation Worship. I will resist Satan and surrender my mind to my Father by declaring those words here. All praise and glory and honor be to Him!

> Beneath the surface, of my anxious imagination, beckons a calmness, that is found in You alone; It washes over, every doubt, every imperfection. Jesus, Your presence is the comfort of my soul; There's nowhere I'd rather be, when You're singing over me, I just wanna be here with You. I'm lost in Your mystery, I'm found in Your love for me. I just wanna be here with You; Here in the waiting, I won't worry about tomorrow, no need to focus, on the things I can't control; All my attention, on the wonder of this moment. Jesus Your presence is the comfort of my soul; There's nowhere I'd rather be, when You're singing over me, I just wanna be here with You, I'm lost in the mystery, I'm found in Your love for me, I just wanna be here with You. So let all that I am, be consumed with who You are, all the glory of Your presence, What more could I ask for? (Repeat twice) There's nowhere I'd rather be, when You're singing over me, I just wanna be here with You!

Hear me loud and clear, Satan. I belong to Jesus, all of me. I resist your lies and the fear that they peddle. I resist you in Jesus's mighty name. Should anyone ever wonder why I come to this place each morning or question whether God meets me here and speaks to me, I implore you to cast aside all doubt. He does and He longs to do likewise with you. Please take Him up on His offer. It is a matter of the utmost importance.

June 25, 2020

Many mornings, my dear friend Arzie sends me a scripture passage that usually arrives before I awake around 6:00 a.m. It has been several days since I have heard from him, so I was pleased this morning when my phone dinged at 4:20 a.m. to deliver Psalm 121:1–2, "I lift my eyes to the hills—where does my help come from? My help comes from the Lord, the Maker of Heaven and earth." From time to time, I also receive passages from other brothers and sisters who are special to my heart, although not with the frequency of those from Arzie. This was such a morning. At about 7:30 a.m. one of those brothers sent me, you guessed it, Psalm 121:1–2. I always strive to be attentive to the Holy Spirit so as not to miss anything that He is purposing that I receive. Today did not require any deep spiritual insight on my part. My Father is leaving no doubt that He has something to say to me and to you. I have to be honest and say that my first thought was to wonder what is before me that God would need to remind me of where my help comes from. While I learn new truths seemingly each day, knowing from where my help is derived is pretty well established within me. Will a need arise today such that a reminder is necessary? The answer to that question is yet to be revealed. Almost immediately, after that initial contemplation, I felt the Spirit direct me to read Psalm 121 in its entirety.

> He will not let your foot slip—He who watches over you will not slumber; indeed, He who watches over Israel will neither slumber nor sleep. The Lord watches over you—the Lord is your

shade at your right hand; the sun will not harm you by the day, nor the moon by night. The Lord will keep you from all harm—He will watch over your life; the Lord will watch over your coming and going both now and forevermore." (Ps. 121:3–8)

I have read and stood upon the words of this psalm many times. It contains powerful promises from God. Assurances that are mine, and yours, every day. Today, in particular, He desires to specifically impart them to us. Like all other days, we have no idea what this one will hold. Its significance may never be fully revealed. However, what I do know for certain is that whatever it may bring, we will be covered throughout it with the help of our Lord. That He who never sleeps nor slumbers will be watching over our coming and our going, not allowing our feet to slip and keeping us from harm all day. And He will do the same tomorrow and the next day and the next and forevermore. All that we have to do is lift our eyes to Him, our Helper. Thank you, Father, for specifically reminding us of the promise of your help and protection on this particular day.

June 27, 2020

I return to Matthew chapter 6 focusing on verses 19 through 24, which are under the subheading "Treasures in Heaven." Jesus continues to teach His disciples on a mountain, soon after calling them, with the common theme seemingly being to live in a manner that honors God and not themselves. Conducting their lives in a way that advances His kingdom and not their own. Today's teaching is no different.

Do not store up for yourselves treasures on earth, where moth and rust destroy, and where thieves break in and steal. But store up for yourselves treasures in heaven, where moth and rust do not destroy and where thieves do not break in and

steal. For where your treasure is there your heart
will be also. (Matt. 6:19–21)

One's first impression upon hearing Jesus's words would be that
He is speaking of material treasures. A conclusion that I immediately arrived upon and one which the Holy Spirit is showing me
is partially, but not wholly, correct. Tangible possessions (money,
property, etc.) most certainly and easily capture our attention and
our devotion. They quickly captivate our every regard and shift our
passion. They become our treasure, and they rule our heart, leaving
no room for Jesus. Here is the problem with material treasures, one
which Jesus warns us against. They are shallow and fleeting. They are
subject to decay and loss. They cannot be trusted or counted upon.
They leave one's heart susceptible to damage. In addition, the Spirit
of God is revealing that the earthly treasures to which Jesus is speaking are not limited to tangible possessions. That intangible benefits
such as comfort, pride, fame, and acclaim can just as easily capture
our hearts and rule our passions and thus distract us from the One
who rightfully is deserving of each. Just as with physical treasures,
these are also fleeting and temporary and subject to being taken from
us, not by human criminals but by the leader of all thieves, Satan.
Likewise, they cannot be trusted or depended upon. As He always
does, Jesus provides us with an alternative. A spiritual answer to the
worldly dilemma that confronts us. One based in truth. One that we
can trust and count upon. One sent from God Himself. "Store up
your treasures in Heaven." But wait, how do I deposit my money or
obtain a title to my property there? What can I do with my fame or
my proud accomplishments in heaven? The answers are, you can't
and nothing. That is because the treasures that Jesus is instructing
us to store up are different from those of the world. They include
generosity, compassion, service, humility, love, selflessness, peace,
joy, and relationship to name a few. Such possessions do not decay
and cannot be stolen, not even by Satan. They are founded in Jesus
and, therefore, can be trusted and counted upon. They focus on our
Father and not upon ourselves. Later, Jesus declares, "What good will
it be for a man to gain the whole world, yet forfeit his soul?" (Matt.

6:26). Then He closes today's portion of His teaching with this: "No one can serve two masters. Either he will hate the one and love the other or he will be devoted to one and despise the other" (vs. 24). I intend to serve one master by storing up my treasures where He directs and by loving and being devoted only to Him.

June 29, 2020

Chapter 6 of Matthew's gospel concludes with his recounting of Jesus's teaching to His disciples regarding worry. Verses 25–34 are actually entitled "Do Not Worry." As is often the case, I was first led to research the definition of "worry" and, upon doing so, found that it is "to give way to anxiety or unease; to allow one's mind to dwell on difficulty or troubles." Jesus begins in verse 25 with this seemingly simple instruction: "Therefore I tell you, do not worry about your life…" In other words, do not give way to uneasy or anxious thoughts by allowing your mind to dwell on difficult or troubling matters in your life. Sounds easy enough, except in my experience it is not. Worry is a direct relative and best friend of fear. I have come to realize that where you find one, you usually will discover the other close by. I asked the Holy Spirit to show me why I struggle with worry so much more than other areas of my life, and His answer was clear and decisive. It is because I am afraid. Most of the time I cannot even tell you of what. And I am certain that I am not alone. Virtually all of us fear something. I once polled a Bible group that I was leading regarding fear. Without any hesitation each member recited their lists of things that caused them fear. Fear is rampant. Worry is the outward manifestation of fear, and it has the potential to debilitate us both physically and spiritually. Our Father is very well aware of the negative effects that accompany fear and worry. That is why He commands us time and again to not be afraid. With worry and fear traveling hand in hand, it stands to reason that God desires just as greatly that we do not give way to anxiety and unease, that we not dwell on troubles and difficulties. That sounds great, but just how do we win that battle? We don't; He does! The opposite of fear is trust, and the answer to worry and anxiety is surrender. Jesus's words on the mountainside near Galilee reiterate our need for both. Your Father feeds and clothes the birds of the air and the lilies of the field. Can we not trust Him to take care of us who are "much more valuable than they" (vs. 26)? Do we not believe that our Father knows just what we need? (vs. 32). God is fully aware of whatever it is that you are fearful of and thus what causes you to worry. He wants you to replace that fear with trust, with the assurance that He loves you and will work out, for your good, that of which you are afraid. He also wants you to substitute surrender for the worry that accompanies that fear. Jesus declares this: "Seek first His Kingdom (Him) and His righteousness (right relationship) and all these things will be given unto you as well" (vs. 33). That includes the gift of carrying that which burdens you and causes you to worry. Jesus defeated fear by restoring our relationship with the only One who takes it away. Then He commands that we not give way to or allow our mind to dwell upon it. In other words, that we should not worry. Is that always easy? No! Not for me at least. Am I always successful? I am not. But I have discovered that when I focus on the truth and do not dwell on the lies, I am better able to trust my Father to carry the burden that causes me to worry.

July 5, 2020

I have mentioned that the blueprint for my proceeding during this season has been simply to arise in the early morning; come to this place at which my Father is waiting for me; surrender to and seek Him; and then be still, wait, and listen for what it is that He is pleased to speak into my heart, my mind, and my spirit. My single most important desire before ever writing a word on these pages is that I be as certain as possible that that which I impart is from Him, is His truth, and not of my own volition. Better that no word or thought be espoused than that it be spoken from any other source than the mouth of God. There have been instances when uncertainty on my part has led to hesitation. Indecision that is not of His making and temporarily impedes the purpose for which I have been called to this place. It is through such times that my Father is teaching me to listen for and recognize His voice. During those moments, He is revealing the absolute necessity that I learn to trust in and surrender to Him and to His will. That He increases while I decrease. Oh, that I would never advance a thought that did not come from Him. That I would take no step that He did not direct or pen no truth that He did not impart. Rather that I would remain still and wait and not ever move devoid of His presence and His direction. That my heart's cry would never cease to be, "All glory and honor and praise be to my God!" I share this morning select words from a song written and performed by Cody Carnes, Kari Jobe, and Elevation Worship. It is entitled "The Blessing," and the Spirit of God has been singing it to me throughout the night. Our Father desires for someone, or many someones, including me and possibly you, to hear these words. My prayer is that you will receive and be blessed by them, as have I, this morning.

> May His presence go before you; And behind you, and beside you; All around you, and within you; He is with you, He is with you, He is with you, He is with you. In the morning, in the evening; In your coming, and your going; In your weeping and rejoicing; He is for you, He is for you, He is for you, He is for you.

Our God is with us, and He is for us. Never doubt or forget it!

July 6, 2020

I have spoken of my awesome brother, Kim, on other occasions herein. God has given Kim a depth of wisdom and understanding that greatly blesses everyone who encounters him, including me. Yesterday, Kim sent me a text and advised that he had been led to read Luke 7:11–17. Then he asked me why he had no recollection of the account written there. Immediately, I went to my Bible and read the passage. I too had no memory of reading or of hearing it spoken upon. It became instantly clear that the Holy Spirit wanted Kim and I both to contemplate the words espoused by Luke. Later,

I felt God's leading to share the passage here. Luke recounts Jesus's encounter with a mother who, along with many others in a burial procession, is in the midst of laying her only son to rest. As one would imagine, the scene that Luke is depicting is filled with great sorrow and sadness. He tells us that as Jesus saw the mother, He was filled with much compassion ("His heart went out to her..."), and He told her, "Don't cry." Then He approached the coffin, touched it, and declared, "Young man, I say to you get up!" Right away, the dead man sat up and began to talk. Needless to say, everyone was filled with awe and praised God, declaring, "God has come to help His people." Luke concludes by informing that "This news about Jesus spread throughout Judea and the surrounding country." What an incredible story of the love and power of Jesus. But why were Kim and I being drawn to it by the Holy Spirit? It is not as if we had not read of Jesus raising the dead to life before. Both Kim and I were instantly shown that this was different. In almost every other such miraculous instance, the person raised or healed was either brought to Jesus or to His attention by others. People came to Jesus looking for a miracle. These folks did not. He approached them with a miracle to give. How amazing is that. Kim and I discussed this, and here is what we each believe that God wants us to see. Jesus brought healing through one of two means: (1) By the faith of the people seeking it or (2) Out of His great compassionate desire to show mercy. Regardless of which motive initiated the movement of God, the result was the same. Jesus was revealed, God was glorified, and the good news was spread. Our Father adores each of His children, and His eye is constantly upon us. He is fully aware of our every need, and whether it is our faith or His mercy that stirs His compassion, we can rest assured that He is moved to meet each in either case.

July 8, 2020

As I sit here in the quiet peacefulness of my Father's presence, the chaos and troubles of the world around me are raging. The Covid-19 pandemic intensifies daily, spreading fear, panic, death and heartache everywhere it travels. Simultaneously, a movement is rising up within this country that I call home. One whose purpose is to attack the established principles of freedom, authority, and faith upon which it is based and recreate a new existence devoid of any of the same. Wherever one turns, they are presented with depravity, death, and destruction along with the fear, despair, and negativity that accompany each. All of which are perceived through the limited perspective of the human lens. When viewed in such light, fear rules and Satan takes ground. Our focus is distracted from the truth. Anxiety, worry, and even panic replace the assurance and promises that are securely ours in Jesus. Truth, the urgency, necessity, and importance of which our Father has declared herein for over a year now. The Holy Spirit is asking me, and you, a series of questions this morning: "Are you going to merely read what your Father is revealing and proclaiming or are you going to live it out? Will you walk by faith in Me or by that which your eyes see? Are you not one with Jesus as He is one with Me? Did He not overcome the world? Did He not conquer sin, death, and the grave? Do I not adore you? Are you not mine? Is this place where chaos and trouble abound your home? Do you believe for one moment that I do not see what is happening or that I am caught off guard by it? Do you believe, even for a second, that I will not take perfect care of my children? That Satan, along with the fear and lies that he peddles, has not already been crushed beneath My feet?

To those of us who are His children, the answers to these questions are clear. When viewed through the lens of faith, trust, hope, and surrender, the chaos is turned to peace, joy overcomes heartache, and love casts away fear. The hymn writer wrote, "Turn your eyes upon Jesus, Look full in His wonderful face, And the things of earth will grow strangely dim, In the light of His glory and grace."

July 13, 2020

> Just as each of us has one body with many members, and these members do not all have the same function, so in Christ we who are many form one body, and each member belongs to all the others.

We have different gifts, according to the grace
given us. (Rom. 12:4–6)

We, who are many, form the Body of Christ with each being graciously given a gift. God has bestowed upon you and upon me a benevolence that is essential to the function of His body as a whole here on earth. Certain of those gifts may appear, to our human eye, to be more important or significant than others. Our Father wants us to know with certainty this morning that such is not the case. That each member and the role given them is critical to the successful completion of the work of His church as a whole. He is asking us this: "Do you perceive your gift and your role as insignificant or less important than other more visible callings? If you do, then transform and renew your mind. Am I not God and did I not create all that is before you with all of its splendor and intricacy? Do I make mistakes? Do I not adore and promise to honor you? That to which I have called you is of great importance and value to me. Glorify and worship me by faithfully exercising the gift that I have bestowed upon you."

I am led by the Holy Spirit to share the Word of God found in Acts chapter 6 verses 1–7. There we learn that a dispute arose in the early church over the distribution of food. The disciples gathered and, led by God, decided to appoint seven men to, in their words, "wait upon tables." Not a very spiritual calling to our human understanding. But wait, we are then told that the disciples directed that the seven to be chosen were to be full of the Spirit and wisdom. The job is beginning to look more attractive. The chosen included Stephen, who is described as a man full of faith and of the Holy Spirit. Stephen's service for God is well documented and amazing. The truth that the Spirit desires to impart is found in verse 7: "So the Word of God spread. The number of disciples increased rapidly, and a large number of priests became obedient to the faith." The kingdom of God advanced greatly, and it did so because seven Spirit-filled servants of God viewed their calling in light of the importance with which it was bestowed, and then embraced it. God is commanding us to do likewise.

October 30, 2020
(Received on October 30, 2020 and inserted here on December 8, 2020)

In the Gospel of Luke chapter 17 verses 11–19, we are told the story of Jesus's encounter with ten men who had leprosy. Our Lord was on His way to Jerusalem to fulfill His divinely appointed mission, and as He traveled along the border between Samaria and Galilee, He was approached by these men who were in grave and desperate need of pity and healing. Compassion and physical restoration that they had no doubt sought and pursued from all earthly sources to no avail. I am certain that feelings of frustration, hopelessness, and defeat enveloped them. I am also pretty sure that word of this man named Jesus and the miracles that He performed had reached their ears. So overwhelmed with a need that no one else could meet and armed with the information that Jesus was different and extraordinary, they went to find Him. We are not told for how long or for how far they pursued Jesus but only that they found Him. Isn't that just how our Lord works? We have a need, we seek His help, and He is there. Oftentimes, we don't even ask for His assistance, and He is there all the same. Whether these ten men went searching for Jesus or He simply came to them is not of great importance. What does matter is that He had, no, He was the answer to their need; and He was completely willing to and desirous of meeting it. All they needed to do was ask. We need only to do the same. "I tell you the truth, my Father will give you whatever you ask in my name… Ask and you will receive…" (John 16:23–24). The exchange between the lepers and our Lord was not extensive or elaborate. It did not have to be. He knew their need and desired to meet it. "Jesus, Master, have pity on us!" they cried out. They declared who He is and asked for His help. His response was equally as simplistic. "Go, show yourselves to the priests." As they did so, their answer and His favor arrived almost immediately. "And as they went, they were cleansed" (vs. 14).

What an incredible story and example of Jesus's mercy and compassion, of His power, and His love. But it is from the four verses that follow that the Holy Spirit desires to speak to you and to me this morning. There we are told of the responses of the ten lepers to this life-altering gift from heaven. One would certainly believe and expect that each man would immediately stop at nothing to find Jesus and fall at His feet in gratitude for this incredible benevolence. Isn't that exactly what each of us would do? Wouldn't we spare no costs to get back to Jesus? Would not our heart's desire be to praise Him in a loud voice and throw ourselves at His feet? To thank Him personally for His attention to and mindfulness of us as the one leper did? Or would we respond as did the other nine, ungratefully going on our way focused on the gift and not the giver, the healing and not the healer? Conscious only of ourselves and that which is before us and not in any manner mindful of from where we came or of He that so graciously delivered us therefrom. It seems unfathomable that nine out of ten people divinely touched by the hand of God would respond in such a way. But they did. I dare say that we too have at some time responded in the same manner. I pray that if such be the case, we will heed the lesson that our Father longs for us to hear this morning. That we shall set our hearts to follow the example of the one grateful leper. That we would "be transformed by the renewing of our minds" (Rom. 12:2). Father, I pray that you would give me, and each of your children, a heart filled with gratitude and praise and a constant awareness to bring each of those gifts of sacrifice to you daily.

July 19, 2020

My Father, His Son, and His Spirit continue to join me daily at this place that has been established for Them, not once ceasing to love me; to comfort me; to hear my cries and my petitions; and/or to answer me with truth, knowledge, and understanding. I continue to strive with all that is within me to honor and worship Them by serving both Them and those around me and by fulfilling the plan and the purpose to which I have been called. My earnest prayer is that They will find my sacrifice and my offering to be pleasing in Their sight. That They would continue to increase in my life, and that as They do, I would decrease. In my spirit, I am beginning to sense a completion to this assignment from heaven. While acknowledging that God's ways and thoughts are not mine and that this charge is His to do with as He sovereignly wills, I do discern that my Father is soon pleased and purposed to fulfill the dream and the vision that He has birthed within me by completing the good work that He has begun in this season of my life. I am overwhelmed, humbled, and filled with excitement and joy all at once. Today God will finish His teaching with regard to Matthew's gospel with a focus upon chapter 7. There we are provided with the final instructions imparted by Jesus from a mountainside in Galilee. You will recall that up to this point in His sermon, our Lord has provided those gathered, and subsequently His church throughout time, with new instructions regarding how to live a life that honors and pleases our Father. The common theme of His message is clearly that whatever we do, whether in word or in deed, must be to glorify God and not ourselves. Jesus is establishing the foundation for the New Covenant that He has come to usher in and, in so doing, is fulfilling all that God has spoken to this point in time. In chapter 7 Matthew records Jesus's teaching regarding "Judging Others"; "Ask, Seek, Knock"; "The Narrow and Wide Gates"; "A Tree and Its Fruit"; and "The Wise and Foolish Builders."

First, judging others. Our Lord is clear that we are not to judge unless we ourselves wish to be judged. If you are like me, being judged is not a prospect you welcome. Believe Jesus when He declares that whatever you observe in your brother's eye is only a fraction of that which is in your own. Your issues are more than enough to occupy your time, so it would be wise to focus your attention inward and stay out of your brother's business.

Next, Jesus encourages and promises that if we ask, and keep on asking, we will receive; if we seek, and keep on seeking, we will find; and if we knock, and keep on knocking, we will be let in. First Thessalonians 5:17 says pray continually and keep on praying. Accordingly, never hesitate or seek to approach your Father with your requests, and when you do, be persistent and expectant.

Our Father has spoken to us before regarding the narrow and wide gates. Therefore, all that I am led to do here is to remind that there is but one way that leads to life, and His name is Jesus. Please never lose sight of that truth!

Jesus next cautions that we are to be aware of and to avoid those peddling a false gospel. He reveals that the real gospel and the genuine truth contained therein bear only good fruit. It is incapable of producing anything bad. If the fruit that you are witnessing is rotten, if it does not acknowledge that Jesus is Lord and glorify God, then avoid and flee from it. And rest assured that in this world there is bad fruit, and you will encounter it.

Finally, in my favorite portion of His sermon (vs. 24–27), Jesus summarizes His teaching by way of contrasting two types of foundations upon which one can build their house, or in this instance, their life. Build it upon a rock (hearing and practicing the truth of His words); and when the storms of life come, and they will come, it will stand strong. On the other hand, build it upon the sand (fail to listen to and practice what Jesus says), and those same storms will bring it crashing down.

Matthew concludes chapter 7 by noting that the crowds who heard Jesus's words throughout His sermon were amazed because He spoke as one with authority. That is because He has been given all authority by His Father in heaven. Authority that should compel us to heed His every word. It is my intention and my conviction to make every effort to do just that. My prayer is that you will do likewise.

September 2, 2020

Very few, if any, of God's children have experienced and/or fully comprehended His willingness and power to restore more than Peter. Although the other disciples lived in the same closeness to and intimacy with Jesus, their denial of Him (except for Judas) was not so blatant, so public, or so emphatic as was Peter's. Paul's conversion was dramatic and extreme, yet he had no relationship with our Lord prior to his encounter on the road to Damascus and, thus, no need for restoration. Peter had not only experienced the joy and privilege of being in intimate relationship with Jesus but had boldly proclaimed that he was ready to go to prison and to death with Him (Luke 22:33). Jesus responded that such would not be the case. We all know Who got it right. At His most dire moment, Peter denied His Lord, not once but three times, and he did so publicly, before the unbelieving world. Immediately upon doing so, Peter heard the rooster crow and instantly remembered Jesus's prediction. To say that he was crushed might be the greatest understatement of all time. Luke tells us that Peter went outside and wept bitterly (Luke 22:62). We are not told so, but I am certain that this was not the last time that he did so. Over the days and weeks that followed, Peter must have experienced the overwhelming pain, heartache, and despair that accompanies a sense of separation from Jesus. I am convinced of Peter's despondency because I too have experienced it. Maybe you have too. It is a place filled with feelings of failure, loneliness, and hopelessness that I would wish on no one. To have known the richness of fellowship with our Lord and to have then turned away from and denied Him is a burden too heavy for our human shoulders to carry. What Peter soon discovered, and what so many of us have since experienced, is that our Father is a God of restoration and of second, third, and numerous chances. A Father whose love and desire for relationship with His children far exceeds His disappointment in our neglect and denial of or our inattentiveness to Him. In the twenty-first chapter of his gospel, John describes how Jesus, before returning to His rightful place in heaven, made a point of reinstating Peter to right relationship with Himself and with His Father. He was purposeful and intentional in doing so, accomplishing the same publicly, before the other disciples, in order that they and each of His children to come would witness the extent to which He would go to reclaim and restore those who had been given to Him. Assuring Peter, and each of us, that His love, His compassion, and His mercy were greater than our sin—even the transgression of turning our back on and denying Him. If that were not amazing enough, the Holy Spirit has shown me that by reinstating Peter, Jesus also established his true identity and revealed the purpose for his life. While restoring relationship with him, our Lord proclaimed Peter to be His. He declared him to be adored and chosen by God to fulfill a purpose long before established. A calling to feed His lambs and His sheep, to shepherd the flock that would be placed under his care, and, most importantly, to follow Him (John 21:19). Jesus declared to Peter, "You must follow me" (John 21:22). He is declaring the same to each of us. Regardless of whether or not we need our relationship with Jesus restored, and I pray you do not, we must follow Him. It is essential! And before we do, it is necessary to know Him personally and intimately, in order that He can establish our identity in Him and reveal His purpose for our lives. I pray that the realization of all three will explode into and over your lives, as it has mine, from this day forward.

The Last but Not the Final Chapter, What's Next?

After declaring the harvest to be plentiful but the workers few, Jesus called His twelve disciples to send them into the harvest field. Before releasing them, He gave each authority over evil spirits, disease, and sickness. He also provided them with specific instructions regarding the manner in which they were to proceed (Matt. 10). It was during that discourse that Jesus proclaimed what I have found to be one of His most difficult and challenging teachings:

> Anyone who loves his father or mother more than me is not worthy of me; anyone who loves his son or his daughter more than me is not worthy of me; and anyone who does not take his cross and follow me is not worthy of me. (Matt. 10:37–38)

For most of my life, I struggled greatly to receive and walk in this truth uttered straight from the mouth of God. Did I love Jesus? Of course, I did. Did I love Him more than my parents? Maybe, but arguably not. Did I love Him more than my children, the bone of my bone and the flesh of my flesh? I did not. Was I willing to give up everything (take up my cross) for Him (follow Him)? I definitely was not.

Jesus declared that I must love Him more than the most important things in my life. But how could that be? Not only was this concept outside of my capacity to comprehend but fulfilling it seemed impossible. The problem was not with loving Jesus but was instead with the degree to which He was calling me to do so. More than my parents, more than my children, more than my wife, my job, my money, my house, my hobbies and my passions—in a word, more than my life. How could I do that? It just didn't seem possible. What I have since discovered is that it was and it is. The answer can be found in that which the Holy Spirit has revealed to me and then had me write on these pages for the last year and a half.

What I have learned, and hopefully what God has revealed to you as well, is that loving Jesus more does not require loving my mom and dad or Daniel and Hannah or Sarah and Shane or Megan any less. It simply means loving my beautiful, amazing Lord more greatly, more intimately, more passionately, and more completely. I believed that loving Him more meant loving those most dear to me less. It did and does not. He simply meant what He said: Love me more.

What Jesus is asking is that we go on a journey with Him. That we take up our cross (sacrifice what we believe to be important) and follow Him. Amazingly, if we accept His offer, along the way, the "loving Him more" directive not only appears attainable but becomes our passion and a way of life. I have experienced such a transformation firsthand and have been afforded the privilege of testifying to the same both here and in the future. What a high honor. Glory and honor and praise be to His name!

At the beginning of this journey, my Father led me through a twenty-one-day prayer and fasting experience. During those three weeks, I drew closer to Him, and He did likewise to me. He began the process of restoring my relationship with Him, His Son, and His Spirit; of revealing who He declares me to be; and of unleashing His plan and His purpose for my life. He has continued to do so from that time forward.

Recently, He led me to participate in another twenty-one-day prayer and fasting encounter during which I went to my church and joined others there and throughout the world in worshiping and seeking God for healing, deliverance, protection, wisdom, knowledge, and understanding, among other things.

What I immediately experienced on day one, and then on each and every day that followed, was the overwhelming, all-encompassing, and completely fulfilling presence of His Holy Spirit. I could not enter that auditorium without being overtaken with emotion and humbled by His presence. I could hardly speak. Each time I tried, I simply felt Him with me. He showed me that I didn't need to say anything. He already knew what I needed. It was Him. I just needed Jesus, and nothing else would do.

The Holy Spirit revealed Jesus to me so clearly and so intimately. He allowed me to see my Lord's unspeakable suffering, His heartbreaking loneliness, and, in particular, His unmatched love; and it broke me. When I could manage words, they were simply, "I am sorry." Then He showed me Jesus in all His glory, in all His majesty, and all His power; alive and seated on His throne, ruling over His Father's kingdom and, most importantly, loving and protecting, providing and caring for me and you and for all those who are His. And then all I could utter was "Thank you!"

For twenty-one straight days, He gave and I received. Its impact was profound and has remained with me ever since, leaving me to ponder what I am to do with this life-altering revelation from heaven. The answer is clear. I am to share it. First, here and then anywhere else that He leads. Such is my purpose, and yours is the same. He has revealed who Jesus is to me, who He really, truly is; and I cannot hold on to that. I must share it!

In his book *Love Does*, Bob Goff states, "That is what Jesus does, He points us toward Himself. We are God's plan and we always have been, and we complete our purpose by pointing people toward Him" (Goff 2012). For almost four years now, I have been pointed toward Jesus. Why? So that I can in turn point others to Him. That is my purpose, and it always will be.

Today, this particular season of my journey to fulfilling that purpose comes to an end. (This time I am certain.) For as long as my Father pleases, there will be other assignments, callings that I am fully convinced will be authored by Him, directed by His Spirit, and purposed to point others to His Son. Ones that I anticipate with great excitement.

While I am unsure of exactly where such commissions will lead me, I know with certainty that I will travel there with my relationship with my Father, His Son, and His Spirit fully restored, my identity in Him established, and His purpose for my life clear. Oh, what great joy, and peace floods my heart, my mind, and my spirit.

Before I close this chapter of my sojourn with my Lord, there are three things that I would like to share. First, this has been an experience that I did not see coming and yet one that has changed my life. If someone had asked me two years ago what I envisioned that I would be doing in the future to serve the kingdom of God, writing a book would certainly not have been my answer. Such an assignment never crossed my mind. But that is how our God works. He sees things that we do not. Gifts that He has placed within us to advance His kingdom. In His perfect timing, He takes us on a journey during which He reveals the gift, along with His plan related thereto, and empowers and invigorates us to complete and fulfill that divine assignment. What an amazing God we serve. I am so very humbled, blessed, and thankful that He has chosen me and declared me to be His.

Secondly, I would like to share a portion of one of the most powerful and incredible messages that I have ever heard spoken. The speaker is the late pastor S. M. Lockridge of Calvary Baptist Church in San Diego, California. Receive his words that, more than any others that I have ever heard proclaimed, capture the essence, the splendor, and the magnificence of our Lord Jesus.

That's My King! Do You Know Him?

My King was born a King.
The Bible says my King is the King of the Jews.
He's the King of Israel.
He's the King of Righteousness.
He's the King of the Ages.
He's the King of Heaven.
He's the King of Glory.
He's the King of kings and the Lord of lords.
That's my King.

·wonder do you know Him?

My King is a sovereign King.
No means of measure can define His limitless
    love.
He's enduringly strong.
He's entirely sincere.
He's eternally steadfast.
He's immortally graceful.
He's imperially powerful.
He's impartially merciful.
That's my King.

Do you know Him?

He's the greatest phenomenon that ever crossed
    the horizon of this world.
He's God's Son.
He's the sinner's Savior.
He's the centerpiece of civilization.
He's unparalleled.
He's unprecedented.
He is supreme.
He is the loftiest idea in literature.
He's the highest personality in philosophy.
He's the fundamental doctrine of true theology.
He's the only one qualified to be an all sufficient
    Savior.
That's my King.

I wonder if you know Him?

He supplies strength for the weak.
He's available for the tempted and the tried.
He sympathizes and He saves.
He strengthens and sustains.
He guards and He guides.
He heals the sick.

He cleanses the lepers.
He forgives sinners.
He discharges debtors.
He delivers the captive.
He defends the feeble.
He blesses the young.
He serves the unfortunate.
He regards the aged.
He rewards the diligent.
And He beautifies the meek.

I wonder if you know Him?

He's the key to knowledge.
He's the wellspring of wisdom.
He's the doorway of deliverance.
He's the pathway of peace.
He's the roadway of righteousness.
He's the highway of holiness.
He's the gateway of glory.
That's my King.

Do you know Him?

Well, He's the master of the mighty.
He's the captain of the conquerors.
He's the head of the heroes.
He's the leader of the legislators.
He's the overseer of the overcomers.
He's the governor of governors.
He's the prince of princes.
He's the King of kings.
And He's the Lord of lords.

His promise is sure.
His life is matchless.

HE MUST INCREASE; I MUST DECREASE

His goodness is limitless.
His mercy is everlasting.
His love never changes.
His Word is enough.
His grace is sufficient.
His reign is righteous.
And His yoke is easy.
And His burden is light.

I wish I could describe Him to you. Yes

He's indescribable!
He's incomprehensible.
He's invincible.
He's irresistible.
You can't get Him out of your mind.
You can't get Him off of your hand.
You can't outlive, and you can't live without Him.
Well, the Pharisees couldn't stand Him,
but they found out they couldn't stop Him.
Pilate couldn't find any fault in Him and Herod
    couldn't kill Him.
Death couldn't handle, and the grave couldn't
    hold Him.

That's my King.
He always has been and He always will be.
I'm talking about He had no predecessor and
    He'll have no successor.
There was nobody before Him and there'll be
    nobody after Him.
You can't impeach Him and He's not going to
    resign.

That's my King!
Praise the Lord!

That's my King!
The glory is all His!
The power is all His!
And the Kingdom is all His!
Forever, and ever and ever!
Amen!

How amazing is that! It is even more incredible to listen to. You can find it on the Internet by searching either the title of the message or Pastor Lockridge's name. (Lockridge 1976) He too is my King. That's my Jesus. The One that the Holy Spirit so clearly revealed to me during those twenty-one days of prayer. The One who has completely captured my heart, my mind, my spirit, and my soul. The One whose presence I crave and whose favor I long for. He to whom no one or nothing else compares. The One that our Father is purposing to reveal to us. My prayer is that you have or will come to know and to see Him as He truly is.

Finally, it would be my honor and my privilege to pray over each of you who have taken this pilgrimage of the highest honor along with me. Words do not seem adequate to express the emotions that are flooding my heart, my mind, and my spirit at this moment. My hope is that this supplication in some way does.

> I pray that the overwhelming richness of God's presence and favor would be with you and rest upon you all the days of your life. That the immeasurable depth of His unlimited love for you would capture your heart, mind, and spirit and never let go. That you would open your heart to and receive the guidance, wisdom, and truth that is freely yours through the amazingly powerful Holy Spirit that dwells within you. That you would embrace your God-declared identity and walk forward in the freedom and the privilege that it affords you. That Jesus would be your constant companion. That whatever you

do, whether in word or in deed, you would do it in His name, giving thanks to God the Father through Him. And I pray that He who is the only way to the Father, that He in whom dwells all that is true, and that He through whom eternal life is freely available may *increase* and ascend to His rightful place upon the throne of your life as you all the while *decrease*. To Him be the glory, to Him be the honor, and to Him be the praise! In His mighty name, I pray! Amen!

Thank you and God bless you greatly!

Journal Entries Topic Guide

A Glimpse of Heaven: 1/30/20
A Good Husband: 3/11/20
A Good Wife: 3/15/20
A Hero: 6/21/20
A Restless Spirit: 4/22/20
Abiding: 12/24/19; 1/13/20
Armor of God: 2/27/20
Battles: 1/24/20; 5/2/20; 5/24/20; 6/17/20
Be Still, Wait, Listen: 5/17/19; 7/21/19; 10/20/19; 12/18/19
Bearing Fruit: 11/21/19
Bearing with One Another: 5/18/20
Bearing Your Cross: 12/5/19
Being Bold and Intentional: 4/26/20
Blind Bartimaeus: 1/15/20
Clinging to God: 4/23/20
Correction and Direction: 6/13/19
Death: 2/26/20
Discipleship: 4/30/20
Distractions: 12/17/19; 6/6/20
Earthly Authority: 2/4/20
Endurance and Encouragement: 10/30/19
Faith: 5/10/19; 5/14/19; 11/18/19; 12/13/19; 5/13/20; 6/5/20
Fear, Anxiety, and Worry: 9/5/19; 9/12/19; 10/23/19; 3/10/20;
    3/16/20; 6/5/20
Forgiveness: 3/24/20
Giving and Generosity: 5/24/19; 5/5/20
Giving God Our Best: 8/21/19
God as Father: 6/16/19

References

Battistelli, Francesca and Steffany Gretzinger. 2018. "Defender." California: Bethel Music Publishing. https://bethelmusic.com/publishing/.

Barrett, Pat. 2018. "Better." Lyrics by Chris Tomlin, Pat Barrett, and Edward Martin Cash. *Pat Barrett*. Capitol Christian Music Group. https://www.capitolcmglabelgroup.com/videos/pat-barrett-better-official-lyric-video.

Bethel Music and Jenn Johnson. 2019. "Goodness of God." Lyrics by Jason Ingram, Ed Cash, Brian Mark Johnson, Jenn Louise Johnson, and Ben David Fielding. *Without Words: Genesis*. California: Bethel Music Publishing.

Bethel Music and Kari Jobe. 2020. "Surrounded (Fight My Battles)." Lyrics by Ellyssa Smith and Alyssa Smith. *Peace*. California: Bethel Music Publishing.

Building 429. 2019. "Fear No More." Lyrics by Jason Roy, David Blake Neesmith, and Riley Lee Friesen. *Fear No More* EP. Friesen House Music, Songs For Full Circle Music.

Carnes, Cody, Elevation Worship, and Kari Jobe. 2020. "The Blessing." Lyrics by Christopher Joel Brown, Steven Furtick, Cody Carnes, and Kari Brooke Jobe. *Graves into Gardens*. North Carolina: Worship Together Music, Capitol CMG Paragon, Kari Jobe Carnes Music, and Writers Roof Publishing.

Church of the Highlands. 2001–2021. *Freedom Curriculum*. https://freedom.churchofthehighlands.com/curriculum.

Cooke, Graham. 2017. *The Newness Advantage* (First Edition). Vancouver, Washington: Brilliant Book House.

Elevation Worship. 2018. "Hallelujah Here Below." Lyrics by Christopher Joel Brown and Steven Furtick. *Hallelujah Here*

Below. North Carolina: Elevation Church, Elevation Worship Albums.

Elevation Worship. 2020. "See A Victory." Lyrics by Ben Fielding, Christopher Joel Brown, Jason Ingram, and Steven Furtick. *Graves into Gardens*. North Carolina: Universal Music Publishing Group.

Elevation Worship (feat. Tauren Wells). 2020. "Never Lost." Lyrics by Christopher Joel Brown, Steven Furtick, and Tiffany Hammer. *Graves into Gardens*. North Carolina: Essential Music Publishing.

Elevation Worship. 2019. "With You (Paradoxology)." Lyrics by Christopher Joel Brown, Steven Furtick, and Tiffany Hammer. *Paradoxology*. North Carolina: Be Essential Songs.

Elevation Worship (feat. Isaiah Templeton). 2020. "What Would You Do/" Lyrics by Steven Furtick and Isaiah Jamaal Templeton. *Graves into Gardens*. North Carolina: Be Essential Songs.

Fairchild, Mary. 2020. Holy Week Timeline. Last modified: April 17, 2020. https://www.learnreligions.com/holy-week-timeline-700618.

Furtick, Steven. 2010. *Sun Stand Still: What Happens When You Dare to Ask God for the Impossible*. Colorado Springs, Colorado: Multnomah Books.

Goff, Bob and Donald Miller. 2012. *Love Does: Discover a Secretly Incredible Life in an Ordinary World*. Nashville, Tennessee: Thomas Nelson.

Guzik, David. 2018. Enduring Word Bible Commentary. https://enduringword.com/bible-commentary/amp/.

Hedges, Brian G. 2014. "What Does It Mean to Abide in Christ?". https://www.christianity.com/bible/bible-study/what-does-it-mean-to-abide-in-christ.html?amp=1.

Hillsong Young & Free. 2018. "Hindsight." Lyrics by Michael Fatkin, Benjamin Hastings, Aodhan King, and Alexander Pappas. *III*. Sony / ATV Music Publishing LLC.

Hillsong Worship. 1993. "I Surrender." Lyrics by Matt Crocker. *Stone's Been Rolled Away*. Australia. https://hillsong.com>lyrics>worship>i-surrender.

Hillsong Worship. 1995. "King of Kings." Lyrics by Geoff Bullock. *Friends in High Places*. Australia: So Essential Tunes, Shout! Music Publishing, Hillsong Music Publishing Australia.

Housefires (feat. Pat Barrett). 2016. "Build My Life." Lyrics by Matt Redman, Pat Barrett, Brett Younker, Karl Martin, Kirby Kaple, and Karl Andrew Martin. *Housefires III*. California: Bethel Music Publishing. https://bethelmusic.com/publishing/.

Holcomb, Justin. 2013. "What Is Grace?" https://www.christianity.com/theology/what-is-grace.html?amp=1.

Johnston, Julia H. 1910. "Grace Greater Than All Our Sin." Illinois.

Lockridge, S. M. 1976. "That's My King." https://m.youtube.com/watch?v=ZKsN-AeqJPO. Uploaded by Albert Martin. Posted: July 23, 2008.

Lucado, Max. 2018. *Unshakable Hope: Building Our Lives on the Promises of God*. Nashville, Tennessee: Thomas Nelson.

Rend Collective. 2020. "Your Name Is Power." Lyrics by Chris Llewellyn and Gareth Gilkerson. *Choose to Worship*. Capitol CMG Paragon, Rend Family Music.

Shane and Shane. 2018. "Holy, Holy, Holy (We Bow Before Thee)." Lyrics by Kevin S. Foster, Reginald Heber, and Shane Barnard. *Hymns*, vol. 1. Well House Records.

Spurgeon, Charles H. 1995. *Morning and Evening*. Illinois: Tyndale House Publishers.

Stanley, Charles. 1985. *How to Listen To God*. Nashville, Tennessee: Thomas Nelson.

About the Author

Most of what someone may want or need to know about Jeff can be found on the pages of this book. For the majority of his life, he presented as happy, successful, prosperous, and content to those around him. A model for and pillar of the societal, professional, and spiritual communities in which he lived. A perception that he relished and thrived upon. An approach to life that placed him squarely on the throne of his own existence while simultaneously both disappointing and breaking the heart of his heavenly Father.

Enter Jesus with a life-changing invitation. An offer to go with Him on a journey that would open the eyes of Jeff's heart, his spirit, and his mind to the richness and the truth of God's promises of restoration, identity, and purpose.

What is important to know about Jeff now is that, after accepting Jesus's invitation, he is completely changed. He is no longer the man that conformed to the patterns of this world, but instead has been transformed by the renewing of his mind. He is who his Father says that he is. He is blessed, redeemed, forgiven, blameless, holy, and righteous. He is adored and chosen by God to be a member of His family and of His household. He is called by his Father to serve Him, to serve others, to fulfill His plan and purpose for his life and thus please Him. Those callings now impassion and drive him. Jeff no longer sits on the throne of his life but has surrendered that position to the One who always was and continues to be worthy of being there. To use a line from the documentary series on the life of Jesus entitled *The Chosen*: "I (Jeff) was one way and now I am completely different and the thing that happened in between was Him."

CPSIA information can be obtained
at www.ICGtesting.com
Printed in the USA
BVHW051339230822
645281BV00005B/128